THE
EAGLE ABOVE

CHRONICLES OF AN AMERICAN FIGHTER PILOT

STAN CORVIN, JR.

"The Eagle Above: Chronicles of an American Fighter Pilot"
Copyright © 2020 by Stan Corvin, Jr.

The information contained in this book is the intellectual property of Stan Corvin, Jr. and is governed by copyright laws of the United States and international convention. All rights are reserved. No part of this publication, neither text nor image, may be used for any purpose other than personal use. Reproduction, modification, storage in a retrieval system, or retransmission, in any form or by any means, electronic, mechanical, or otherwise, for reasons other than personal use, except for brief quotations for reviews or articles and promotions, is strictly prohibited without prior written permission by the author.

ACKNOWLEDGMENTS:
Design Services: Melinda Martin – MartinPublishingServices.com
Aviation Technical Advisor – Major General Carl G. Schneider, USAF (Ret.)
Fleet Finch 16B Cover Photo: GoldenAgeSimulations.com
Headstone Photographer: Shawn Richendollar – www.shawnrichendollar.com

ISBN: Paperback 978-1-7348118-6-5, Hardback 978-1-7348118-5-8, eBook 978-1-7348118-4-1
PUBLISHED BY: Southwestern Legacy Press, LLC
P.O. Box 1231
Gallatin, TN 37066
Email: swlegacypress@gmail.com

LIBRARY OF CONGRESS CATALOGING NUMBER (LCCN): 2020907417

LIBRARY CATALOGING:
Names: Corvin, Jr. Stan (Stan Corvin, Jr.)
"The Eagle Above: Chronicles of an American Fighter Pilot"
322 pages 23cm × 15cm (9in. × 6 in.)

Description: *"The Eagle Above: Chronicles of an American Fighter Pilot"* is the remarkable true story of Colonel Stanley E. Corvin, Sr. who went to Canada in 1941 at age nineteen and enlisted in the Royal Canadian Air Force where he trained as a fighter pilot and flew in WWII. Going to England, he became a Flight Officer in the legendary 121st Eagle Squadron, a British fighter aircraft unit made up exclusively of Americans. Flying British Supermarine Spitfires, Hawker Hurricanes, and P-51D Mustangs, Corvin flew fighter sweeps and escorted bombers into Germany on their sorties to attack the enemy. After his unit was transferred to the USAAF, then Captain Corvin flew P-51Ds in North Africa, Sicily, and from Iwo Jima on attack missions into Japan becoming an American "Ace." In November 1950, he was sent to South Korea, where he flew F-86 Sabres on combat missions against the North Korean, Russian, and Chinese communists. Returning home to Austin, Texas, in 1951, he graduated from the University of Texas and continued his USAF career. In mid-1954, he was assigned to Tsuiki AFB, Japan, as an instructor pilot teaching Japanese pilots how to fly the T-33 jet aircraft. His first student was Lieutenant Colonel Kenshi Ishikawa, the WWII commander of Japanese forces for Osaka and who personally shot down seven B-29 bombers killing seventy American airmen. His last student was Major General Minoru Genda, who helped plan the attack on Pearl Harbor. Colonel Corvin's career included becoming a test pilot at Edwards AFB and certifying the supersonic T-38 Talon and flying the first F-4 Phantom IIs to Germany as nuclear weapons platforms. Finally, in 1974 he retired after thirty-three years of combined RCAF, RAF, USAAF, and USAF service.

Key Tag Words: World War II, RCAF, RAF, American Eagle Squadron, Supermarine Spitfire, Hawker Hurricane, Messerschmidt Bf-109G, USAAF, Iwo Jima, P-51D Mustang, Japanese A6M Zero, US Fighter Aircraft, Korean War, Mig Alley, Kimpo AFB, Suwon AFB, Tsuiki AFB, Nellis AFB, Williams AFB, Webb AFB, Craig AFB, Edwards AFB, Randolph AFB, Bitburg AFB, Wiesbaden AFB, James Connally AFB, Twelfth Air Force, F-86 Sabre, T-33 Thunderbird, T-38 Talon, F-100 Super Sabre, F-4 Phantom, Vietnam War, Vietnam Pilots, Eighth Air Force, Twelfth Air Force, General Curtis LeMay, Colonel Eddie L, Skelton.

Chapter 12 MiG Alley 145
            Wars End for Me 155
Chapter 13 Craig Air Force Base 159
Chapter 14 Williams Air Force Base............................ 173
Chapter 15 Tsuiki Air Force Base 181
            Daily Flying..192
            Major General Minoru Genda................197
Chapter 16 Webb AFB 207
            General Curtis LeMay 213
Chapter 17 Edwards AFB, Test Pilot 217
Chapter 18 Randolph AFB... 227
            3510th FTW 230
Chapter 19 Bitburg AFB 241
            Paris, France...244
            Wiesbaden AFB Hospital........................255
            Broken Arrow 258
Chapter 20 Waco, Texas 265

Epilogue: The Eagle I Knew.......................281
About The Author: Stan Corvin, Jr. 283
Appendix A...291
Appendix B...299
Bibliography...301
Notes 305

CONTENTS

Foreword v

Introduction vii

Chapter 1   Crash Landing! 1
                     RCAF Flight Training, August 1941 8

Chapter 2   RAF, March 1942 15

Chapter 3   The War in Europe 23

Chapter 4   Calais to Dunkirk Mission 31

Chapter 5   Eagles No More 39

Chapter 6   Ferrying Fighters 49

Chapter 7   Joy Estelle Heath 61

Chapter 8   Hell to Pay on Iwo Jima 81
                     Attacked by Wolves 89
                     Chichi Jima Incident 92
                     Homeward Bound 99

Chapter 9   USAF Reserves 1946–1950 103

Chapter 10   Recalled into the USAF 111
                     Nellis Air Force Base 113
                     F-84G Thunderjet Training 115
                     F-86A Sabre Jet Training 125

Chapter 11   The Korean War 133
                     Communist AN-2 Bi-Plane 138
                     MiG-15 141

FOREWORD

Major General Carl G. Schneider, USAF (Ret.)

I never met Colonel Stan Corvin, Sr., but in a sense, I've known him from the time I joined the United States Air Force (then called the USAAF) in 1946, which was five years after he joined the Royal Canadian Air Force. Stan Corvin, Jr.'s book *The Eagle Above: Chronicles of an American Fighter Pilot* about his father's USAF career also captures the story of thousands of brave young men who answered the call of duty to serve their nation during World War II and subsequent wars. Their lives were upended and thrown into chaos as they left home and fought for the very freedoms we cherish today, "…life, liberty and the pursuit of happiness" embodied in the words of the Declaration of Independence.

The story of Colonel Corvin's pilot training in the RCAF in 1941 and his transfer to the American Eagle Squadrons serving in Debden, England, before the United States entered the war, provides a rare glimpse into a little known, but important, fighter pilot group helping the British combat the Nazis. The three squadrons (the 71st, 121st, and the 133rd) originally had a total of two-hundred-fifty-three American fighter pilots flying Supermarine Spitfires and Hawker Hurricanes. They primarily escorted Allied bombers into France, Germany, and the Netherlands. The young American pilots, many only nineteen or twenty years old, were protecting the bombers against the older and more experienced Nazi pilots flying German Bf-109 Messerschmidts. Only one hundred and three pilots were still alive two years later when they all were transferred into the United States Army Air Force in September 1942. A little known fact is that more American pilots and crew members were killed in WWII than all of the Marines who landed on the beachheads in the Pacific.

Ironically, although we never met, Colonel Corvin (then a captain) and I served in the Korean War together at Kimpo (K-14). His unit, the 4th Fighter-Interceptor Wing, was located at the north end of the runway flying F-86 Sabres while my group was at the opposite end flying F-80 Shooting Stars. They flew much needed high altitude CAP missions, protecting us from marauding North Korean MiG-15s, as we provided close air support for the American and NATO ground troops.

Stan Corvin, Jr.'s book *The Eagle Above: Chronicles of an American Fighter Pilot* is wonderfully written in a straight-forward style putting the reader in the cockpit with his father as he flies in two wars then on a very unique and historic assignment in Japan teaching former enemy pilots how to fly jets. The book is chock full of flying stories and detailed airplane specifications, which aviation enthusiasts will find especially interesting.

I am very familiar with Stan Corvin, Jr.'s writing abilities because besides being a good friend and a multi-published author, he helped me write my own book, *Jet Pioneer: A Fighter Pilot's Memoir*.

Finally, I highly recommend *The Eagle Above: Chronicles of an American Fighter Pilot*. As the old TV ad used to say fifty years ago, "Try it—you'll like it!"

—**Major General Carl G. Schneider, USAF (Ret.)**

INTRODUCTION

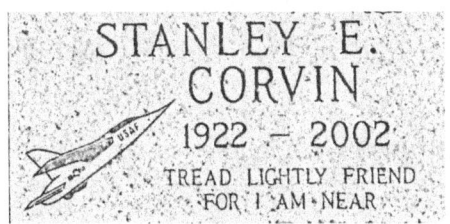

Dad's Headstone

"*Tread lightly friend for I am near*" are the wry words inscribed on my dad's granite tombstone at his gravesite in Moriah cemetery located east of Oak Hill, Ohio. Stanley E. Corvin was born on August 8, 1922 and was the oldest child of Carl Stanley Corvin and Ethel May Corvin. His father, my paternal grandfather, was born in 1899 and died at age 90 in 1989. "Grandpa," as I called him, was born in Wytheville, Virginia. During the American Civil War, his grandfather, my great-great-grandfather, served at Harpers Ferry, West Virginia, with the 116th Infantry Brigade nicknamed the "Stonewall Brigade." As a young infantry private, he took part in the guarding of famed abolitionist John Brown, who was hanged for treason against the Commonwealth of Virginia. Brown was the first person convicted of treason in the history of the country, and the surprise raid on the arsenal was considered a dress rehearsal for the Civil War.[1]

Charles Edward Corvin, who was my great-grandfather, was born on a farm in Black Lick, Virginia, in 1867. At the age of thirty-one, he volunteered to serve in the U.S. Army with Teddy Roosevelt's

Rough Riders in Cuba for one year during the Spanish-American War of 1898. Returning home from the war, he resumed his career as a railroad construction engineer and later supervised the building of the first railroad from 1909 to 1911 through the Great Dismal swamp south of Norfolk, Virginia.

For two years, my great-grandfather Charles and my grandfather Carl, who was age ten through twelve years old at the time, lived in a railroad caboose car furnished as a mobile office and living quarters. It contained a built-in lift top desk, three beds with corn husk mattresses, a table with some chairs, and a small woodburning stove. All of their meals were cooked by an eighty-year-old African-American man and former slave named Pap. The three of them lived in the car, which moved daily down the line, while the tracks were being laid. During the summertime, many workers died from yellow fever and other swamp related and mosquito-borne diseases. My great-grandfather Charles insisted that their bodies be buried alongside the track, so the construction project was not delayed by taking them back to their homes. Grandpa once told me that his father was a hard man accustomed to hard ways, but the hazardous swamp environment and grueling nature of railroad construction work required it of him.

Grandpa served for two years in the U.S. Navy as an enlisted sailor during WWI from 1917 to 1918 as part of the American Expeditionary Force (AEF). His naval ship transported troops, horses, cannons, and war material from Norfolk, Virginia, to Saint-Nazaire, France, carefully avoiding the German U-boat submarines prowling the Atlantic sea around Brest, France. The United States suffered more than 320,000 casualties in the First World War, including over 53,000 killed in action (KIA) and over 63,000 non-combat related deaths, due mostly to the influenza pandemic of 1918.

later, in 1938, in city-wide local balloting, he was elected as the county tax assessor-collector. The 1940 census showed his annual income of $2,000. He also owned a small car dealership and had one new Buick sedan parked and displayed in a small glassed-in showroom located in downtown Oak Hill.

During Grandpa's election for public office, he sent my sixteen-year-old father to drive the Buick around town, pick up voters, take them to the polls, and return them home after voting. If they voted for Mr. Carl, Dad gave each of them a crisp new one-dollar bill from the cigar box he carried on the car's front seat. As the county tax assessor-collector, Grandpa purchased a lot of property for the delinquent taxes that were owed and became quite wealthy through his real estate transactions. Fiercely loyal to FDR, he was a life-long "yellow dog" Democrat, a term generally defined as someone who would rather vote for a yellow dog than a Republican.

Dad's family had the first television in town, an Emerson console model, which was mounted in a large wooden cabinet with a round twelve-inch screen pointing straight up. A mirror attached to the lid was what you looked at, and it reversed the image, so the picture was displayed correctly. On Saturday evenings in the summertime, they placed the TV on their raised front porch and hooked up the antenna. Then friends and family sat on spread-out quilts and blankets under the big oak trees on the front lawn, ate watermelon, fried chicken with fixings, drank beer, and watched but mostly listened to the fuzzy and snowy Cincinnati Red's baseball game on the tiny twelve-inch round screen. As the oldest son of a prominent civic leader with a secure paying federal job, life was good for my dad living in a small southern town before America entered World War II.

After his mother died early in his senior year, Dad graduated from

After the war, Grandpa moved to Oak Hill, Ohio, and married my grandmother in 1921. Born in Oak Hill in 1898, Ethel May Dunn, was her maiden name. She died of cancer in 1940 when Dad was eighteen years old. Managing a small grocery store which she owned, her annual income was $1,000 according to the 1940 census records. Many of Dad's aunts and uncles lived nearby in the adjacent houses, and I remember him telling me that frequently as a child, after playing with his cousins all day, he ate dinner at their homes instead of going to his own.

My dad was a star athlete in high school as a halfback on the football team. Years later, an avid fan of college football, he especially enjoyed watching The Ohio State University and The University of Texas football games because he had attended both schools. As a child, a favorite pastime of his was hunting squirrels with his father in the Wayne National Forest south of town, and frequently they came home with a sack full of the furry creatures for his mother to clean and cook for supper.

I also remember him telling me about fishing on the banks of the nearby Ohio River at Gallipolis when he was six years old. Early one summer morning, while standing by the river's edge, his father tied a rope around his waist and threw him out into the water to teach him to swim. After going underwater several times and being dragged back to the bank by Grandpa, my dad finally got the hang of it and learned to swim; it was a sort of a do-or-die situation. At least that's what he thought at the time. What he didn't know until many years later was that his father could not swim at all, though he frequently was on the water in his small rowboat and was an avid fisherman.

Grandpa was the United States Postal Service's Postmaster in Oak Hill, appointed by President Franklin D. Roosevelt in 1934. Four years

The EAGLE Above

Oak Hill high school in May 1940 and enrolled at The Ohio State University in Columbus, Ohio. He was the first person in his family to go to college. However, as the war raged on in Europe between England and the Axis powers, American movie theaters began showing newsreels of the vicious battles being fought and the horrific atrocities being committed by the German Wehrmacht and the infamous Gestapo.

Seeing the romanticized Tyrone Power and Betty Grable movie, *A Yank in the RAF,* my dad decided he wanted to fly fighters in combat and fight the Nazis. So in late May of 1941, after completing his freshman year and without telling his father, he sold all of his possessions, left school, and traveled alone on a train to Montréal, Canada. There he joined the Royal Canadian Air Force (RCAF) and began flight training at Hamilton Station, an airfield located near the town of Mount Hope, Ontario, Canada, forty-one miles west of Niagara Falls.

Several weeks later, he was given a day pass and walked to the Western Union office in town and sent a telegram to his father saying, *"Left college STOP Joined the RCAF and going through fighter pilot training STOP Will call you before leaving for England STOP."*

Angry and upset because my dad left college and joined the RCAF, Grandpa never responded to his telegram and refused to talk to him when he called before his departure overseas from Halifax, Nova Scotia. They did not speak again for three years until the summer of 1944 when Dad returned to the United States to ferry P-51D fighters from Arlington, Texas, to Coronado, California, en route to his deployment to the Pacific theater of operations and Iwo Jima.

What you are about to read is the story of my dad's remarkable military career as a fighter pilot from 1941 through 1974 when he retired as a United States Air Force colonel. He told me many stories of his childhood growing up in Oak Hill and of his time training and flying with the RCAF/RAF and deployments with the USAAF to England, North Africa, Sicily, and Iwo Jima during World War II. He also shared other stories with me about flying F-86 Sabre's on combat missions for one year and one hundred and two missions in the Korean War from Kimpo and Suwon, South Korea.

Unlike most military veterans who returned from war and never talked about what they experienced, my dad freely discussed it (but only when asked), and over the years, I asked him a lot of questions about his service. He never glorified the events but matter-of-factly recounted them as part of his *"just doing my job"* attitude. Being somewhat stoic like most men of his generation, he never talked about fear, although I imagine there were times when he was afraid while flying in combat.

During flight training in Canada, Dad bought a Kodak 35 mm rangefinder camera known as the Model 35. He carried it throughout his flying assignments during World War II. Frequently trading a bottle of whiskey for 35 mm film, he had an ample supply to use in his camera. Unfortunately, the thousands of black and white photos he took and stored in a custom-built aluminum footlocker were lost when someone at the moving company stole the container after he and my mother returned to the United States from Bitburg, Germany, in 1969.

As a boy living with my parents, I remembered occasionally being allowed to look at the piles of neatly stacked photos held together by rubber bands. I was fascinated by the grotesque images of dead German, Italian, and Japanese enemy soldiers, destroyed trains, airfields, and airplanes on fire. I have no idea how Dad shot some of the photographs while flying an airplane. At the time, I wondered if I would ever be in a war and how I would react in combat. In 1968 I found out while flying helicopters for the U.S. Army during the Vietnam War, and I describe my experience in my first book, *Vietnam Saga: Exploits of a Combat Helicopter Pilot*.

I'm telling my father's story from his perspective and point of view, as he told it to me over several years and many beers long ago. Throughout the book, I have changed most of the names of individuals, but not all of them. The dialogue and conversations between my father and his family, friends, and pilot buddies are historically accurate but not verbatim. Primarily because I was not there to hear most of them. However, they do give additional insight and clarity to specific events and circumstances.

For the aviation enthusiasts who read this book, I have included considerable detail regarding airplane specifications and flight characteristics. In 1963 as a student at Texas Technological College, I began flying at Reece Air Force Base's flying club when I was eighteen years old. Within a year, I received my private pilot license then an instrument rating one year later. Since then, I have logged a total of 13,009 hours, including 7,437 hours of flying time in a dozen different types of helicopters from a small two-seat Bell 47G model featured in the TV series *Mash* to large Boeing twin-engine CH-47C Chinooks. I also have 5,592 flying hours in about the same number of airplanes ranging from a tiny two-seat Cessna 150 to turbine-powered twin-engine Beechcraft King Air 90s.

To write this book, I have done extensive research on WWII, RCAF, RAF, and USAAF airplanes, Korean War jet fighters, and various post-cold war aircraft my dad flew for the remainder of his distinguished USAF career. Although I offer no conclusion as to which airplanes or helicopters are the best, I know one thing for sure: it's great fun to fly high and fast and low and slow!

The image of the Fleet Finch 16B and the F-4 Phantom used on the front cover design were provided by GoldenAgeSimulations.com. A special thank you to them for allowing the use of their beautifully crafted images.

Finally, as I tell this story, I will indeed endeavor to "tread lightly," for I have never felt closer to my father, Stan Corvin, Sr. than I do at this moment.

Dad, I love you, and I think if you were alive, you would like what I've written. You truly were one of the founding fathers of the greatest generation!

—Stan Corvin, Jr., Chief Storyteller

DEDICATION

For all the men, women, and children who have suffered the painful separation of multiple military deployments and sometimes the heartbreakingly ultimate sacrifice and loss of a loved one in war, I dedicate this book to you and your courageous efforts to maintain a normal family life under challenging circumstances.

And to my parents, Stan and Joy Corvin, who died long ago, I offer my heartfelt gratitude for instilling in me an indomitable spirit, resilience, and Texas grit, which allowed me to survive my own combat situations where I very easily could have perished.

Finally, I must acknowledge the incredible encouragement and support of my wife, Peggy, whom I love beyond measure. Thanks, babe, you are the best!

May God bless you all, and God bless America!

—Stan Corvin, Jr., Author

CHAPTER 1

CRASH LANDING!

Slowly regaining consciousness, I leaned back from my slumped over position in the small cockpit and tried to open my eyes. All I could see was deep red darkness and briefly thought I was blind. A few minutes earlier, I was flying my Fleet Finch 16B bi-plane low over the water, buzzing a large flock of Canadian geese floating on the lake. Turning my head to the right to watch them as I went by, laughing at their frantic attempts to fly, I looked back over the front engine cowling just in time to see several tall pine trees directly in front of me. Hitting the trees at eighty-five miles per hour, I briefly heard the loud crash as the airplane broke apart. I was knocked unconscious when my head slammed into the overhead metal supports and the Plexiglas canopy. It shattered and sliced through my cloth flight helmet, cutting a six-inch gash in my scalp.

Groaning in pain, I released the lap and shoulder harness buckle, slowly climbed out of the upright cockpit, and fell to the ground where I immediately passed out again. Sometime later, I awoke, clambered out of my seat pack parachute straps, and crawled to the nearby shoreline where I heard the water quietly lapping against the rocks. Removing my canvas flight helmet, I submerged my face in the ice-cold water and carefully cleaned the blood out of my eyes with my fingers. Sitting up, gradually, I saw the surrounding lake come into focus as my eyesight cleared and slowly recovered.

Fleet Finch 16B

Shakily, standing up, I walked over to the twisted frame of my airplane, holding my cloth flight helmet tightly against my scalp to slow the flow of blood running down my face and neck. In the crash, the aircraft's left two wings had been sheared off, and the right two were folded under the bright yellow metal fuselage. The five-cylinder engine with its shattered two-bladed wooden propeller was smoldering, and as I stood there, I felt the heat from the exhaust pipes, relieved there was no fire or flames. I saw gasoline trickling out of the bottom of the engine compartment in a small stream and slowly backed away from the wreckage.

Turning, I staggered to the shoreline, reached into my leather flight jacket pocket, and removed a package of Lucky Strike™ cigarettes and my Zippo™. Lighting one, I inhaled deeply and felt the acrid smoke fill my lungs. The surface of the lake was mirror-smooth, and the gentle breeze coming from the water was slightly fishy smelling. Looking around, I briefly thought, *"This reminds me of Dad's fishing cabin on Pickerel Lake in Northern Wisconsin."*

I had been on an afternoon solo cross-country to build my flying time when I decided to dive down to the water and scare a flock of geese who were gathered near the edge of a small island in the middle of the remote lake—one of the thousands in the Ontario province. Regrettably, I did not realize how close I was to the trees until I hit them. Flicking my cigarette into the water, I walked over to the aircraft, reached into the cockpit, and from under the front metal seat, removed a square canvas survival gear bag and small first aid kit. Taking it out and opening a paper wrapper containing a large gauze bandage, I placed it on the top of my head and tightly tied the long attached strings under my chin to stop the blood flow. Searching the shoreline, I found several dry pieces of driftwood, stacked them in a pyramid shape near the water's edge, took a long stick, and held it under the stream of gasoline seeping from the airplane. Going to the firewood, I lit the gas-soaked stick and built a big bonfire. The warmth from the flames felt good, and I moved my parachute over and sat on it.

Although it was late August, as the sun began to set, the temperature was falling, and the air was crisp and chilly. The accident happened so quickly that I had not made any "Mayday" call on the radio, so no one at my unit knew that I had gone down. I thought, "When I don't return tonight, I imagine a search party will be sent out tomorrow, and I'll be picked up then." However, I was very wrong.

Opening the survival kit, I took out an olive drab green square tin container labeled EMERGENCY FLYING RATIONS, MK II and peeled back the metal top with the large attached key. Inside were twelve hard biscuits, two chocolate bars, twelve milk chocolate tablets, and four packages of chocolate cocoa powder. All of the food was concentrated, and the instructions printed on the tin lid said to eat it slowly. Rummaging through the survival equipment, I found a box of halazone water purification tablets on the top and below them, a square signal mirror with a leather lanyard wrapped around it. I set it aside where I could easily find and use it if an airplane flew nearby.

"Tomorrow morning at first light, I'll build a bigger fire and place green pine branches on it to create a smoke column."

Removing the rations and placing them in the cloth survival kit bag, I took the tin container, knelt by the edge of the lake and filled it with water then put a halazone tablet in it. Sitting on my parachute by the fire, I ate a biscuit and one-half of a chocolate bar and drank the cold water. Then I lit another cigarette. My scalp bandage was already soaked with blood, so I replaced it with a fresh one and took two aspirin from the first aid kit and swallowed them with a drink of the lake water. Although the gash in my head was painful, I didn't have much of a headache, so I didn't think I had a concussion.

Zipping up my fleece-lined leather jacket and pulling on my flight gloves, I stretched out by the crackling fire and carefully rested my head on the parachute. Soon after closing my eyes, I heard the clear call of a loon. It was one of the most beautiful sounds I had ever heard. Its mournful wail reverberated over the still water, and for a moment, I felt a twinge of homesickness. Then its mate called from farther down the shoreline, and the two birds began a duet that lasted for a while. I fell asleep, exhausted from the crash and my head injury. Sometime in the night, I awoke when I heard a loud splash in the water a short distance away from me.

"Maybe I can catch a trout in the morning with the fishing tackle provided in the survival kit," I groggily thought as I moved closer to the

Slowly retrieving the fishing cord in, I waited for something to strike the bait. Several throws later, I felt a hard jerk, and a big fish took off with the lure. Tightening my grip on the line, I set the hook and began to haul the splashing and jumping fish to me. Finally, as I pulled it ashore, I saw that it was a large Northern Pike.

"Holy crap!" I exclaimed aloud as I held the vigorously thrashing fish up and admired its glistening black speckled skin. Striking it on the head with a rock, I killed it and took it back to the fire. The survival kit contained a sharp knife inside a leather sheath, and I cleaned the fish leaving the skin on one side of the fleshy pink fillets. Finding several large rocks and placing them on each side of the fire, I trimmed several green pine branches and lay them on top of the rocks several inches above the hot coals. Then I placed the two large fish fillets, skin down across the branches. Soon the meat was sizzling, smoking, and smelled wonderful. After thirty minutes, I removed the steaming white fillets from the fire and, with my bare fingers, ate them and a survival kit hard biscuit.

Although not feeling well, I spent the remainder of the day maintaining the fire and adding green pine branches so that it would produce lots of smoke. I did not see any other airplanes in the sky nor boats on the lake. I was beginning to run a fever, so I rested most of the afternoon. That evening I shivered continuously and was chilled even though I had a roaring bonfire next to my makeshift bed, which I had made from layering multiple soft pine needle branches down on the ground. The night was uneventful, and at dawn the next morning, I added more driftwood logs to the fire. Hearing a nearby splashing noise, I faintly saw in the fog the shadowy outline of a large swimming moose with huge bifurcated horns on its head.

Remaining very still, I watched it swim past the small island and

brightly glowing embers of the fire.

At dawn, I awoke and added several large driftwood logs to the fire. Wisps of fog were slowly rising from the glassy surface of the lake as I stood by the shoreline and watched the sun cast golden rays of light through the pine trees and onto the glistening water. My head had mostly stopped bleeding, and after removing the bloody bandage covering the gash, I opened a paper packet of sulfa (sulfonamide) antibiotic powder and sprinkled it in the open wound. I replaced the dressing with a fresh one. My upper body was bruised, and I ached all over, apparently from banging around in the cockpit of the airplane after crashing into the trees.

Opening a package of chocolate cocoa powder, I mixed it in the tin with freshwater and another halazone tablet and placed it on the glowing coals to warm. After a few minutes, I put on my gloves, removed the tin, and sipped the steaming hot beverage while smoking a cigarette. Then I heard the faint sound of a distant airplane engine and hurriedly stood up and put more wood on the fire and several pine branches I had broken off of a nearby tree to create a grey smoke column. Searching the skies for the aircraft, I finally saw it several miles away; however, it continued in a northeasterly direction and then disappeared. Somewhat dejected, I sat down on the parachute and wondered how long it would take for me to be rescued.

Throughout the day, I kept the fire burning and put more green pine branches on it to produce a sizeable grey smoke column. At noon, I removed the fishing line from the survival kit and on the end of it tied a shiny silver spoon lure with a large hook. Holding several large loops of the line in my left hand, I walked to the water's edge and, with my right hand, quickly twirled two feet of the fishing cord with the silver lure on it and cast it as far out into the lake as I could.

disappear into the mist. Sitting on my chute, I drank more cold purified water, swallowed two aspirin and two antibiotic sulfa tablets, and then lay down because I was running a low-grade fever.

Suddenly I heard a voice on the water yell, "Bonjour, monsieur. Comment allez-vous?" *(French: "Hello, sir. How are you?")*

Jumping up, I excitedly waved my hands when I saw a white homemade birch bark canoe containing two Canadian Indians with black braided hair hanging down the sides of their faces paddling in my direction. Enthusiastically shaking their hands when they came ashore, I explained that I was an American pilot who had crashed my airplane on the island two days earlier. The men spoke broken English and said they were from the Mohawk tribe and lived in a nearby village across the lake.

Pointing at my head and indicating for me to lean over, the older man gently examined the blood-soaked bandage covering my scalp wound and muttered. "Mon Dieu! C'est vraiment tres mauvais. Monsieur, vous avez besoin d'un médecin." *(French: My God! That is indeed very bad. Sir, you need a doctor.)* From my limited high school French, I understood what he said, so after extinguishing the fire, we loaded my gear into the canoe, and they began to paddle us back across the lake.

After two hours, we arrived at their small lakeside village, and they took me to a one-room log building that was their tribal infirmary. Inside, a grey-haired middle-age woman, wearing a crisply starched white uniform and neatly folded nurse's cap pinned to her hair, cleaned and bandaged the wound and said something to the two men in rapid French. Then helping me to a narrow bed next to a window, I laid down, feeling feverish and exhausted. She sat down in a chair next to the bed, gently patted my shoulder, and, in English, said the two men would drive me back to my unit. Thanking her, I promptly fell asleep.

Sometime later I awoke when I heard a noise at the front of the building. The two men who found me, a father and son, came inside and said they would take me back to my base. When we walked outside, I saw they had a wooden horse-drawn buckboard wagon with my flight gear in the back and a gray cornhusk-filled mattress so that I could lie down during the trip. I climbed aboard, and several hours later, just before sundown, we arrived at the main gate of my flight unit RCAF Hamilton Station. The two uniformed military police guards looked over the sideboards at me then immediately called for an ambulance to take me to the hospital. A few minutes later, the ambulance arrived. I shook hands with the two Mohawk men, thanked them, and was then loaded onto a stretcher in the vehicle and driven away.

RCAF Flight Training

August 1941

At the hospital, the emergency room nurse gave me a tetanus shot and some penicillin tablets, shaved my scalp around the wound, and the doctor sewed thirty stitches in my head after deadening the area with novocaine. Later that night, my commanding officer came by, and I lied to him when I said that as I was flying over the lake, my engine quit from carburetor icing, and I was forced to crash land on the island. He did not question me anymore, and after a few days' stay in the hospital, I went back to my unit and resumed my fighter pilot flight training without any further incidents. Although, I did get some good-natured ribbing from my buddies for wearing what looked like a white turban on my head. While on the training flights, I wore a headset containing earphones over the gauze bandages. After several weeks I did not need them anymore; however, the stitches were still very tender to the touch when I wore my cloth flight helmet.

RCAF Flight School Entrance

Typically, I had classroom instruction for half a day and flew the Fleet Finch 16B the other half. The schedule rotated each week. Some mornings I went to ground school classes where I studied airplane flight characteristics, Morse code (sending and receiving at least eight words per minute was required), powerplant characteristics, and hydraulic system mechanics.

Dead reckoning navigation was critical knowledge for pilots, and I learned how to use the E-6B manual flight computer, also known as a circular slide rule and nicknamed the "whiz wheel." It was invented and patented in the United States by Navy Lt. Philip Dalton in the late 1930s, and the name comes from its original part number for the U.S. Army Air Corps. The E-6B was introduced to the Army in 1940, but it took Pearl Harbor for the Army Air Forces (as the former "Army

Air Corps" was renamed on June 20, 1941) to place a large order. Over 400,000 E-6Bs were manufactured during World War II.[2]

Meteorology, the theory of flight, and aircraft armament were the other courses we were taught. In the afternoon, we flew one and one-half hours with an instructor pilot who generally had four students assigned to them. Students that failed the academics or did not solo by the tenth hour were washed out of flight training and then sent to RCAF infantry units as ground soldiers. After sixty hours of elementary instruction, I was ready for my next training assignment.

An interesting fact about recruiting the Americans into the RCAF as student pilots was that the mandatory oath of allegiance to the current reigning King George VI had been waived because he was the great-great-great-great-grandson of George III who was the British monarch during the Revolutionary War with the United States colonies.

Dad at 19 years old sitting in a Fleet Finch IIB

Graduating in early March of 1942 in the top thirty percent of

carrying my duffle bag while also holding a cloth OD green bag over my shoulder that contained my leather flight jacket, lace-up boots, gloves, helmet with an oxygen mask, headphones, and throat microphone. I finally reached my assigned room and opened the door.

Inside the small smoke-filled stateroom were seven young RCAF pilot officers who were going to England to fly for the British units. I was the only "Yank" in the room, and we all introduced ourselves and shook hands. There were two large metal bunks bolted to the floor, each containing four beds. The last remaining unoccupied mattress was on top, so I threw my duffle bag and gear bag on it and climbed up and stretched out.

Pilot Officer Oliver White lying on the top bunk across from me said, "Stan, where are you from in the US?"

"I'm from a small town in southern Ohio called Oak Hill. Where is your home?" I asked.

"I'm from Downsview, Canada, near Toronto, and my dad is a design engineer at the DeHavilland Aircraft Company and works on the Mosquito 'B' model MkIV light bomber. That's how I became interested in flying. What brought you to RCAF flight training, Stan?"

"My father is the postmaster at the local post office, and in 1932 when I was ten-years-old, he took my mother, younger sister, and me to the county fair in Jackson, Ohio. There was a barnstorming pilot giving rides in his WWI Curtiss JN-4 Jenny airplane for a dollar a person. After pleading with my dad to let me ride, he relented, and the pilot put my sister Sue and me together in the back seat and flew us around for about ten minutes. From then on, I knew that someday I was going to be a pilot. After attending Ohio State University for one year, I heard about the Canadian flight training program and signed up for it, and here I am."

my flight training class, I was commissioned a Pilot Officer, which was the equivalent rank of a USAAF second lieutenant and my pay increased from $2.25 per day ($67.50 monthly) to $6.25 per day ($187.50 monthly). I traveled by troop train to Halifax, Nova Scotia, arriving at the Cunard ship terminal located at Pier 21. The train trip from Hamilton, Canada, was eight hundred six miles and took nearly eighteen hours. It was an exhausting trip sitting on the hard wooden bench for that length of time as we passed through Ottawa, Montreal, and Quebec City, but I was excited to be going overseas, so I quietly endured the journey. After waiting two days in a large metal shed the length of two football fields, I boarded the RMS Queen Mary, bound for Southampton, England.

The enormous ocean liner carrying fifteen thousand Canadian military personnel plus two thousand crewmembers was part of a large naval convoy of hastily built Liberty ships traveling together and zig-zagging along the way because of the fear of being torpedoed by German U-boats patrolling the North Atlantic in wolf packs. Adolph Hitler had placed a reward of $250,000 on the mighty ship for any Nazi commander who sank her. The trip took nearly two weeks, although the Queen Mary was capable of making the ocean crossing in four days if she had been sailing alone and did not have to elude enemy submarines. Painted a dull grey color to avoid easily being seen on the horizon, she was nicknamed the "Grey Ghost." All of her luxurious furnishings, including paintings, carpet, crystal chandeliers, and draperies, had been removed as she was stripped down to accommodate the troops.[3]

Wearing my heavy blue RCAF overcoat with a bright yellow cork-filled Mae West life preserver around my neck, I pushed my way through the crowded main deck corridor of the immense ocean liner

Then I asked, "When will we get to eat something? I haven't had anything since early this morning at Pier 21's troop canteen, and I am hungry."

Oliver answered, "Probably not until tomorrow morning at breakfast because the dining room is closed until then as we get underway. It's located several floors below us and, once opened, will operate twenty-four hours a day as everyone eats in shifts. I've heard there is a nicely furnished lounge for officers somewhere on the main deck. Do you play bridge?"

"No, but I'm willing to learn if you will teach me," I replied.

Then we began to feel the deep vibration of the enormous engines as the ship pulled away from the dock. Over a loudspeaker mounted in the hallway, we heard, "Attention, everyone. Attention. In thirty minutes, you will hear three loud blasts coming from a klaxon, which is the signal for an abandon ship drill. You will proceed to your designated area and wait for the all-clear message to be given to you. In the event of a real emergency, you will hear an announcement saying, 'Abandon ship. Abandon ship. Abandon ship. This is no drill.' You must then quickly proceed to the lifeboats. They will only hold twenty-five percent of the passengers and crew, so the remainder of you will need to climb aboard any available inflatable rafts or float in the water in your Mae West life jackets. If you are among the unfortunate ones to be floating in the ice-cold water, you will only have approximately fifteen minutes before you can no longer move because of hypothermia. Then, you will lose consciousness and drown."

Suddenly, the grim reality of war struck me, and I was no longer hungry. I also vowed to do whatever was necessary to get in a lifeboat and not end up being one of the unfortunate ones floating in the water. Over the next two weeks, emergency drills were called both day and night, and we all quickly scrambled to our designated areas wearing our life preservers.

The next morning at 0400 hours, breakfast was announced over the loudspeaker, and we prepared to move to the dining room as our meal shift number was called. However, it was three hours later before my cabin mates and I were finally able to eat. The food was delicious, filling, and plentiful, and I stuck an apple and a banana in my overcoat pockets to eat later. Afterward, we went out on the deck, smoked, and watched the immense number of ships surrounding the RMS Queen Mary traveling eastward to the British Isles.

Later we found the officers' lounge, and Oliver and two other of our cabinmates taught me how to play bridge. For the remainder of the voyage, our days consisted of sleeping, eating, responding to abandon ship drills, and playing bridge in the officers' lounge. By the time we docked at Southhampton, England, I was reasonably good at the card game and continued to play it throughout my life.

CHAPTER 2

RAF, MARCH 1942

From Southhampton, where the RMS Titanic departed on her ill-fated voyage in 1912, I rode a crowded smoke-filled troop train for about two hours (eighty-nine miles) northeast to Waterloo train station in central London. It was a huge railway terminal with twenty-four separate platforms built under an opaque glass, and steel beam reinforced roof. One year earlier, during the London blitz, approximately ten thousand Londoners sought shelter in the nearby underground bunker facility during the fifty-seven days of continuous bombing by the German Luftwaffe.

Changing trains, I traveled for another hour, only covering nineteen miles and arrived at my new assignment in Debden, England. Opened in April 1937, it was first used exclusively by the Royal Air Force. Two hard-surface runways were laid in 1940, although we usually took off and landed using the large grassy areas adjacent to them.

On January 28, 1941, the station was visited by King George VI and Queen Elizabeth. Ironically, the following month, during a heavy rainstorm and low visibility, a German Luftwaffe pilot landed his Bf-109 Messerschmidt airplane on the main runway and taxied to the control tower, at which point he realized his mistake, and hurriedly turned around and took off from the concrete taxiway. He disappeared into the clouds and was never seen again.

At the Advanced Flying Unit 287 RAF Squadron Training Unit #5, I checked in at the headquarters building. I was assigned a metal bed in a long concrete pilot barrack, which had coal-fired pot-bellied stoves arranged every twenty feet along the walls to provide warmth. Next to the bed was a tall steel wall locker where I hung my extra uniform and flight clothes. I had no civvies, since all American Eagle pilots were required to wear only their RAF uniforms everywhere on and off the station. My "kit," as the British called the rest of my clothing, and shaving gear was stored in a footlocker under the bed.

After unpacking and settling in, I went to the pilot's lounge next to headquarters, where I met several other American pilots who had just returned from flying Spitfires on bomber escort missions over France. Deep leather chairs were placed against the walls of the lounge, and there were about a dozen wooden card tables with straight back chairs arranged in the middle of the room. The large windows were covered with blackout curtains, and three black double-ring dartboards were mounted between several of them. A regulation size pool and a billiard table was located at one end of the room with balls and cues neatly arranged in a wall-mounted holder. Several tables had chess, checker, and backgammon sets on them. Two large coal-fired pot-bellied stoves warmed the area. The pilot lounge was the center of activity whenever pilots were not flying, sleeping, or eating in the nearby officers' mess hall. Although not as large, it reminded me of the old student union building at Ohio State University, which I had attended two years earlier.

About an hour later, I began to hear the increasingly loud sound of many fighter aircraft (called "kites" by both the British and Americans)

Heavily armed with one thirty-millimeter MK-108 cannon firing through the propeller shaft with a cyclic rate of fire of 650 rounds per minute and two thirteen-millimeter MG-131 machine guns mounted in the cowling with a cyclic rate of fire of 900 rounds per minute, the airplane was a formidable fighter aircraft responsible for shooting down many British and American airplanes. My training aircraft had only one British Vickers .303 caliber machine gun with a cyclic rate of fire of 500 rounds per minute which was used for gunnery practice, so we were woefully outclassed by the enemy airplane's superior armament, and its ability to fly one hundred forty-four miles per hour faster than we could.

Similar to my Canadian flight training schedule, the new American pilots and I alternated between having classroom instruction in the morning and flight training in the afternoon. The advanced training took about eighty hours, and the primary focus was on combat aerobatic maneuvers, dead reckoning navigation, aerial gunnery, instrument landings, and enemy aircraft recognition. Critical to my wartime survival was my complete mastery of the fighter combat aerobatic maneuvers. Those included performing inside and outside loops, slow rolls, snap rolls, verticle reverses, chandelles, Immelmans, split Ss, and Cuban 8s. Assigned to an experienced RAF flight lieutenant (pronounced leftenant) instructor pilot who was the equivalent to a USAAF captain, we flew for two hours every day except when the heavy rain and low visibility prevented it.

returning to the airfield. Going outside, I watched as dozens of Spitfires and Hawker Hurricanes entered the traffic pattern and began to land in a single file on the paved runways. Then I was surprised to see many planes landing three abreast on the open grassy area next to them. The kites slowly taxied toward us and soon sat on the grass parking area near the flight operations building. Once their engines were shut off, British ground crews called fitters hurriedly drove to the airplanes and began to refuel each one from large tanker trucks. Enlisted personnel arrived in three-ton lorries, and from large wooden ammo boxes began to rearm the machine guns and twenty-millimeter cannons with long rows of metal linked ammunition. Others removed the elliptically shaped gun camera film canisters and replaced them with fresh ones.

After refueling and rearming the kites, the fitters stuck a large screwdriver in the ground next to the left landing gear tire to signify the airplane was ready to fly combat missions again. I was impressed with the speed and efficiency of the whole operation and soon met the pilots as they boisterously came into the lounge. Most of the American pilots were in their early twenties like me. However, there were several older ones in their thirties who I learned were former airline pilots and crop dusters who had sprayed chemicals low level over farm fields, mostly in California and the southern United States.

In a few days, I began flying the Miles Master with an instructor. It was a tandem-seat monoplane, which was a fully aerobatic high-performance trainer with an eight hundred seventy horsepower engine and a top speed of two hundred and forty-two miles per hour. Because I now was in the war zone, my instructor and I had to be very careful and extremely watchful while flying training missions so as not to encounter any German Bf-109 Messerschmitts, which were capable of flying three hundred eighty-six miles per hour.[4]

RAF Student Classroom

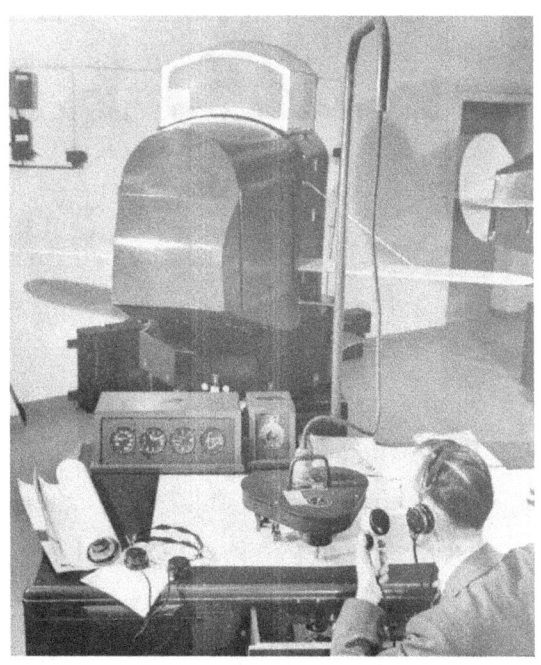

Link Instrument Trainer

One afternoon on a solo flight, I flew over Sherwood Forest (of Robin Hood fame) near Nottingham, and to my amazement, there were three tall oil well drilling rigs below. Circling low-level overhead, I saw each one had a hardhat roughneck crew busily working on the raised wooden platform under camouflage netting. On my third pass above them, someone below fired a red Very pistol flare close in front of my propeller, and I immediately departed the area, deciding that discretion was the better part of valor. Many years later, after retiring in Waco, Texas, I learned the drilling crews were a small group of forty-two American oilfield workers from Oklahoma who had been recruited and secretly brought to England to increase the oil production output and support the British war effort.

Known as "The English Project," it was completed in March 1944 when the Americans finished drilling one hundred six new wells with ninety-four producing oil. England's petroleum production increased from three hundred barrels a day to more than three thousand barrels per day, thanks to the hard-working and diligent "Yanks." Living in Kelham Hall, a nearby isolated Anglican Monastery, their cover story was that they were building a movie set to film an American western starring John Wayne and Maureen O'Hara. That was a great story but completely false.[5]

Total flight training time was approximately two-hundred hours for the complete RAF fighter pilot course, then I transitioned into the Spitfire, which lasted another sixty hours. Early model Spitfires had a manually operated hydraulic pump to raise and lower the landing gear. Immediately after taking off, I had to hold the control stick in my left hand while I vigorously pumped the landing gear handle up and down with my right hand to raise the landing gear; this generally caused my aircraft to porpoise wildly through the air for a while.

Before landing, the same procedure occurred while I pumped the gear down. Soon new models of the Spitfires arrived with electric-actuated, hydraulically-driven landing gear, which eliminated the strange takeoff and landing behavior of the first model. In May of 1942, I completed all of my flight training and, at a graduation ceremony, was given my RAF wings and promoted to the rank of Flying Officer (equivalent to a 1st Lieutenant).

Typical presentation of RAF wings ceremony.

Initially flying Hawker Hurricanes and later Supermarine Spitfires, it was quickly followed by Number 121 RAF Squadron in May 1941 and then No. 133 RAF Squadron in July 1941. Before their transfer to the USAAF, the three Eagle Squadrons had a total of one hundred seven pilots killed and thirty-four captured by the Germans, a fifty-eight percent loss ratio.

Miles Masters over Debden, England

CHAPTER 3

THE WAR IN EUROPE

*"Never in the field of human conflict
was so much owed by so many to so few."*
WINSTON CHURCHILL, 1940[6]

From the first part of May through September 29, 1942, RAF Debden airfield was used by Number 71, 121 and 133 Eagle Squadrons who were later transferred to the United States Army Air Force's Eighth Air Force and assigned the USAAF designation of Station #356. It was nicknamed "The Eagle's Nest" because the three American fighter squadrons, containing two hundred fifty-three pilots, were all based there.

The Eagle Squadrons were RAF fighter squadrons, manned by American's who volunteered to serve as pilots before Nazi Germany declared war against the United States in December 1941. At the time, U.S. citizens were prohibited from serving in the armed forces of a foreign power, upon penalty of losing their citizenship. The first unit was accepted by the RAF in July 1940, and Number 71 RAF Squadron was formed in September 1940, becoming operational in February 1941.

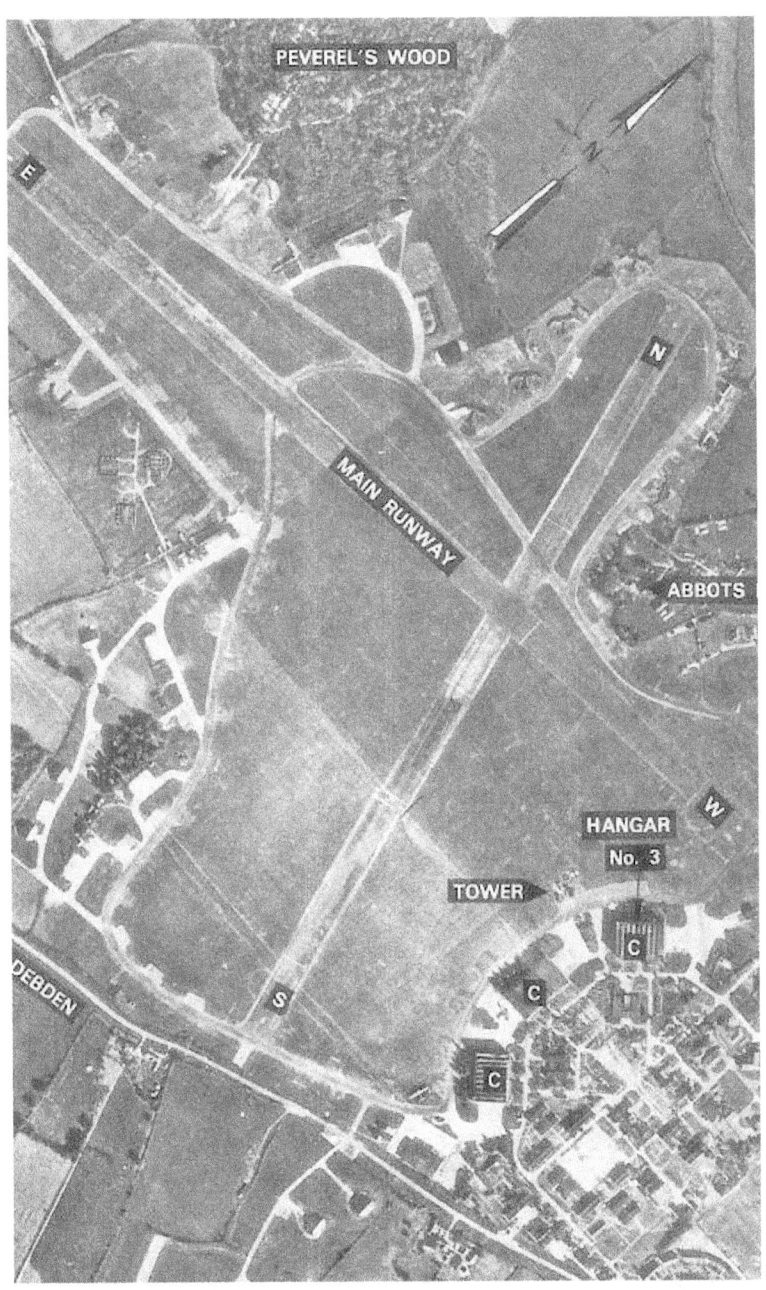

RAF Debden Airfield

Eagle Squadron Patch

Stan Corvin (left) is 20 years old.

Supermarine Spitfire

Dense fog was a serious problem for pilots landing at Debden airfield because there were no instrument landing systems (ILS) or ground control approach (GCA) available at the time. Generally, at night the runways and surrounding area were under a mandatory blackout restriction, so the runway lights were never to be used. Landing after dark was a dangerous and harrowing experience, and several pilots died after crashing on the darkened airfield.

Bad weather plagued us all the time and restricted our flight capabilities. Britain has a temperate maritime climate, which means that it has mild temperatures generally no lower than 32ºF in winter and no higher than 90ºF in summer. It also means that year-round it is very humid with lots of fog. The proximity to the Atlantic Ocean, its northern latitude, and the warming of the waters around the landmass by the Gulf Stream significantly affect its weather patterns since England is an island about the size of Wyoming in the USA. Compared with the other landmasses in the northern hemisphere, it is small. Therefore it is more influenced by the ocean when compared with other European countries because it is surrounded by the Atlantic Ocean to the west, the English Channel to the south, and the North Sea to the east.

The Gulf Stream, also known locally as the North Atlantic Drift, is a warm current that flows across the Atlantic Ocean from the more temperate seas of the Caribbean and makes West-European countries considerably warmer than they would be otherwise. The Gulf Stream is the main ocean current that affects Britain and warms it by about 3º to 7º degrees Fahrenheit. That is one reason why Britain often receives so much wet weather.[7]

The next day after graduation, I traveled northeast by train to Kirton-in-Lindsey, England, and was assigned to the 121st Eagle

Squadron, which had recently moved there along with the 71st Eagle Squadron. I began flying a turbocharged Hawker Hurricane MK IIC fighter equipped with four twenty millimeter Hispanos cannons mounted two in each wing. Capable of firing two thousand four hundred rounds per minute (six hundred per gun), the "Hawker" was a very stable gun platform. Their deadly long-range weapons were responsible for it shooting down more enemy aircraft during the Battle of Britain than the Spitfires.

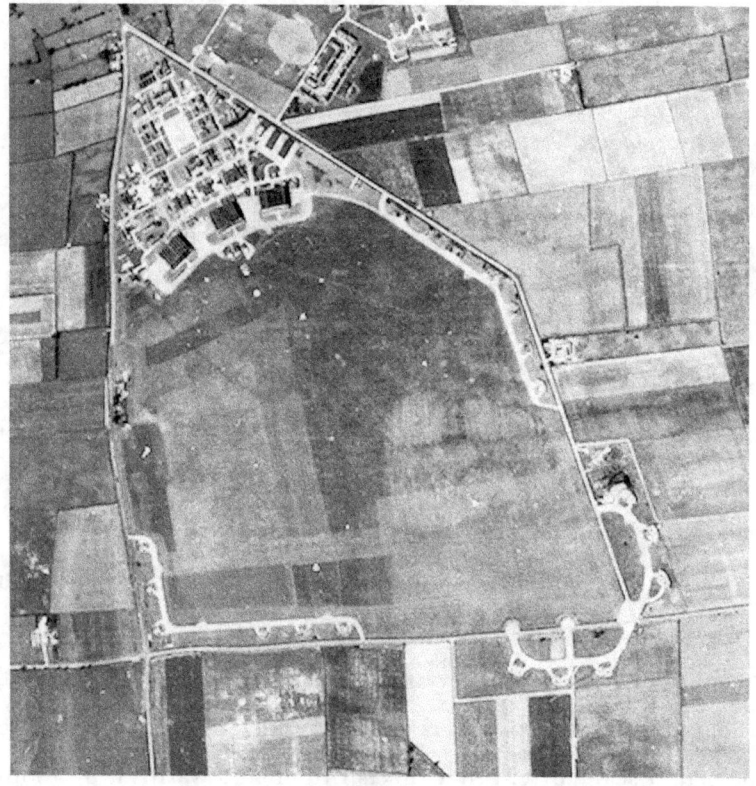

Kirton-in-Lindsey Airfield

The monocoque airplane fuselage was covered in heavy Irish linen fabric painted with butyrate dope and stretched tightly over an oak wooden slatted frame, a construction technique derived from early biplanes. Frequently, a German Messerschmitt's 30-millimeter cannon projectile hitting the fabric and wood supporting structure passed right through without exploding or doing severe damage, and the hole was quickly patched.

After starting the engine, I immediately had to put on my oxygen mask because the noxious fumes coming from the forward-mounted exhaust pipes filled the cockpit. However, my main concern was the large fuel tank that was mounted behind the engine but in front of the cockpit where I sat. If enemy bullets hit it, the ensuing fireball would immediately engulf the cockpit and quickly incinerate me. Once in a dogfight with a German Messerschmitt, one of the pilots in my unit had been horribly burned before he was able to bail out of the aircraft. The pain was so severe he took out his British Webley-Scott .455 caliber pistol and committed suicide while floating down in his parachute.

Hawker Hurricane with four Hispano 20 mm Cannons

The Hawker Hurricane was a very uncomfortable airplane to fly. The cockpit was so narrow that my shoulders rubbed against the sides while I continuously looked from side to side and above for enemy fighters. Although, my chamois lined leather flying helmet, with its dual earphone radio headset, covering my ears was somewhat comfortable, it was tight because a rubber oxygen mask covered my nose and mouth. Containing the radio's microphone, it left deep crease marks on my face when I removed it after flying for several hours.

During the early stages of WWII, the airplane had a De Havilland Aircraft Company propeller with only two pitch settings, take-off, and cruise. That was a drawback in aerial combat because the motor was either overspeeding or else was not being used to its full potential. However, by late 1941, every Spitfire and Hurricane in service had been converted with three-blade constant-speed propellers—1,051 aircraft in all. The new propellers gave the RAF fighter pilots a significant extra performance margin when any slight advantage in altitude, speed, or climb rate could mean the difference between life or death.[8]

CHAPTER 4

CALAIS TO DUNKIRK MISSION

Sitting on my bunk, I pulled on my heavy boots, and fleece-lined leather flying jacket, stepped into my parachute harness securely fastening it, then put on my inflatable Mae West life preserver. I had a light breakfast of coffee, toast, and orange juice then returned to my pilot's barrack. I was definitely keyed-up because today was going to be my first actual combat mission after having completed all of my flight training.

Looking at the bunk next to mine with the mattress rolled up and the springs exposed, I kept thinking about my friend Flying Officer Alan Johnson. He was killed a few days earlier on his first mission flying convoy escort for British ships crossing the English Channel. Flying at 10,000 feet with two other Hawker Hurricanes, his element was attacked from above by nine Focke-Wulf 190 A-3s, part of the German's *Jagdwaffe* (Fighter Force). The Nazi aircraft were equipped with BMW fourteen cylinder radial engines, which had 1,677 horsepower and a top speed at sea level of 352 mph. Their armament consisted of four 7.92 mm machine guns synchronized to fire through the propeller arc. They also had two outboard wing-mounted 20 mm cannons.

Alan's plane was attacked from behind and essentially shredded by the massive firepower of an attacking FW-190. Pilots witnessing the event said the Hurricane immediately burst into flames and spiraled down, hitting the ocean below. Standing by his bed with a lump in my throat, I decided then not to make friends with any other pilots.

Walking over to the dispersal hut, a term the British used to describe our central briefing quonset building, I saw my Red flight group climbing into an open jeep and ran to join them. Driving to the aircraft parking area, we stopped in front of our four Hurricanes, and Flight Lieutenant William Andrews, our leader, along with the other two pilots, and I jumped out. We ran and climbed into our cockpits assisted by our "fitters" (crew chiefs) and started our engines. We were Red Flight, and I was going to be flying on the left (port) side of our leader once we took off from a four-ship echelon formation, which was part of a sixteen aircraft group. My call sign was Red One. To my left was my friend Pilot Officer Donald Williams, call sign Red Two. To his left was Pilot Officer Harold Faulkner, call sign Red Three. Although there were two paved runways, usually large numbers of airplanes took off on the grassy expanses beside them.

It was early July 1942, and we were assigned the duty of flying what was known as a "Rhubarb" fighter sweep from Calais, France, to Dunkirk. The purpose of our mission was to search out and destroy any enemy fixed gun emplacements, anti-aircraft facilities, and heavy equipment along the coastal region between the two towns, which were only thirty miles apart.

The British evacuated 338,200 Allied troops off the beach two years earlier on June 4, 1940, and they abandoned enough equipment to outfit eight to ten Wehrmacht infantry divisions. Left behind were millions of rounds of ammunition, eight hundred and eight

"Red Flight, this is Red Leader, I'll begin my takeoff roll in thirty seconds, and we'll depart in an echelon formation. Watch for my hand signals and maintain radio silence. Out."

Soon he raised his left hand above the open cockpit and held it there, then pumped it up and down and lowered it, which was the signal for us to increase power and begin our rollout for takeoff. With my left hand on the throttle handle, I slowly increased it to three thousand RPMs and then reached over and increased the boost control cutout to twelve pounds of boost while slightly pressing on the right rudder pedal with my boot. I needed to do that to counter the 1,280 horsepower Merlin 12 cylinder engine torque, which tended to pull the aircraft to the left. Within seconds the tail lifted off the ground, and I was looking over the nose of the airplane.

Approaching eighty knots, I saw Red Lead lift off the ground and began to climb. As our speed increased, I maintained my relative position to him, which was to his left and slightly behind approximately one-half an aircraft length. After reaching 15,000 feet in about five minutes, we leveled off, and I reduced my throttle to 2,850 RPM for three minutes to allow the engine to cool down to 90°C. After a few minutes, I increased it to 3,000 RPM for the remainder of the mission as we climbed to 20,000 feet and flew south at approximately 326 miles per hour to London then made a slow left echelon turn to a heading of 125° to Calais, France arriving there one hour after takeoff.

Over the English Channel, the other flight elements departed to their assigned target area of operations (AOs), and we quickly descended to two thousand feet spreading out in a wide combat echelon. Red Lead came on the radio and said, "Arm your weapons, Red Flight."

Immediately I rotated the brass bezel to the fire position on the trigger button at the top left of the round flight yoke allowing me to

artillery pieces, five hundred anti-aircraft guns, eight hundred and fifty anti-tank guns, eleven thousand machine guns, seven hundred tanks, twenty thousand motorcycles, and forty-five thousand cars and lorries. Ironically, at the time of the British evacuation, the total military equipment available in England was only sufficient to equip two infantry divisions.

Once the German high command marched the captured British, French, Belgium, Canadian, and Polish POWs east one thousand miles, they distributed all of the serviceable allied weapons and equipment to Nazi units in anticipation of an imminent attack from England.

We had a pilot briefing at headquarters about our mission before going to our airplanes. Then Flight Lieutenant Andrews met with the three of us at breakfast to discuss how we would conduct our fighter sweep once we arrived in the coastal area of Calais and to tell us which radio frequency we were to be assigned.

The aircraft were equipped with American made Bendix Radio Corporation VHF (very high-frequency) units transmitting and receiving only on four preselected channels A, B, C and D. Utilizing the model TR 5043 radio, the small tuner box was mounted in the upper-left edge of the airplane's instrument panel and consisted of an on/off button on top plus four red push buttons; one for each frequency.[9]

A large black toggle switch at the bottom of the panel allowed me to transmit and receive on the assigned channel. Since all the Spitfires, Hawker Hurricanes, and the towers were equipped with the same communication systems; radio discipline was extremely important so that everyone could talk to each other and the towers as needed without hogging a particular frequency.

fire all four of my Hispano 20 mm cannons at targets.

Hawker Hurrican Stick with Brass Cannon Firing Button

"Let's spread out now and good hunting, mates. We'll rendezvous in fifteen minutes at our departure point (DP) and return to our station."

I dropped down to one thousand feet altitude and began my hunt for the enemy. Seeing railroad tracks near the coastline, I followed them and soon saw a parked train with a dozen cargo cars behind it and several German soldiers standing alongside them. Passing overhead, I saw multiple muzzle flashes as they began to fire their weapons at me and suddenly realized I really was flying in a combat environment. Tightly turning 180°, I lined up in front of the railroad engine and pushed the Hurricanes brass trigger button.

"Holy shit!" I said aloud as I was stunned by the deafening roar from all four 20 mm cannons and saw the tracers hit the ground in front of the engine and then multiple flashes as the exploding one-forth pound projectiles began to hit their target. Passing overhead, I quickly climbed to one thousand feet, performed a split "S" turn, reversed course, and in a steep dive attacked from the opposite direction firing into the cargo cars and the Wehrmacht (*German: Defense Force*) soldiers. Many fell, and others began to run away. Then dozens of soldiers started pouring out of the cars which were being used for troop transports.

Making another split "S" at the top of my one thousand foot climb, I dived towards them shooting continuously as I descended. Suddenly, the four cannons stopped firing, and for a second, I assumed they had malfunctioned. Then I realized that I had run out of ammunition after approximately ten seconds of shooting.

"Well, hell!" I thought as I began to climb up to 15,000 feet and headed out over the water to the British coast. My total time over the target (TOT) was approximately three minutes from finding the railroad train and soldiers, attacking them, and expending all of my ammunition. Because of the German atrocities, I had heard about, I never considered the enemy soldiers as anything more than violent butchers incapable of feeling any human compassion, so I was determined to kill as many of them as I could, and I certainly succeeded.

Circling at the departure point, it occurred to me that if any German fighters attacked me, I was utterly defenseless. I reached up and flipped the black transmit toggle switch on my radio saying, "Red Lead, this is Red One. I am at the departure point. Over."

"Roger, Red One, climb to the assigned altitude and wait while we rendezvous with you. Out," Red Lead responded.

Soon I saw two Hurricanes approaching from the Dunkirk area of the beach. Red leader and Red Three pulled alongside me and lead pointed to the northeast, indicating we were to head back to England. My friend Donald Williams was not with them.

After flying over the English Channel for a few minutes, we encountered a massive rain storm on the leading edge of a cold front moving in from the North Atlantic, and Red Lead keyed his microphone briefly, saying, "Mates, tuck in close to me. Out."

We moved closer until our wingtips were only two or three feet apart and flew that way on a direct heading to our airfield at Kirton-in-Lindsey. Approaching our airfield after an hour's flight, visibility was very poor. I was sweating profusely from the stress of flying in such a tight formation and had a severe crick in my neck from staring intently at Red Lead's aircraft a few feet to the right and in front of me. Reaching the base, he indicated with a hand gesture for us to lower our landing gear, and through the rain and broken cloud cover below, I saw the grassy open airfield.

Simultaneously touching down, all three Hurricanes taxied to the parking area, and we shut off our engines. Three canvas-covered lorries and a refueling truck pulled up to our aircraft, and the fitters jumped out and began to work quickly, refueling and rearming the planes. A big ruddy-faced British crew chief climbed up on my wing and unfurled a large black umbrella while indicating for me to open the canopy. After sliding it back, he casually saluted with his left hand. After returning it, I stiffly climbed out of the cockpit, ran over to the covered lorry, and got in, sitting down beside Flight Lieutenant Andrews.

"What happened to Red Two, Pilot Officer Donald Williams?" I asked.

Staring down at the wooden floor he quietly said, "I saw Donald in a nearly vertical dive attacking a German fixed gun position in the dunes near the Dunkirk beach. Then a Mauser Flakvierling *(German: quadruple flak)* quad-mounted 37 mm antiaircraft gun, which was hidden under a nearby camouflage net opened up on him. The one-pound ten-ounce exploding projectiles hit his canopy area, killing him instantly. I saw his kite prang almost on top of the gun position and explode in a fireball. I rolled in and fired all of my cannon rounds at the AA gun, destroying it and killing the German soldiers who were operating the gun."[10]

Leaning back against the truck's slat sideboards, I grimly thought, "This isn't nearly as glamorous as Tyrone Power's movie a *Yank in the RAF* I saw in the theater at Columbus, Ohio." Arriving at the dispersal hut, the three of us got out of the lorry and went in for a debriefing by the intelligence officer. Because it was still raining heavily, we were unable to take off and return to the Calais and Dunkirk beaches.

For the next two months, our missions included escorting bombers into France and Germany, flying more rhubarb and circus sorties, and flying maritime convoy escort patrols. Then on July 31, 1942, I was part of a one hundred thirty-three aircraft flight of Spitfires and Hurricanes escorting an enormous bomber formation to Abbeville, France. Over Berck-sur-Mer, located twenty-nine miles north of the target area, we were attacked by a large group of Messersmith Bf-109s. In the ensuing dogfight Luftwaffe "Ace" Oberleutnant Rudolf Pflanz, who had previously shot down fifty-two allied aircraft was himself, shot down and killed. We learned that bit of information from the intelligence officer debriefing after we returned to our base at Kirton-in-Lindsey. I have no idea how they knew so quickly. Still, it told me that there must have been excellent coordination between the British and the French underground resistance fighters. Probably because General Charles de Gaulle, who had been evacuated two years earlier to London, England was in charge of all "Free French" forces and had secret lines of communications with them.

CHAPTER 5

EAGLES NO MORE

On September 12, 1942, the three Eagle Squadrons (71st, 121st, and the 133rd) transferred to the United States Army Air Forces (USAAF), becoming the 334th, 335th and 336th Fighter Squadrons in the 4th Fighter Group, which was part of the Eighth Fighter Command. Of the three fighter squadrons, only one hundred forty-six pilots were still alive, and thankfully I was one of them. Notwithstanding our heavy losses, we ultimately destroyed more enemy aircraft in the air and on the ground than any other fighter group in the Eighth Air Force. My unit the 121st became the 335th fighter squadron, and I transitioned (learned to fly) into the Supermarine Spitfires. Upon being transferred to the American group, I was also promoted to a first lieutenant.

Left: Eagle Squadron 121st Chiefs
Right: 335th Fighter Squadron Chiefs

*Transfer of the RAF 71st, 121, 133 Eagle Squadrons
to the 8th USAAF September 1942.
Stan Corvin, Sr. is standing somewhere in the formation.*

*Debden Control Tower,
USAF Officers waiting for the return of the 4th FG aircraft.*

> **OVER TO YOU**
> 10 Stories of Flyers and Flying
> **BY ROALD DAHL**
>
> Here are ten vivid penetrating stories which serve to introduce a fine new talent to the American public. Wing Commander Dahl is a writer whose direct experience of the flyers and the flying of which he writes is tempered by the strength, control and projection of the true craftsman.
>
> All of the stories are concerned, directly or indirectly, with the war in the air and its psychological effect on the gallant young men who deserted the schools, the farms and the factories to fight for the civilized world against the incursions of fascism.
>
> Roald Dahl portrays them with great honesty and brilliance in their moments of tension, fear and courage (as in the moving and savage *Katina*, and *Death of an Old Old Man*), as well as in their moments of relaxation and escape from the rigors of battle (see the touching and hilarious *Madame Rosette* and *Someone Like You*).
>
> It should be emphasized particularly of this sequence of stories, many of them concerned with the fortunes of a common group of characters, that they are not so much stories about the flying of airplanes as they are about a group of human beings with whom, through the author's skill, the reader becomes intimately acquainted. It is more than probable that several of these stories will in the course of time take an honored place in the permanent literature of the air. $2.50

Captain Corvin's signature in a book he carried during WWII.

Spitfire Of the 31st Fighter Group 309th Fighter Squadron

Mostly our missions were to escort Boeing B-17 Flying Fortress bombers and Consolidated B-24 Liberator bombers that were attacking industrial factories, submarine pens, V-2 rocket sites, and other targets in France and Germany. Sometimes we went out with a small number of bombers to intentionally draw up the enemy's fighters so we could destroy them in aerial dogfight combat. As a flight leader now, at times with two other aircraft, I attacked the German Luftwaffe infrastructure by strafing and dive-bombing their airfields and planes. We also hit numerous enemy ground troops, Panzer tank columns, supply depots, bridges, rail lines, and trains.

In early November 1942, I was assigned to the 309th Fighter Squadron, 31st Fighter Group, which was part of the new 12th Air Force. We were soon deployed to the RAF airfield at Gibraltar as part of the *Operation Torch* invasion force, where we lived in squad tents, and flew out of former Vichy French airfields in Algeria. Then advancing east across Algeria and Tunisia during the massive North African Campaign, we supported the United States Fifth Army, which stopped Field Marshal Rommel's tank corp advance against the allied positions.

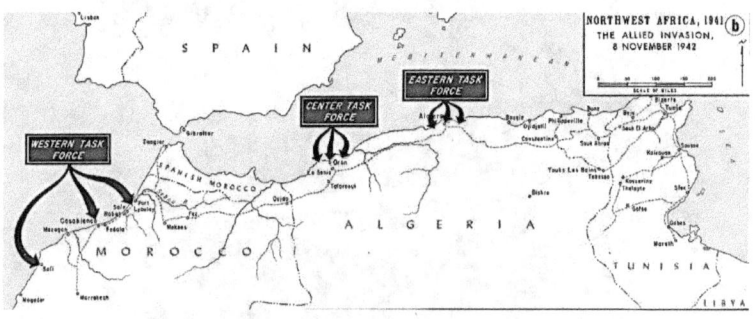

Operation Torch Invasion Plan

From November 8–10, 1942, the United States and Britain launched an amphibious operation against North Africa, at the Vichy French-held territories of Algeria and Morocco. That beach landing, code-named "Operation Torch," was the result of British and American planning about the future course of the Allied war strategy. This amphibious action postponed their landing in France until June 6, 1944, "D" day. Still, it allowed the United States to complete the mobilization of its vast industrial and manpower resources for the air and ground battles of 1944.[11]

My squadron and I flew British RAF marked Supermarine Spitfires providing air support for Allied Forces as the invasion of Italy began with the capture of Sicily and the landings by Allied forces in Fascist Italy. Moving north with the ground troops, we supported the Fifth Army during the Italian Campaign. Allied bomber forces operating from Italy began bombing Axis petroleum and communications facilities in central Europe, and the squadron was re-equipped with the North American P-51D Mustang to replace the shorter-ranged Spitfires.

Next to the towering Rock of Gibraltar, we sat on benches in a large tent with its sides folded up training for the Mustang, which consisted of a one-hour classroom orientation of its starting procedures, aircraft takeoff, and landing specifications. The outside air temperature (OAT) was about 60°F, so all the pilots were wearing their shearling-lined leather flight jackets. After the instruction, thirty pilots and I walked approximately one-quarter of a mile to the flight line where all the aircraft were parked. We were instructed to take off in a single file and fly by ourselves for approximately two hours over the Gibraltar strait to familiarize ourselves with the flight characteristics of the high-performance airplane. It was significantly faster than anything that I had flown up to that point, and I had a lot of fun practicing rolls, loops, Immelmans, and other acrobatic maneuvers out over the Atlantic Ocean and the Mediterranean Sea before returning and landing at the airfield.

Equipped with a 1,380 hp Rolls-Royce licensed Packard twelve-cylinder engine, it became known as the high altitude Merlin-Mustang. The radiator containing a mixture of 70% water and 30% ethylene glycol coolant was pressurized; however, it was mounted on the underbelly of the fuselage and was very susceptible to being hit by enemy ground fire. If struck by bullets, the engine would seize up within a few minutes as the coolant was lost. So there always was a danger of my having to bail out anytime I attacked gun emplacements or truck convoys, which usually had quad mounted anti-aircraft weapons accompanying them.

RAF/USAAF Spitfires at Gibraltar Airfield - Operation Torch

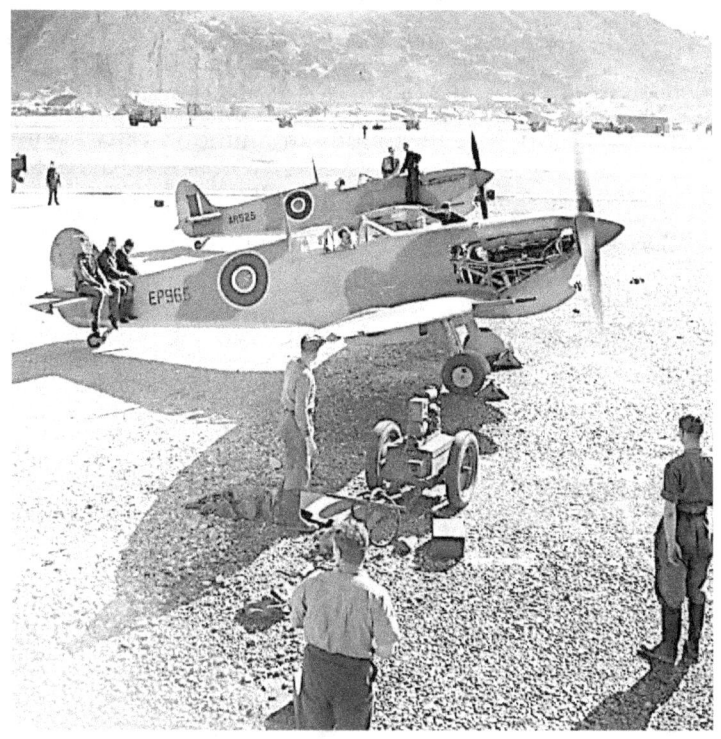

USAAF flown Supermarine Spitfire Mark Vs in Gibraltar for Operation Torch undergoing an engine test before the invasion on November 8th.

The Mustang had a maximum speed of 440 mph at 25,000 feet and cruised at 362 mph. So with a range of 1650 nautical miles (with small external tanks), I could fly for approximately four and one-half hours before refueling. The service ceiling of 41,900 feet allowed me to engage successfully in high-altitude dogfights with German Messerschmitt Bf-109s. Over Tunisia, I shot down my first one by attacking from above and behind him as he and a wingman flew in close air support of a large German "Afrika Korps" troop transport column. One week later, over southern Italy, I shot down my second enemy fighter, a Fascist Italian Macchi C202 Folgore.

The P-51D was equipped with six machine guns, three in each wing. The guns were manually charged on the ground and fired simultaneously when the gun trigger switch was pressed on the front of the control stick grip. The maximum ammunition capacity was four hundred rounds for each of the inboard guns and two hundred seventy rounds for the center and outboard guns for a total ammunition load of one thousand eight hundred eighty rounds. The guns were adjusted on the ground for various convergence points based on the tactical needs of the mission. Usually, the convergence point was set to three hundred yards in front of the nose of the airplane. With a rate of fire of six hundred rounds per minute, I had approximately three minutes total shooting time at targets before running out of ammo. Equipped with the K-14 gunsight, mounted on the instrument hood centerline, the sight contained both fixed and gyro-actuated optical systems. It computed the correct lead angle for targets at ranges of 200 – 800 yards.

I continued flying daily fighter sweep missions with the other pilots of the 309th Fighter Squadron, 31st Fighter group until November 1943, when I was promoted to captain. I received new orders to report immediately to the VII Fighter Command, 15th Fighter Group, at Hickam Field in Hawaii. In order to get to my new assignment, I returned to RAF Gibraltar, caught a flight on a C-47 to London then departed on the troopship RMS Queen Elizabeth back to New York City. From there, I flew on a military C-47 to Little Rock, Arkansas, and then to Williams Army Airfield in Chandler, Arizona. Staying overnight in the transit bachelor officer quarters' (BOQ), I left the next day and flew on a military aircraft to San Diego, California, where I boarded a troop-carrying ship that took me to Honolulu.

Arriving there on Christmas Eve 1943, we soon began to receive

a few North American P-51D Mustang fighters and trained for very long-range (VLR) bomber escort missions. One afternoon a few weeks later, my commanding officer Major Darrell Oakes sent a jeep for me along with two other pilots, and we met in his office.

With the three of us sitting in front of his desk, the CO said, "Gentlemen, today I am sending you to Dallas, Texas, to the North American Aviation plant located in nearby Grand Prairie at Hensley Field. You'll begin ferrying new P-51Ds to Coronado, California, where they will be loaded on the aircraft carrier USS Kalinin Bay and taken to the Mariana's islands for offloading and then taken to the nearby Tinian airfield. You will accompany the aircraft, and all be assigned to the 506th Fighter Group or other units, where they will assign you to one of their fighter squadrons. Do you have any questions? If not, you need to pack and go to the operations building at the airfield and catch a flight back to the mainland in three hours."

CHAPTER 6

FERRYING FIGHTERS

On the afternoon of Friday, March 3, 1944, I arrived on a USAAF C-47 at the former Hensley Army Airfield, which one year earlier was renamed Naval Air Station Dallas (NAS-Dallas). Carrying my B-4 bag and flight equipment duffel bag to the operations office next to the tower, I checked in with the major who was the officer in charge (OIC). I explained to him that I was to begin ferrying new P-51Ds from the Grand Prairie North American Aviation factory to the Naval Air Station – North Island, which was located at Coronado, California, in San Diego Bay.

Checking my written orders, he said. "Captain Corvin, you'll be assigned to the Fifth Ferry Group and will fly with about thirty other pilots taking planes to the West Coast. You can stay in the bachelor officer quarters (BOQ). In two days, plan on coming back here Monday morning at 0500 hours for a weather and flight briefing, and then you and four other pilots will take a group of fighters to San Diego. It's 1,232 miles there and will take you approximately four hours total flying time at 10,000 feet. With two seventy-five gallon drop tanks, your range is about 2,000 miles, so you can easily make it there without refueling. You will return here the same day aboard a military C-47. Let me know if you need anything." Then he went over to his desk and sat down.

The plant was called North American Aviation-NAA #1 and had a large cafeteria, a barber and beauty shop, indoor recreational areas with basketball courts, dry cleaning, and laundry facilities that I could use while ferrying the P-51Ds to the West Coast. It operated twenty-four hours a day with three shifts producing twenty-five of the fighters daily.

I walked out front and got into a jeep with a sergeant who took me to the BOQ. There I checked in and was given a room where I unpacked my clothes and hung them up in a closet. It felt strange not to be in a combat zone sleeping in an oil smelling tent next to a noisy flight line. But I was grateful to have the room even if it was only for a few months. Laying down on the bed and pulling my hat over my eyes, I was surprised at how comfortable it was and soon fell asleep fully clothed.

Later that evening, I awoke and went down the hall to the bathrooms where I shaved and showered then put on my slightly wrinkled uniform. Walking about three-quarters of a mile to the side entrance to the plant facility, I showed my USAAF military ID to the guard and entered the biggest building I had ever seen. At nearly 1,000,000 square feet, it was constructed of steel and concrete, and since it was windowless, it was completely air-conditioned and artificially lighted. At the time, it was the largest freestanding climate-controlled structure in the United States. While walking to the cafeteria around the interior perimeter, which was 1,000' by 1,000,' I noticed dozens of people riding three-wheeled bicycles carrying brown paper boxes containing aircraft parts in large baskets mounted in front of the handlebars and attached over the rear wheels. They were carefully peddling between the two long rows of new fighters being built. *"Now, that's not something you see every day,"* I murmured to myself.

Grand Prairie, TX North American Aviation Plant Facility #1

North American Aviation Plant #1 - P-51D Assembly Line 1944

Going by a glass door that said Dry Cleaners/Laundry, I made a mental note to bring my two other uniforms and dirty clothes there after eating. I entered the cafeteria and was astonished at its size. There probably were a thousand men and women sitting at tables eating, laughing, and enjoying themselves. These were the first American women I had seen up close in three years. That was a long time for a twenty-two-year-old guy, so my interest was definitely piqued by these women who appeared to be about college-age.

On my way to the cafeteria line, I passed a table where five young women sat. They all stopped talking and stared at me as I walked by in my pinks-and-greens uniform, crusher hat with a gold eagle on the front and captain bars on each shoulder.

I smiled and said, "Hello, ladies." Then picking up a tray, I began to slide it along the three stainless steel bars in front of the many containers of steaming food thinking, *"Apparently, because this is an aircraft manufacturing plant, wartime food rationing does not apply to this cafeteria."*

Looking around the large room, I saw there were no other military servicemen. There were a few women wearing Women's Air Corps (WAC) uniforms who probably were the airfield tower operators I had seen walking near base ops. Since it was later in the evening, I assumed most of the ferry pilots had already eaten.

After piling two pieces of chicken fried steak smothered in cream gravy with mashed potatoes, green beans, and corn on my plate, I picked up a large slice of pecan pie then paid the cashier. The total cost was ninety-five cents, and the coffee was free.

Looking for a place to sit down, I saw one empty chair at the table where the five young women were quietly whispering to each other and furtively looking at me. Walking over, I politely asked, "May I sit with you, ladies?"

"Sure, have a seat, Captain," the pretty brunette in the middle chair said confidently as she reached out her hand to shake mine.

"I am Joy Heath, and these are my coworkers Ethel, Nancy, Babs, and Mary."

"I'm Stan Corvin, pleased to meet you," I said with a smile as I sat down and reached across the table and shook everyone's hand.

Beginning to wolf down the food, I suddenly realized I was hungry since I'd not eaten anything in almost twenty-four hours.

"Stan, how long have you been a pilot?" Joy asked after leaning over and looking at the wings above my left breast pocket.

"Nearly three years now."

"But the United States has not been at war that long. How's that possible?"

In between bites, I quietly said, "I know. But I joined the Royal Canadian Air Force in Canada about three years ago before the Pearl Harbor attack took place. And after graduating from flight school near Ottawa, I flew for the British Royal Air Force's 121st American Eagle Squadron in England before the US entered the war, and it became the USAAF 335th Squadron."

The girls murmured their approval, and I could tell they were impressed.

"Stan, what are you doing here in Dallas?" Joy asked.

"I just arrived this afternoon, and in two days, I'll begin ferrying the new P-51Ds from here to Coronado, California."

Pausing a moment to think and allowing me to take several bites of food, she said, "Tomorrow is Saturday, my day off, but there's a dance here with a big band tomorrow at 6:00 p.m. in the recreation center. Would you like to go with me? Nearly everyone that works here goes to it."

Surprised and somewhat amused at her directness, I answered, "Yes, I'd like that; however, I need to have my uniforms and laundry done first so I'll have something clean to wear."

"If you'll take them to the cleaners after eating, they will have them ready tomorrow afternoon."

"Where is the recreation center located?"

"It's at the opposite end of the building from here about one-fifth of a mile away. Are you staying in the BOQ near the runways?"

"Yes, I am."

"Then why don't I pick you up at the BOQ at 5:45 p.m., and we will drive to the parking lot outside the rec center entrance."

"You have a car?" I asked incredulously.

Smiling shyly, she said, "Yes, I do. Last year in May, my daddy gave me a new 1940 Chevrolet special deluxe two-door convertible when I graduated from college. It's black with a cream-colored top and interior."

Joy Estelle Heath

The Eagle Above

Leaning back in my chair, now I was the one impressed. A loud buzzer on the wall sounded, and all five of the girls stood up and said they had to return to their jobs. They waved to me, and before leaving the table, Joy smiled broadly and said, "I'll pick you up tomorrow evening at 5:45 p.m.. See you then." And she ran to catch up with her girlfriends. Reaching them, they all laughed and twittered, then she looked back at me and waved.

Sitting there, I could not believe my good fortune at having met a pretty brunette who was taking me to a dance the next evening in her convertible! Finishing my pie, I stood up, carried my tray back to the food line, emptied the leftovers on my plate into a large metal garbage can with a sign on it that said EDIBLE GARBAGE and placed the plate and tray on a nearby stack of dirty dishes. Chuckling to myself, I thought, *"The hog farmers around here must love this place and have a huge supply of free slop for their pigs."*

Walking to the entrance of the cafeteria, I stopped and watched a man unhook a bright yellow Case airplane tug from the tail wheel of a P-51D. Looking at me, the driver waved and said, "Hey, Captain. How about a lift?"

Quickly walking over to him, I happily said, "Sure. Thanks a lot."

Hopping on the back of the little vehicle, he drove me to the opposite side of the building and dropped me off at the door where I had first entered. I walked back to the BOQ, gathered up all of my dirty clothes, and took them back to the dry cleaners and laundry. Afterward, I returned to my room and went to bed.

The next morning I awoke, shaved and showered and dressed in my cleanest dirty uniform, and walked over to the operations center next to the control tower where I poured myself a cup of coffee. Checking the weather for the Monday morning flight, I saw that my route from NAS-Dallas to Coronado was going to be clear all the way or as pilots frequently say "CAVU" meaning "Ceiling And Visibility Unlimited."

The operations officer gave me all of the sectional charts I needed to plot my headings to the California airfield and then said, "Captain Corvin, you're going to be the flight leader of a five-aircraft group going to the West Coast. Do you need any help planning this exercise since you haven't flown in the United States before?"

"No, sir, I don't think so. All of the radio and tower frequencies we need are printed on the maps, so we'll fly west on a heading of 270° until we hit the Pacific Ocean," I said with a smile. "Recently in North Africa and Tunisia I flew some long-range combat fighter sweeps over hundreds of miles of desert sand dunes using only dead reckoning computations. The maps we had were ancient British and French ones with not much detail, so I think we should be okay."

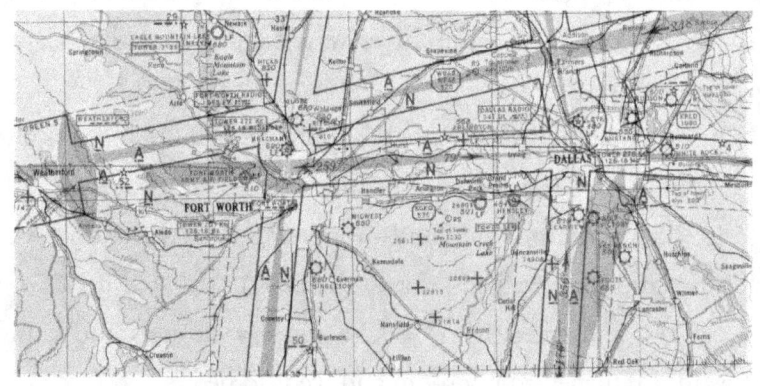

1944 Sectional Map of NAS - Dallas

NAS North Island - Coronado, CA (US Navy Photo)

"It sounds like you'll easily handle the ferry missions, but let me know if I can help you in any way," the major said as he walked away.

The route I plotted showed several military airfields along the way, including New Mexico's Alamogordo Army Airfield (renamed Holloman AFB) and Arizona's Williams Field (renamed Williams AFB) in Chandler in case we needed to make an emergency landing. We were to fly at 10,000 feet to avoid the need to continuously wear our oxygen masks and use only our throat microphones to communicate on the radios. That altitude also put us below the newly coined German term known as the *Strahlströmung* (literally jet current) or "jet stream" in English. Beginning at approximately 20,000 feet, this strong current of prevailing westerly winds, averaging one hundred-ten mile per hour, can significantly slow the ground speed of an airplane flying into it. It also can greatly increase the airspeed if the plane is flying in an easterly direction with its flow.

Finishing my dead reckoning calculations and drawing the course line in pencil on the maps, I realized I would be able to use them repeatedly as we flew the same route each time we delivered new fighters. The four other pilots and I were scheduled to return the same day to NAS-Dallas aboard a military C-47, which had a cruising speed of one hundred sixty miles per hour. That meant that it would take us roughly nine hours to get back. With thirty ferry pilots, I ended up flying five or six days in a row, had a day off, and then repeated the schedule. That was my routine for approximately four months until I left on July 17, 1944, for the Marianas Islands in the Pacific Ocean and, ultimately, Iwo Jima.

Stopping by my room at the BOQ, I dropped off the sectional charts and walked over to the cafeteria to have breakfast. After eating bacon, eggs, hashbrowns, and something the locals called grits, I went into the barbershop, got a haircut, had my shoes shined, then stopped by the laundry facility and was surprised to learn that my uniforms and laundry were ready. Carrying everything back to my room, I spent the rest of the day napping and reading a new book I had picked up in England sent there by an American library in Charlotte, North Carolina. It was Ernest Hemingway's 1940 edition of *For Whom the Bell Tolls*. I had already read *The Sun Also Rises* and *A Farewell to Arms*, so I was a big fan of his writing.

At 5:00 p.m., I showered again and dressed in my clean pinks-and-greens uniform and walked outside after putting on my crusher hat. It was a beautiful day with no clouds but cool at 60°F. Lighting a cigarette, I thought, "*I wonder if the brunette will have the top down on her convertible today. What did she say her name was? Oh, yes, Joy.*"

Nervously chain-smoking and pacing on the sidewalk in front of the BOQ, I realized that it had been three years since I had dated in

my first year at Ohio State University in 1941. Then from down the street, I saw a shiny black convertible with the top down driving fast toward me.

Braking hard and pulling up to the curb, Joy, who was wearing sunglasses, a pink silk scarf over her hair and tied under her chin lowered her shades, looked over the rims, and said, "Hey, GI, are you going my way?" Then she laughed.

Smiling, I got in the passenger seat and answered, "I'm going to a dance with the prettiest girl in town." And with that being said, our whirlwind romance began.

CHAPTER 7

JOY ESTELLE HEATH

Parking near the center recreational door of the massive building, we got out of Joy's convertible and walked inside. She had removed her scarf, and after shaking her head, her dark hair flowed down over her shoulders, perfectly framing her slender face. Wearing a tight beige cashmere sweater and a navy pleated skirt with short white rolled down socks and brown and white saddle oxfords, she looked like a young college girl. To say that I was smitten is an understatement.

Standing at the door, I saw there were several hundred men and women already mingling together, many standing beside cloth-covered tables where huge punch bowls were located with paper cups stacked next to them. A large band was warming up their instruments on the stage off to one side of the room.

Leaning over to Joy, I said, "It's been a long time since I've been to a dance, and I've never been very good anyway, so I'm going to apologize to you upfront if I accidentally step on your toes."

Reaching her right arm around my left one, she giggled and said, "That's okay, Stan, I'm pretty light on my feet after taking music and dance lessons for several years in high school, and college, so I think I can avoid having my toes crushed."

Suddenly with a loud trumpet flourish which startled me, the band began playing Benny Goodmans popular song *Sing, Sing, Sing*. Joy squealed gleefully, grabbed my hand, and said, "Let's dance, handsome."

For the next thirty minutes, we stayed on the dance floor, where she tried to teach me the swing dance to fast Big Band music but without much success. After Glenn Miller's famous song *In The Mood* finished, Artie Shaw's version of *Begin the Beguine* started to play, and I put my right arm around her slender waist, and we began to slow dance. It felt wonderful to hold a girl in my arms again as we rhythmically danced the foxtrot step to the music. We slow danced for several songs, then she took me by the hand, and we walked over to the punch bowls where she filled two paper cups while the band took a break.

"Joy, do you live somewhere around here?" I asked.

"No, I live in Dallas with my mother's two younger sisters, Hazel Sutton and Louise Clower. They both work here too. Aunt Hazel works in the small airplane parts department with me, and aunt Louise works in the accounting department. We all work the same hours, so I drive us to and from our house because neither one of them drives," she said.

"They don't have a driver's license?" I asked.

"Yes, they do; however, two years ago, while they were taking my grandmother shopping one day, they were in a car accident that killed their mother. So they immediately sold their automobile and decided never to drive again," she replied.

"I'm sorry to hear that. Were all of you living together then?" I gently asked.

"No, I was living in the women's dormitory at East Texas State Teachers College in Commerce while I finished my degree. I graduated last year in May with a bachelor's of arts degree in elementary education and music. My mother and father live in Colorado City about two hundred miles west of here. My mother stays home and takes care of my two younger sisters and my little brother. Daddy is in the oil business and drills wells on ranches all the way to the New Mexico border," she answered.

Joy Heath, College Graduation Photo

"Isn't that a pretty tough and dirty job for a man his age handling all the oily pipe?" I asked. Thinking back to the oil rig workers I had seen in Nottingham Forest.

Smiling with brilliant white teeth and laughing, she punched my arm and said, "Silly man. He owns the company. I didn't mean that he physically works on the eleven drilling rigs he has."

Feeling foolish, I said, "Oh. Sorry, I misunderstood what you said."

Lifting her face to mine, she kissed me on the left cheek then wiped away the bright red lipstick with her thumb saying, "It's okay. Let's dance some more." The band began to play Johnny Mercer's *G.I. Jive*, she took my hand and led me out to the dance floor. We danced until 9:00 p.m. when the bandleader announced that it was time to shut everything down and go home.

Leaving the building, Joy held my hand as we walked out to her car. It was a very still starry night with a bright waxing gibbous moon, and standing beside the passenger door we kissed. Holding her close, I asked, "What is that perfume that you are wearing? It smells wonderful."

"It's called Evening in Paris, and I bought it this morning at the Neiman-Marcus department store on Main street in downtown Dallas," she whispered. Then we kissed again.

Driving back to the BOQ, Joy asked if I wanted to go to Sunday lunch with her the next day.

"Yes. I would like that very much, but I have no transportation," I answered.

"I'll pick you up at noon, and we will go to a great Mexican restaurant that is near to my house. You do like Mexican food, don't you?" She asked.

"I've never had it before, but I'm willing to try anything if you think it's good," I said.

"Where do you come from that doesn't have Mexican restaurants?" she asked, looking a little shocked.

"I'm from a small town in Southern Ohio, and we don't have many restaurants there and certainly no Mexican ones," I said with a laugh.

Thinking, *"I really like this girl a lot. She's fun, straightforward, and*

"I'm ready to try some of your Mexican food, but you will have to explain what I'm eating," I replied.

We drove out the north main gate of NAS-Dallas and headed east to downtown Dallas and the El Fenix restaurant located on lower McKinney Avenue. Arriving there, I got out of the car came around and opened the door for Joy. She thanked me, and then we walked in the front entrance holding hands. The inside was huge, with tables scattered around the edges of a dance floor with a low stage at one end. Strange sounding music was being played by a roving group of five Mexican men who wore black and silver brocaded sombreros and tight-fitting "vaquero" costumes playing the guitar, violin, and trumpet. Joy said they were called "Mariachis."

After being seated at a white cloth-covered table, we were brought glasses of water and a basket of triangular-shaped corn chips, which she said was something new the restaurant had begun serving called a "tostada." Taking a chip and scooping it into a nearby bowl of red sauce, I ate my first bite of Mexican food, and immediately my eyes started watering, and I coughed because of the hot chili spices. I quickly drank some water, and then we both began to laugh.

"So. How do you like it?" she asked while smiling.

"It's great. But is everything else so hot?" I asked.

"No. Probably not, but it depends upon what you order. Why don't you try the beef enchiladas, refried pinto beans, and rice."

"Sounds good to me."

The waiter came over, and Joy ordered our food, including something called "guacamole" and "queso." While waiting for the food to arrive, I noticed there were many businessmen dressed in suits at the restaurant. Later I learned that both the Adolphus and Baker Hotel located a few blocks away regularly brought their guests to the

smart. Oh, and she's got a rich daddy too!" Arriving at my quarters, we kissed again, then said our goodbyes.

Early the next morning, I awoke, showered, and shaved and put on another clean uniform. *"Dammit, I don't have any civvies to wear today,"* I thought. *"Oh, well, I'll make do with what I've got on."* Then I walked over to the cafeteria, drank coffee, and ate a light breakfast while sitting and talking to three other pilots who were there. We all agreed that this was a pretty cushy job, ferrying the fighters to San Diego.

Two of the pilots who were considerably older than me had been flying crop dusters in Alabama and Mississippi before the war. After USAAF pilot training, they became flight instructors in the North American Aviation AT-6. They were excited to transition into the P-51D and finally have a chance to fly in combat. The third pilot who was also a first lieutenant, had recently returned from Burma and China flying P-40 Kittyhawks for General Claire Chennault and the "Flying Tigers." Other than me, he was the only one that had any combat experience at all. We sat in the cafeteria telling the other two pilots war stories until midmorning, then I left and went back to my room and finished reading my Hemingway book.

At noon I walked outside and waited for Joy to arrive. Ten minutes later, I saw her black convertible turn on to the street and drive to the BOQ. Pulling to the curb, she waved me over to the passenger seat, and I got in. She was wearing a blue silk scarf over her hair, which was tied up in a ponytail and a heavy pale-blue cashmere sweater and white slacks with brown penny loafers, and she looked stunningly beautiful.

Leaning over to me, we briefly kissed, then she said, "I am famished. Let's go eat."

restaurant. Once the food arrived, I dipped a chip in the dark green guacamole and carefully took a bite of it, preparing to drink some water if I needed to.

"Wow. That stuff is really good," I exclaimed in between bites.

"I know. It's one of my favorite dishes, and I think you'll like the other food too, she said as she began to eat."

For the next hour, we talked about her growing up in a small town in West Texas and my coming from a small town in Southern Ohio, joining the RCAF and flying fighters in England, North Africa, and Sicily. I also told her that in a few months, I would be leaving for the Marianas Islands in the Pacific and begin flying combat missions against the Japanese and mainland Japan.

She became very quiet and reflective, finally saying, "I wish you didn't have to leave so soon."

"Well, we can enjoy our time together while I'm here, and maybe I'll come back someday." That didn't seem to make her feel better.

I motioned for the waiter to bring me the check, and he came over saying, "Captain, your bill has already been paid by a group of businessmen who were eating when you and the young lady came in." Looking surprised, I thanked him, and we left the restaurant.

Starting her car, Joy said, "Would you like to see some of Dallas? And then maybe we can go to White Rock Lake and watch the sailboats on the water."

"Sure. That sounds great," I answered.

"First, I need to run by my house and get a jacket because it's a little cooler today than I thought it would be. My home isn't far from here in Highland Park."

A few minutes later, we pulled into the driveway of her home at 3509 Euclid Avenue. She ran into the house while I waited in the car.

A few minutes later, she came out wearing a stylish black fur jacket, carrying a homemade patchwork quilt and closely followed by two middle-aged women whom I guessed were her aunts.

Stepping out of the car, I said, "Hello ladies. I'm Stan Corvin."

Shaking hands with me, the tall, thin one said, "I'm Louise Clower, and this is my sister Hazel Sutton. We are pleased to meet you, Stan. We have heard a lot about you."

"Oh, Louise, you have not," Joy said while blushing self-consciously.

We talked for a few minutes with Hazel telling me about her son Bob who was a corporal in the US Army and stationed at Fort Leavenworth; then, Joy said, "We need to be going. I'll be home later."

Driving downtown, I was impressed with the size of the skyscrapers and all the traffic on the streets. Finally, we turned east on Mockingbird Lane driving until we reached White Rock Lake Park, where we got out of the car, and I spread the quilt on some grass near the water. A white school bus with iron bars on the windows and large black POW letters painted on the side passed by on the street and continued around the lake.

Shocked, I asked, "Oh, my God, who are those people on the white bus?"

"They are German prisoners of war who are staying at the POW camp on Winfrey Point on the southeast side of the lake. Recently *The Dallas Morning News* ran an article about them being brought here from Mexia, Texas, where they were originally sent four months ago. It said they were part of Field Marshal Rommel's *Afrika Korps* recently captured in Libya and Tunisia."

Frowning, I said, "Joy, you're not going to believe this, but on a daily basis, six months ago, I was flying P-51D fighter sweeps in those exact areas shooting and killing their comrades."

Her face paled, and then she quietly said, "Oh, I had no idea." Tears quickly welled up in her eyes and began to roll down her cheeks. Removing a clean handkerchief from my hip pocket, I gave it to her, and she dabbed her eyes.

We stayed at the lake for about an hour, quietly talking and watching all the sailboats, and then Joy drove me back to NAS-Dallas and the BOQ. Before getting out of the car, I asked her if I could see her again. Reaching into her purse without answering me, she took out a fountain pen and wrote DL3875 on the palm of my right hand.

"That's my home telephone number. Why don't you call me tomorrow night after you get back from California and we will talk? I'm going to be working the morning shift from now on." Then she leaned over, and we kissed goodbye.

At 0330 hours the next morning, my alarm went off, and I quickly showered, shaved, and dressed in my flight suit and boots. Carrying my gear to the operations building, I poured myself a cup of coffee and filled out a flight plan to Naval Air Station - San Diego. The other four pilots arrived, and we were given the weather and flight briefings. The AVG pilot had entered first, and I asked him if he would fly in the number two slot as my wingman. Then I told the other three pilots they would be number three, four, and five. I explained we would fly in a trail formation with everyone following me.

Spreading my maps out on a large table, I showed them our penciled route over New Mexico, Arizona, and into Southern California. Everyone agreed that it was going to be an easy flight, although fairly long. I chose our inflight VHF frequency, which we would use to communicate with each other and then wrote the frequencies of the tower and our rudimentary flight following services in ink on the back of my left hand.

Looking at my watch, I saw that it was nearly 0545 hours, so with the other pilots, we picked up our seat parachutes from the "ready room" and attached them to our harnesses, then we walked to the flight line, and I went over to the first parked P-51D. North American Aviation technicians and mechanics were standing by a gas-engine auxiliary power unit (APU) rated at 28.5 Volts and four hundred amps in case it was needed to assist with the engine start. Once I finished the preflight inspection, I climbed into the cockpit and waited for everyone else to finish theirs.

P-51D Cockpit

Soon the other pilots were looking at me. Raising my right hand, I made a twirling motion indicating that they were to start their engines. The two ground crew at the front of my airplane slowly walked the propellers around a few times. I set the parking brake, moved the fuel selector valve to the drop tanks, turned the ignition switch on, and turned off the two magnetos checking that the fuel mixture was

hold short because we have a Navy SNJ on final. The winds are from the Southwest at 15 knots, and the altimeter setting is 2937. Over."

Adjusting the altimeter's Kollsman window for the actual barometric pressure, I said, "Roger, 2937, ma'am. Mustang 375 will hold short of one eight until the SNJ lands and clears the runway. Out"

Looking over at my wingman, I raised my right fist for a moment then rapidly pumped it up and down, indicating I was about to taxi. Releasing the small red parking brake handle, I slowly increased the throttle until the airplane started to roll. Differential braking was needed to turn the aircraft while taxiing, so after forty yards, I tapped the left brake pedal and made a slow 90° turn paralleling the runway. Pulling the stick all the way back locked the tail wheel in the forward position, and I increased my ground speed slightly until I reached the end of the taxiway where I pushed the stick forward and tapped my right brake slowly, turning 90° to the end of the runway where I stopped. Sitting there, I increased the RPMs to 1800, performed a magneto check, and reduced the power down to idle. Making my cockpit check beginning on the left with the mixture and power setting handles and scanning to the right of the instrument panel, I waited for the Navy trainer to land.

After it touched down and pulled off the 8,000-foot runway, the WAC tower operator said, "Mustang Lead 375, 'suh, you are cleared for takeoff, and a right crosswind departure to your heading of 270°. Please contact Fort Worth center on 122.15. Have a good flight, and y'all be careful now. Out."

Smiling to myself at hearing her southern drawl, I said, "Roger that. Out"

Taxiing to the middle of the runway, I slowly turned to the right on a heading of 180° and stopped until the other four aircraft had

rich and the propellor was set. Pushing the two carburetor induction system handles to the forward operating position, I set the rudder trim to almost 5° to the right, the aileron trim to zero, turned the battery, generator, and fuel boost switches on and loudly yelled, "Clear."

Flipping up the red protective cover, I lifted the starter toggle switch, and the big four blades began to turn slowly clockwise. After the fifth rotation to get the oil and fuel flowing, I turned on both magnetos, and the big Merlin V-12 roared to life, then I reduced the throttle to idle and slowed the engine to 1100 rpm.

"God, I love the sound of that engine, and I've missed it!" I thought as I began turning on the radios and checking the engine instruments to make sure everything was in the normal operating range.

After a radio commo check with the other four pilots and setting the altimeter at 484 feet, I switched to the tower frequency of 126.18 and said, "NAS tower, this is Mustang leader 414375 ready for taxi and takeoff. Over."

WAF Tower Operator Painting

A strong, very southern female voice replied, saying, "Roger, Mustang Lead 375. Y'all can taxi to runway one eight, 'suh, but please

moved up to the edge of the runway beside me in a trail formation. Cranking the bubble canopy closed, I pulled the stick back, locking the tail wheel in position, and then slowly advanced the throttle to 3,000 RPM with 40 inches of manifold pressure and began to roll down the runway. At seventy-five miles per hour, the tail was off the ground, and I could see Mountain Creek Lake in front of me. Accelerating quickly to one-hundred miles per hour, I lifted off, raised my landing gear, and began my ascent while banking right to a heading of 270°. Over my shoulder, I could see the other four fighters start to take off behind me. Climbing at 3,200 feet per minute, it only took three minutes to reach 10,000 feet. Throttling back to 2,400 RPM, I leaned the fuel mixture, adjusted the propeller, and air induction system, trimmed the airplane again, and began to cruise at 300 miles per hour. Then I called Fort Worth Center for flight following.

Behind me, I could see the other four aircraft strung out for a couple of miles. After flying for ten minutes, I saw the fourteen-story Baker hotel in downtown Mineral Wells, which was seventy-one miles from NAS - Dallas. Tempted to buzz it, I remembered the last time when I buzzed something and crashed in Canada, and so I decided to maintain my altitude. *"Taking chances in combat is enough excitement for me now,"* I thought.

From Mineral Wells, we flew four hundred ninety-two miles to Alamogordo, NM. From there, we flew four hundred forty miles to Chandler, AZ, and I changed our course to 260° for the final three hundred miles leg of our journey to the Naval Air Station San Diego (renamed US Naval Air Station, North Island in 1955) where we landed. Our total flying time was about four hours and ten minutes. The flight was uneventful, and the terrain was quite beautiful as we crossed the vast West Texas plains of the Llano Estacado, White

Sands National Monument, the snow-topped mountain ranges of the Southern Rockies, and finally the Sonoran desert with its expanse of saguaro cacti at Williams Field.

During World War II, Coronado, California's North Island was the main U.S. military base supporting the Allied forces in the Pacific, including over a dozen aircraft carriers docked at its piers. Operating around the clock, it became home to the majority of the local aircraft factory workers and dependents of the large base.

We parked the airplanes at base operations, gathered our flight gear, and went inside the Spanish style building next to the tower. Signing the paperwork transferring the five P-51Ds to the NAS – San Diego flight operations section, I walked into the snack bar at base operations and sat down with the other four pilots and looked at my watch. It showed 1000 hours, so we had to wait for two hours to catch our return flight. We were scheduled to leave at noon on a C-47 going back to Grand Prairie, Texas, and the North American Aviation plant at NAS - Dallas. The "Gooney Bird" as it was nicknamed, can carry twenty-eight passengers or six thousand pounds of cargo at a cruising speed of 160 mph, over a range of about 1,600 miles. It was going to take us about seven and three-quarters hours to fly the 1,232 miles, so we were going to land around 2000 hours.

"I wonder what Joy is doing now at the plant?" I thought to myself, sitting at the table drinking coffee. Clearly, I was infatuated with the pretty brunet girl and looked forward to our next meeting; if there was going to be one. *"I need to remember to call her tonight when I get back to the BOQ."*

For the next two hours, we sat in the pilot's lounge talking and reading page worn magazines killing time. Then at 1145 hours, I heard an aircraft taxi to the front of the building and shut down its engines. It was our bird, which was going to take us back to the plant in Grand Prarie.

Filling out a flight plan to Texas, the "Goony Bird" pilots motioned for us to board the plane. Inside there were fold-down seats arranged along the sides and several large tied down stacks of spare airplane parts that were going back to the plant. Stowing my flight gear near the back, I sat down, leaned back, and promptly went to sleep. Two hours later, I awoke when the airplane hit a pocket of turbulence. Looking out the window, I could see the Sonoran desert below. *"We still have a long way to go,"* I thought as I settled down in the seat and propped my feet on several wooden crates in the center cargo floor.

Six hours later, we landed at NAS-Dallas and taxied to the base operations building. Checking in with the ops officer, I saw that we were scheduled to fly out the next morning at 0600 hours. Five more ferry pilots were added to the flight so that a total of ten airplanes were going to be flown to California the next morning.

"How was your first flight to San Diego, Captain Corvin?" the operations officer asked.

"No problem, sir. It's a piece of cake. Unless there is an aircraft problem or bad weather, I don't see any issues that will prevent us from doing this every day," I said.

"Good. That's what I like to hear. Tomorrow you will be leading a group of ten aircraft to Coronado. I'll see you at 0500 hours." Then he sat down at his desk behind the counter.

Taking my parachute back to the "ready room," I hung it up, left the building, and walked back to the BOQ. After dumping my flight equipment on the floor, I walked down the hall to a pay phone mounted on the wall and called the number Joy had given me. After a few rings, her Aunt Hazel answered the phone, and I asked to speak to Joy.

After a few minutes, she said, "Hello. Is this Stan?"

"Yes, it is. I just got back in from California. How was your day?"

"Okay. I like working the morning shift now, and I've been moved into another department where I am distributing rivets, screws, and brads. How was your first flight?"

"No problem. It was pretty routine but a little boring. When can I see you again?" I hesitatingly asked.

"Would you like to go to a movie with me this Saturday afternoon?"

"Yes, I would. I'll be flying the rest of the week but will be finished on Friday at 8:00 p.m.."

"Why don't I pick you up on Saturday at 3:00 p.m.? Then we will go eat before the movie starts at 6:00 p.m. *Casablanca* with Humphrey Bogart and Ingrid Bergman is showing at the Lakewood theater on Abrams Road. Oops! I forgot that you probably don't know where that is." She giggled girlishly.

At that moment, I fell in love with Joy and decided I would come back to Texas and marry her after the war if she had not met anyone else.

The next morning I arrived at base operations at 0500 hours and briefed the five new pilots about our route to the Southern California naval base. As I had done the previous morning, I led the group out to the aircraft, and after preflighting and starting them, we took off and flew the plotted course west then returned the same day on another C-47. For the remainder of the week, that was our daily routine.

On Saturday morning I awoke, shaved, showered and dressed then went to the cafeteria for breakfast. Later I went back to my room and finished reading Roald Dahl's book *Over to You,* which was a group of short stories about British RAF pilots flying in combat. Shortly before 3:00 p.m., I walked outside and waited for Joy to arrive. A few minutes later, she pulled up to the curb, waved at me, and I got in the passenger seat. Leaning over, we kissed, and I realized then that everything was going to be okay between us.

Joy took me to the Southern Kitchen restaurant on Northwest Highway. I ordered my favorite dish, a fried shrimp and oysters plate, and it was some of the best seafood I had ever tasted. Afterward, we drove to Abrams Road in East Dallas to the Lakewood theater. It was a marvel of technological achievement with RCA high fidelity sound equipment, the first air-conditioning system for a theater in Dallas, and thickly upholstered auditorium seating. The ceiling rose one hundred feet and had 7,000 watts of power for its lighting. I was impressed with its Art Deco styling and lavish furnishings. There even was a bar in the foyer serving liquor. Once the movie was over, we went to Joy's house on Euclid Avenue and played bridge with her aunts Hazel and Louise.

Over the next several months, I fell into a routine of working during the week and dating Joy on the weekends. Then on Saturday, June 3, 1944, after she drove me back to the BOQ and we parked, I asked her, "Will you marry me?"

"When?" she immediately asked.

"After the war, when I return home," I said.

"No! Let's not wait until then. Let's get married on July 3rd, and I'll call my parents tomorrow morning." Then smiling broadly, she threw her arms around my neck, kissed me, and gently rubbing her nose against mine said, "Yes. I'll marry you, Captain Corvin."

> Mr. and Mrs. Jesse H. Heath
>
> announce the marriage of their daughter
>
> Joy
>
> to
>
> Lt. Stanley Everett Corvin
>
> United States Army Air Force
>
> on Monday, the third of July
>
> Nineteen hundred and forty-four
>
> Dallas, Texas
>
> 3509 Euclid Ave.
> Dallas 5 Texas

Joy and Stan's Wedding Invitation

The next thirty days was a whirlwind of activity as she and her aunts and mother, Olivia Maude Heath, organized everything. Since it was such short notice and most of the churches were booked marrying couples before the husbands went off to war, Joy decided that the service needed to take place at her home in Highland Park. Mrs. Heath ordered the wedding invitations from a local printer who inadvertently demoted me to 2nd lieutenant, which we did not notice until it was too late to correct the mistake. So on July 3, 1944, at 2:00 p.m., Joy and I were married by a local minister who agreed to come to the house and perform the ceremony.

As a wedding present, her father Jesse H. Heath paid for the honeymoon suite at the Adolphus Hotel in downtown Dallas for three nights. Using room service to order food the entire time, we never left the hotel until we checked out.

After taking four days leave from my unit, we drove to base operations to see when I would be flying to California again. A new operations officer said, "Captain Corvin, we just received orders yesterday that in fourteen days you are to proceed to NAS - Coronado and board the USS Kalinin Bay aircraft carrier. Then you will go to Guam in the Mariana Islands, where you will be assigned to the 7th Fighter Command, 21st Fighter Group in the Pacific. You are now officially relieved of duty with the Fifth Ferry Command. You can take two weeks leave before you have to depart for California."

Stunned, I thanked him, and he handed me a large manila envelope with the written orders inside. Glumly I walked out to the car and sat down.

Joy looked at me and could immediately tell something was wrong. She anxiously asked, "When are you delivering more planes to California?

"I'm not. In fourteen days, I'm being reassigned to the 7th Fighter Command in the Pacific and will be flying P-51Ds against the Japanese Air Force's Zeros on their mainland."

She paled visibly, losing all facial color, her chin began to quiver, and her face contorted as she began to sob softly.

"This isn't fair. We just got married. Isn't there any way you can get the orders changed?" she angrily asked while slamming her fists on the steering wheel.

Holding her close as she cried on my shoulder, I said, "No, honey. This is what I signed up for three years ago, and I have to go where I am assigned."

We went to the BOQ and packed all of my belongings then loaded them in her car. Then we drove to her house and unloaded everything in her bedroom. I lived with Joy, Hazel, and Louise until I departed from Dallas two weeks later.

On July 17, 1944, fourteen days after Joy and I were married, she took me to Fort Worth Army Airfield (renamed Carswell Air Force Base in 1955), where tearfully, we said our goodbyes at the departure gate outside. I boarded a military C-47 and flew to Coronado, California, landing at the Naval Air Station on North Island at dark.

CHAPTER 8

HELL TO PAY ON IWO JIMA

Four days after arriving at NAS – North Island along with about fifty other fighter pilots, I boarded the USS Kalinin Bay, and we left for Pearl Harbor, Hawaii. We stayed there for several weeks before continuing to the Marianas Islands and arriving on Guam in October 1944. The flight deck of the aircraft carrier was filled with new P-51Ds, many of which I had brought to the West Coast naval base.

*USS Kalinin Bay Aircraft Carrier P-51Ds
Headed to Guam - July 1944*

Assigned to the officers quarters below the aircraft carriers flight deck, I carried my B-4 bag and flight gear duffle bag to a large open bay filled with triple-stacked bunk beds where I met Second Lieutenant Eddie L. Skelton sitting on a lower bunk. Ed, as he preferred to be called, was born in Polk County, Arkansas, near the small town of Mena on September 17, 1922. After graduating with high honors from college, he joined the USAAF and trained as a fighter pilot. This was his first combat deployment since completing flight school; however, he already had transitioned into the P-51D Mustang and later proved to be an exceptional aviator in many types of high-performance aircraft, including supersonic jets.

Sitting on the bunk next to his, I introduced myself. "Hello. My name is Stan Corvin. What is yours?"

"Sir, my name is Lieutenant Ed Skelton." We shook hands.

"Lieutenant, we've got a long trip ahead of us, so let's dispense with the formalities and just call me Stan, and I'll call you Ed. How about that?" I said with a smile.

He grinned at me and said, "Yes, sir. I mean, Yes, Stan." That initial meeting began a lifelong friendship that spanned the next fifty-six years.

After arriving on Guam, along with the other pilots, we disembarked from the USS Kalinin Bay and were officially assigned to the 7th Fighter Command, 21st Fighter Group, 47th Fighter Squadron. The living conditions were very primitive because the Marines had recently recaptured the island from the Japanese Imperial Army, who had destroyed most of the facilities before fighting and dying to the last man. Large squad tents were set up next to the airfield, and Ed and I shared one with four other pilots. We ate "C" rations until several large mess tent facilities were set up and provided some hot chow.

Since none of the other pilots had been in combat, I was given the responsibility of teaching them gunnery tactics. Our P-51D aircraft were equipped with six Browning M-3 .50 caliber machine guns, three in each wing. Manually charged on the ground, they all fired simultaneously when the gun trigger switch was pressed on the front of the control stick grip. Each firing 600 rounds per minute meant that we only had slightly over three minutes of shooting before we exhausted our ammunition. So, for several weeks I led groups of four aircraft each day to isolated atoll locations so they could practice strafing small targets on the ground approximately three football fields lengths away. We needed to become very precise and accurate in our shooting because soon, we were going to be supporting the Marines who were furiously fighting and dying on Iwo Jima.

At sunrise on the morning of March 6, 1945, Brigadier General "Mickey" Moore, the commander of the 7th Fighter Command, led our 21st Fighter Group to the infamous island where the American flag had been raised atop Mount Suribachi eleven days earlier on February 23. We landed on the south field runway, which was pocked marked with numerous mortar and naval gunfire craters but had been hastily filled in by the newly arrived "Seabees."

The living conditions were atrocious on the small two-mile by eight-mile pork chop shaped landmass. Before the Marine's ground assault, the constant offshore bombardment by naval ships had destroyed all the island vegetation and created huge craters all over the landscape. Unexploded shells and ammunition were scattered everywhere. During the fighting, over twenty-two thousand Japanese soldiers had been killed, and their blackened bloated bodies were left exposed and rotting on top of the ground. The stomach-churning stench of putrified and decaying flesh permeated everything. Many of the enemy soldiers had been burned alive with flamethrowers because they refused to come out of the small caves and caverns near the airfield. As a result, the disgusting smell of cooked meat was pervasive throughout our camp. This also resulted in billions of maggots hatching; with flies covering everything in our encampment, especially our food when we ate.

Until the chow tents were set up, all we had to eat were Australian "C" rations consisting of cans of meat and beans, meat and vegetable stew, or meat and vegetable hash. Periodically, specially equipped C-47 cargo planes flew low-level one hundred feet overhead, spraying huge clouds of DDT insecticide to kill the flies. Notwithstanding its lethal effect on them, all it did was add to our misery as it coated everything with the foul-smelling oily mixture.

Because I already was a combat-experienced P-51D pilot, at 0700 hours on April 7, 1945, along with about fifty other fighter pilots, I took off on our first very long-range (VLR) B-29 escort mission to Yokohama, Japan. It was located just seventeen miles south of Tokyo and the Imperial Palace, where Emperor Michinomiya Hirohito lived. I was excited to finally begin the attack on the Japanese mainland, especially knowing the war in Europe was coming to an end as the Russian army was on the outskirts of Berlin, where Adolph Hitler was hiding in his underground bunker.

The distance from Iwo Jima to Yokohama was seven-hundred-fifty miles, all over the water, and took nearly four hours flying at two hundred ten miles per hour, which was required to reach our target area and have enough fuel left to return safely. Although the cruise speed of the B-29 Super Fortress, which had just been put into service, was two hundred ninety miles per hour, they flew slower to allow our fighters to escort them the entire distance to their targets. *"Hopefully, the war will be over soon, and I can go home to my wife, Joy,"* I thought as I flew in a loose formation with eleven other fighters on the left side of the massive bomber flight.

P-51D Iwo Jima takeoff from PSP Runway

P-51Ds going to Japan on VLR mission from Iwo Jima.

P-51D Headed to Japan From Iwo Jima

Japanese A6M Zero

The Eagle Above

As we approached our target area at ten thousand feet, we began to climb to twenty-five thousand feet to support and protect the bombers. However, warned of our departure by the Japanese long-range radio stations based on Chichi Jima Island, one hundred sixty-five miles north of Iwo Jima, suddenly, in the distance, we saw several large approaching flights of Japanese fighter airplanes. They had been waiting for us at an even higher altitude of thirty-two thousand feet.

The Mitsubishi A6M "Zero" was a light-weight long-range fighter aircraft manufactured by Mitsubishi Aircraft Company and operated by the Imperial Japanese Navy from 1940 to 1945. With a top speed of 410 mph and a cruise speed of 346 mph up to nearly 15,000 feet, it had a range of about 1,900 miles. Although it was not as maneuverable as the P-51D, it still was a formidable airplane that had shot down many allied airplanes.

Flying as the leader of an element of four fighters, I thought, *"To hell with this. I'm attacking now."* With my wingman watching me, I pointed to the enemy airplanes with my gloved hand, dropped my two empty 110-gallon auxiliary wing tanks, and pushed the throttle fully forward to intercept a group of about twenty-five "Zeros" who were diving down to us. I had learned while flying with the 121st American Eagle squadron in England to fly directly at a group of enemy fighters and risk a head-on collision to get them to disperse. The dangerous high speed "chicken" tactic had worked to my advantage each time I used it. Choosing the center enemy airplane as my target, our combined approach speed was approximately 810 miles per hour or stated another way, about 1,188 feet per second; about the speed of a .22 long rifle bullet. Within just seconds, I began firing my .50 caliber machine guns at him and saw that he was too far away for the bullet's convergence point to be effective. Then as he was jinking wildly, he unexpectedly flew into my orange stream of machine-gun tracer fire, and I saw white flashes as the bullets swept through his engine and cockpit. Spinning uncontrollably, the Japanese Zero began a vertical dive into the ocean below, and I saw him crash and explode. Fortunately, other aircraft in my flight witnessed this, and I was officially given my first kill of the Pacific war.

Since all of the Zeros were now far below me, I rolled the aircraft on its back and dived straight to the formation of B-29s. Slowing to their cruise speed, I pulled up level with them and watched as their bomb bay doors opened, and they began to drop their 5,000 pounds of bombs on Yokohama. This mission was the first time fighters had escorted bombers over Japan, and we were credited with having the longest over-water fighter escort sortie to date. During the raid, more than two hundred dogfights took place over Yokohama, with twenty-six Japanese Zero's being shot down and only two P-51D lost with one pilot killed. Over the following months, we continued to escort American B-29s over numerous enemy airfields and engaged Japanese fighter aircraft in high-speed dog fights, leaving intricately woven white contrails crisscrossing the clear blue skies. Later we also flew fighter sweeps attacking military installations, airports, industrial complexes, and railway facilities.

A few days after our second bomber escort mission, Brigadier General Moore issued a command that none of the fighter pilots was to fly more than six very long-range (VLR) escort missions in a single month since they averaged seven and one-half hours per sortie. The physical stress of sitting and flying for that long was enormous, and frequently upon landing, I had to be helped out of the cockpit by my ground crew because my legs were so stiff and cramped up they would not move.

P-51Ds returning to Iwo Jima from Japan on attack mission.

Attacked by Wolves

On March 25, 1945, at 0300 hours, Japanese four-star general Tadamichi Kuribayashi, age fifty-four, quietly led the last remaining group of his three hundred surviving soldiers (called wolves), through our tent area built next to the airfield. All hell broke loose at 0400 hours when they silently began entering the tents and slashed the pilots' throats with their razor-sharp short swords called wakizashi's, which were about eighteen inches long. Soon gunfire erupted as everyone began fighting back against the attacking Japanese soldiers. Asleep on my cot, which was placed at the foot of Lieutenant Ed Skelton's bed, I awoke when suddenly I heard loud machine-gun fire and saw bullets piercing the canvas a few inches above my head. Two of the pilots sleeping on cots next to the tent wall were struck repeatedly and instantly killed.[12]

Ed and I rolled off our cots and lay flat on the wooden pallet floor then began low-crawling to the moonlight doorway entrance. My holstered .45 automatic was hanging from a nail on the center tentpole, and I was unable to reach it because of the enemy bullets flying above me. However, Ed slept with his pistol under his makeshift pillow and had it in his right hand and an extra magazine in his left. Crawling forward, I tightly clutched my Marine Ka-Bar knife in my right hand. Finding a folded wooden-handled entrenching tool next to an empty bunk; I held it tightly in my left hand. We exited the canvas tent door at the same time that seven Japanese soldiers rounded the tent corner beside us. Ed immediately jumped up and began firing point-blank at them. Squatting and slashing the entrenching tool at the legs of the closest enemy soldier, I knocked him down and stabbed him in the throat with my knife before he could recover. Then standing up next to Ed, I began to wildly swing the tool into the closest enemy soldier who was lunging at me with his bolt action 7.7 mm Type 99 Arisaka rifle with a fixed bayonet attached. Dodging his thrust, I forcefully hit him in the face with the sharp edge of the small shovel. I heard the bone give way with a crunch, and he fell to the ground where I repeatedly stabbed him in the upper chest. Suddenly it became eerily quiet except for nearby sporadic shooting at other bivouac areas. Seven Japanese "wolves" lay dead at our feet in the pale moonlight. Ed quickly reloaded his pistol with a full magazine and released the slide, which fed a round into the chamber. I dropped the entrenching tool, leaned over, and removed a Type 14 Nambu 8 mm semi-automatic pistol from the hand of one of the fallen soldiers at Ed's feet. *"How appropriate, if I now kill an enemy soldier with their own gun,"* I grimly thought.

Soon dozens of Marines, ground crew, and members of an army regiment arrived at the tent area with their M-1 carbines, .45 caliber Tommy guns, and Browning Automatic Rifles (BAR). Everyone squatted down as more machine-gun fire was heard close by, and bullets flew a few feet over our heads. Finally, after thirty minutes, the shooting stopped. Ed and I were standing barefoot near the tent entrance in our OD green skivvies, our faces and torsos covered with blood splatter from the carnage all around us. A Navy corpsman (medic) from the 5th Marine Division carrying a flashlight came over and asked if we had been wounded after shining its beam on our bloody faces.

"No. I don't think so, but two of our tentmates were hit by the initial enemy gunfire," I answered.

He went into the tent and came out a few seconds later, shaking his head and said, "They are both dead. I'll have some of our guys bring stretchers and retrieve their bodies and take them to the grave registration people for processing." Then he left. Ed and I watched the Marines carry the enemy bodies a few yards away from the tent and stack them in several large bloody piles. As dawn was breaking a small bulldozer, came by, and the NavySeabees dug a large trench and pushed all the bodies into it, covering them with sand.

We sat down on some stacked wooden pallets, and each smoked several cigarettes although our hands were shaking so badly it was difficult for us to light them. I walked inside the tent and removed a bottle of Johnny Walker scotch from my footlocker. Coming outside, I opened the sealed top and took several long swallows of it then gave the bottle to Ed, who did the same. Neither of us said anything but only sat there in stunned silence while our adrenaline-filled, racing hearts slowly returned to a normal beat.

Twenty minutes later, we walked to the showers and cleaned up, then went to our tent and washed the congealed blood off the cots and wooden pallets we were using as a floor. However, a few days later, we had to replace everything because of the massive fly infestation taking place inside the tent. A lasting bond was forged between First Lieutenant Ed Skelton and me during the attack, and we remained lifelong friends, although we rarely ever spoke about it again.

When the Japanese attack was finally over, our unit, the 21st Fighter Squadron, suffered twenty-one killed, including nine pilots, with fifty wounded. Our group commander Colonel Kenny Powell was one of the wounded and was taken back to the hospital on Guam. Japanese General Tadamichi Kuribayashi and the entire enemy force of three hundred Japanese fighters were killed. His body was never identified among the dead wolves because he had removed all rank insignia and thus blended in with all of the infantry soldiers. Ours was the only aviation unit in World War II to be engaged in ground combat. First Lieutenant Eddie L. Skelton was awarded the Silver Star, and I was awarded the Bronze Star with "Valor" device for our efforts to defend ourselves against the sneak enemy attack. It had been another eventful morning in the sands of Iwo Jima.

Chichi Jima Incident

One of the nearby islands bypassed by the Allies but still occupied by the Japanese was Chichi Jima, located one hundred sixty-five miles north of Iwo Jima. When not flying bomber escorts, we frequently attacked and strafed the enemy garrison there and tried to destroy the tall radio antennas and relay stations built atop several of the mountains in the central part of the island.

Six months earlier on September 2, 1944, Lieutenant (Junior Grade) George Herbert Walker Bush, age 20, led a flight of four TBF/TBM Avenger torpedo bombers, part of Torpedo Squadron 51, from the aircraft carrier USS San Jacinto, attacking the enemy garrison and radio transmission station with bombs. Encountering heavy antiaircraft ground fire, his airplane was repeatedly hit, and the engine burst into flames. Each Navy Avenger aircraft carried a crew of three. By flying a mile offshore, he avoided the Japanese soldiers gathered on the shoreline who were prepared to capture him and his crew. He bailed out and landed in the water, where he inflated his small rubber dinghy and began paddling furiously out to sea. Four hours later, he was picked up by an American submarine. His two crew members in the plane died. All eight of the other captured American pilots and crew were severely beaten, mercilessly tortured, and then eventually beheaded by the blood-thirsty Japanese soldiers.

After being killed, four men had their livers removed as well as large portions of their thighs, and the Japanese officers and soldiers ate these at parties celebrating their victory over the Americans. In 1947 after the war, thirty Japanese military officers and enlisted men were tried for their murder and prevention of honorable burial because, at the time, military and international law specifically did not address cannibalism. Most were executed by hanging or firing squad, but a few of the lower-ranking enlisted soldiers were given prison sentences ranging from five to ten years then released. Many years later, when he was the 41st President of the United States, a reporter once asked him about the incident.

Tearing up and with a quivering chin, he quietly answered, saying, "I think about my two crew members co-pilot Lieutenant White and radioman Delaney every single day, and that's all I will say about the matter."

On June 6, 1945, arriving early in the morning over Osaka, Japan, after escorting 274 bombers, our group of fifty fighters was released to perform individual sweeps over the adjacent sizeable industrial area of the city. While the B-29s began dropping their 1,733 tons of bombs on the Osaka civilian residential housing area, to the east, I descended to two hundred feet, dropped my two newly installed empty 165-gallon auxiliary tanks and took my small element of four P-51Ds in search of targets of opportunity across the bay to the west. Finding a slow-moving train at a terminal with many passenger cars attached, I began strafing it then pulled up to allow the other three aircraft, including Lieutenant Ed Skelton, my wingman, to fire into it. On our second pass, the engine exploded, stopping the train and preventing other rail traffic from using the track.

Flying further north, in the distance, I saw the Osaka Two airport with its parallel runways, multiple hangers on one side, and dozens of Japanese aircraft of various types parked on the grass next to them. Two Nakajima Ki-84 fighters (called "Franks" by the Allies) were scrambling to take off in a two-ship right echelon formation. These aircraft were the newest fighters that recently had been put into service by the Japanese. They were much faster and better armed than the Mitsubishi A6M "Zero." With one 30 mm and one 20 mm cannon installed in each wing, they had enough firepower to destroy effortlessly any single-engine American fighter plane they encountered. However, their main weakness was they had virtually no armor protection for

climbing turn and individually entered the traffic pattern after which we landed. We continued to fly our fighter sweeps and bomber escorts until August 1, 1945, when at a group pilot briefing, we were told that we were not going to fly any more missions over Japan or any enemy-occupied islands. At the time, we wondered what was going on; however, we soon found out.

Five days later, on August 6th, a heavily modified B-29 Flying Fortress named the "Enola Gay" was flown from Tinian Island by Colonel Paul Tibbets and dropped the first uranium 235 atomic bomb called "Little Boy" on the city of Hiroshima, Japan. After not getting a response from the Japanese high command or the Emperor to President Harry Truman's demand for an immediate and unconditional surrender, three days later on August 9th at 1102 hours another B-29 Flying Fortress named "Bockscar" flown by Major Charles Sweeney dropped the second even more massive plutonium bomb called "Fat Man" on the city of Nagasaki.

At noon on August 15, 1945, Japan's Emperor Hirohito announced his country's unconditional surrender in a radio broadcast. The news quickly spread, and "Victory in Japan" or "VJ Day" celebrations broke out across the United States and other Allied nations around the world. Two weeks later, on September 2, the formal surrender agreement was signed aboard the battleship USS Missouri, anchored in Tokyo Bay.

After flying sixty very long-range fighter missions over mainland Japan, World War II was over, and I had survived four years of intense combat flying in two major theaters of war.

"I'll be going home soon," I thought while choking up at the prospect of finally seeing my wife Joy again and my family in Oak Hill, Ohio. *"At twenty-three years old, I have my whole life ahead of me now.*

the pilot or the massive engine. Their top speed was nearly 500 mph, and their rate of climb was 4,000 feet per minute so they could out-maneuver my P-51D.

Advancing my throttle to maximum power and increasing my newly installed K-14 gunsight reticle intensity to its brightest setting, I leveled the aircraft and began to fire at the trailing enemy plane. I watched as the six streams of bullets impacted the asphalt runway immediately behind it, then began to hit the tail empennage, continue up into the canopy, and then into the engine, which immediately burst into flames. Slightly raising the nose of my aircraft, I rapidly closed on and fired at the swiftly climbing lead Frank and watched as the six .50 caliber machine gun's bullets shredded the tail, cockpit area, and engine. Both planes crashed into a warehouse area and exploded.

Lt. Skelton keyed his microphone and excitedly said, "Way to go, Boss. That's fantastic!"

Smiling to myself, I said with mock modesty, "Thanks, it's just all in a day's work, and I do love this work!"

Making a hard right 180-degree turn, we dove back down and continued to strafe the other aircraft parked on the grass, making several passes until we were out of ammunition.

"Everyone, let's return to our rendezvous departure point."

Then I reduced my power and began to climb to 10,000 feet and headed south to meet up with the circling navigational B-29 who was going to lead us back to Iwo Jima. We saw no more enemy aircraft except those we had destroyed on the ground, and my two kills.

Four hours later, we arrived at the airfield, and I called the tower requesting permission for a low-level pass over the runway in celebration of my two kills at Osaka. The tower operator granted permission, and after reaching the departure end of the runway, we began a steep

I'll go back to college. Joy and I will start our new life together. Maybe we will even have a couple of kids in a few years."

The next ten days were spent in preparation for our return to Guam's Anderson Field in the Mariana's. Then early on August 25[th,] after all of the P-51Ds were fitted with two 165-gallon auxiliary tanks, the various flight squadrons began to take off from both airfields on Iwo Jima. I was leading a group of sixteen aircraft and climbed to 10,000 feet following an enormous line of fighters stretching out in front of me for eight hundred and eighteen miles. At the time, I thought this flight would be the last time I would ever fly a fighter airplane. But I was wrong!

Arriving at Anderson Field, we parked our aircraft and soon began to process our paperwork to return to the United States and muster out of the USAAF. Large banks of telephones had been hastily set up in a metal-roofed shed so that pilots, airmen, soldiers, sailors, and Marines could call home. Finally, on my second attempt to call Joy at the number she had given me at her home in Dallas, her aunt Louise Clower answered the phone.

"Hello, this is Louise," she said.

"Hello, Louise. This is Stan. Can I speak to Joy, please?"

"Who is this?" she abruptly yelled while adjusting her hearing aid.

"Louise, this is Joy's husband, Stan. May I speak to her, please?" I shouted.

"Oh, my God! Is it really you, Stan?"

"Yes, it is. Is Joy there?"

Hesitating a moment, she said, "No, Stan. She is living with her parents Maude and Jesse Heath, in Colorado City. Let me give you their number."

Startled and concerned that something was wrong, I asked, "Is she okay? Why is she living with them now?"

Laughing, Louise said, "Yes, everything is okay. She moved there eight months ago when she learned she was pregnant. Congratulations, Stan. You're the father of a three-month-old baby boy!"

"What did you say?" I asked incredulously.

"Stan, you have a three-month-old son now."

Shocked, I didn't know what to say but finally managed to thank her. Hanging up, I stood there a moment then placed another call to the number Louise had given me for my in-law's home in West Texas.

"Hello," Joy said, answering the phone.

"Joy. This is Stan. Are you okay? I just talked to Louise, and she said that you had a baby boy."

"Oh, my God! Is it really you, Stan? It's been so long since we've talked or seen each other. Are you okay?"

"Yes, honey, I am. But what is this about you having a baby?

"A few months after you left, I learned that I was pregnant, but there was no way to tell you. Then for four months, I had severe morning sickness, so I quit my job at the North American Aviation plant and moved back home to Colorado City to live with my parents until the baby was born. You have a healthy son named Stanley Everett Corvin, Jr. There was no way to reach you, so I named him Junior. I hope that's okay." Then she began to cry.

Several GIs behind me started yelling, "Hurry up, Captain. We have family to call too."

"Joy, it's going to be alright. I like his name, and I'll be back in Texas in a few weeks, but I'll call you from Pearl Harbor when I get back to Hawaii in three weeks. I love you." Then I hung up the telephone.

Stunned that I had a child, I walked outside and, with shaking hands, lit a cigarette. Standing there, I said aloud, "I've got a boy! I've got a baby boy! Hey, everybody, I just found out that I have a son!" Shouting joyfully, I yelled, "I have a son!" and pumped my right fist up and down in the air.

Shredding my used cigarette butt, I ran back to the bivouac area where Ed Skelton was waiting for his turn to call home, and I told him the good news about my wife having a baby. Clapping me on my back, he enthusiastically congratulated me and said, "That's great, Stan. I know that you and Joy and the baby are going to be very happy."

Homeward Bound

A few days later, we boarded the Navy troop carrier *USS Admiral C. F. Hughes* bound for Pearl Harbor in Hawaii, a distance of 9,855 miles. We reached our destination in twenty-one days, and Ed Skelton and I caught a taxi to Hickam Field, where I had first been assigned to the VII Fighter Command, 15th Fighter Group nearly two years earlier. I explained to the operations officer that we were returning from Iwo Jima and going home to Texas and Arkansas.

He said, "Captain Corvin wait here just a second I'll be right back." Then he walked over to his desk and made a phone call. "Sir, this is Major Clifton at base ops. I have two P-51D fighter pilots returning from flying one year in combat on Iwo Jima, and I would like to add them to the passenger manifest for the C-47 heading back to San Diego this afternoon. May I have your permission to do so?" Silently listening and nodding his head, he gave us a thumbs up and said, "Thank you, sir," and hung up the telephone. "The old man said it's okay for me to bump a couple of rear-echelon people and add you guys to this afternoon's flight back to the mainland. Why don't you go to the Officers' Club, get something to eat, and then come back here? The plane is scheduled to leave at 1500 hours. The 'O' club also has telephones that you can use to call your families to let them know that you're coming home."

The operations sergeant on duty drove us to the club, and immediately, I called Joy at her parent's home in Colorado City, Texas.

"Hello," Joy said as she answered the phone.

"Is this the beautiful mother of Stan Corvin, Jr.?" I laughingly asked.

"Stan. Where are you?" she asked while squealing with joy. *(No pun intended!)*

"I'm at Hickam Field in Hawaii, and I'll be leaving on a C-47 for San Diego in about three hours. Once I arrive there, I'll call you again and let you know where I'm flying into in Texas. I may be able to come into Abilene Army Airfield on a flight to Fort Worth. But I'll let you know when I get to California. How are you and the baby doing?" I asked.

"We're fine. He's very active and growing like a weed and very cute, according to my mother. But I'm not so sure," she said with a giggle.

"I can't wait to see you both."

"Me too," she said excitedly.

Then she somberly said, "By the way, I got a telegram from the Department of Army Air Force several months ago saying that you were missing in action (MIA) after your airplane crashed into the Pacific ocean. Then about a week later, I got another telegram from them saying that it was a case of mistaken identity and that you were okay. So I have been worried about you ever returning home."

"I'm sorry that happened, honey. But I'm okay, and I'll probably see you somewhere late tomorrow afternoon or the next day. I'm just not sure where. I'll call you again once I have more information. I love you, Joy."

Arriving in San Diego at NAS-North Island at 10:00 a.m. the next morning, Ed Skelton and I said goodbye to each other, and we were able to find standby flights to our homes. He flew to Little Rock, Arkansas, and I caught a Fairchild C-82A Packet (flying boxcar) to Abilene Army Airfield. Before leaving, I called Joy at her home and asked if she could pick me up.

"Of course. My parents, the baby, and I will be there when you arrive. It's only seventy miles from Colorado City to the airfield. So we will leave a couple of hours before your scheduled arrival. Welcome to your new home, Captain Corvin. I thought we would stay with my parents until we decide what our next plans are going to be."

"That's fine with me, honey. Do they have enough room?"

"Yes, my younger brother Jesse has not yet returned from the Navy so we can stay in his room until he gets home. I'll see you later this evening."

At 9:00 p.m., I arrived at the Abilene airfield and was greeted by my mother-in-law and father-in-law Maude and Jesse Heath and Joy, who was holding my son Stan Jr. Afterward, we drove to Colorado City. A few days later, Joy and I drove back to the airfield, and I mustered out of the U.S. Army Air Force. My four-year experience had been a swell adventure, and I had survived where many of my friends, buddies, and fellow pilots did not. I was grateful to be alive and at home. It is said that home is where the heart is, and my heart was finally with my young wife and baby boy in West Texas. World War II was over, and life looked good for us.

Capt. Corvin with his son.

Capt. Corvin with his son.

CHAPTER 9

USAF RESERVES 1946-1950

We lived with Joy's parents for about a month. Then, one evening her dad sat down at the kitchen table with Joy and me and said, "Stan, what do you plan to do now that you're no longer flying?"

"Well, sir. I need to find a job and save some more money then I'd like to finish college," I answered.

Pausing for a moment, he sipped his iced tea and said, "I have twenty producing oil and gas wells scattered around Haskell County, Texas, and need someone living up there to keep track of their daily production. Would you like to go to work for me until you can save enough money to start back to college?"

"Yes, sir. I sure would, but I don't want to leave Joy and Stan Jr. here," I said emphatically.

"No, no! I meant that all three of you would need to move to the town of Haskell and live there. We will find you a house to rent, and you can drive to each of the oil well locations daily to change out the 12-inch paper charts and record their results in a report which you can then mail to me on Monday, Wednesday, and Friday of each week."

"Joy, we will need to sell your convertible and get y'all something else because it will not hold up on the rough dirt roads out in the country."

"Daddy, do I have to sell my car?" she asked tearfully.

"I'm afraid so. It's just not well suited for the job in Haskell County," he said.

Hesitatingly I asked, "Mr. Heath, how much will I get paid?"

"Stan, since you are my son-in-law, I will pay you $200 per month, which is considerably more than the normal wage for an oilfield worker."

"Thank you, sir. As a captain, I was making $210 monthly during the war, so that's about what I was making while flying in the USAAF, and I would like to work for you."

We shook hands on it, and the deal was done.

About a week later, Joy and I drove one hundred miles north to the little town of Haskell (1940 county census population 3,053), and after asking at the local barbershop and the police station, we found a small two-bedroom, one-bath wood-frame house to rent for $35 per month. One week later, Mr. Heath had several of his oilfield workers help us move into the house. He and Mrs. Heath bought a bedroom suite, living room furniture, and dishes to get us started. But with only $165 left each month to live on, we soon realized that Joy needed to teach school to supplement our income. So in September 1946, she began teaching first grade at Paint Creek Elementary School a few miles south of Haskell. Her monthly salary of $132 helped out. But then our issue was who would keep Stan Jr. while we both were working. A month later, the problem was solved when Joy's old-maid aunt, Louise Clower, moved in with us to keep our son. We paid her $30 per month salary; she adored the baby, and she slept on a small twin bed in the same room with him.

We drove to Abilene and traded in Joy's 1940 Chevrolet convert-

monthly payment would supplement my income from Mr. Heath and help pay for our food and gasoline, which cost only $.17 per gallon. Joy and I decided that it was best for our family if I joined, so we immediately drove to Abilene Army Airfield, and I signed up with the reserve detachment headquartered there. A few weeks later, I began flying the North American AT-6 Texan advanced trainer once a month from the airfield while staying overnight in their BOQ. The airplane was manufactured in the same plant at Grand Prairie, Texas, where Joy had worked, and I had ferried the P-51Ds to Coronado, California.

One summer weekend, I picked up a Texan trainer in Abilene and landed on a long stretch of dirt road five miles west of Haskell, where I met Joy, Jesse, Aunt Louise, and Stan Jr.

I took Joy and Jesse each for a ride in the airplane then landed. Aunt Louise was afraid to fly, so she stayed on the ground. Then putting my son on my lap, we took off, and I flew for a few minutes with him excitedly looking around at the instruments, the terrain below, and holding onto the stick with both hands. Having my young son fly with me was an experience I never forgot. After landing and shutting off the engine, I started to carry him over to Joy.

Passing the front edge of the right-wing, he asked, "Daddy, is that the machinegun?" as we walked by the long pitot tube sticking out of it. I laughed and said, "No, son, that makes the airplane instruments work." At the young age of three years old, he was already interested in flying and learning about airplanes.

In the spring of 1948, Joy learned that she was four months pregnant after experiencing morning sickness for several months. At the time, Texas school teachers were prohibited from being in the classroom if they were going to have a baby. Because she was tall and slim, she managed to complete the school year without anyone

ible for a new 1946 four-door Model 463 Jeep station wagon, which was America's first all-steel SUV and featured three-tone paintwork simulating the woodie look. Joy was not happy with the vehicle but knew that it was better suited for our family's needs. Each morning I drove her to school at 7:30 a.m. then began making my rounds to each well location, changing the paper chart and recording the results in a green clothbound ledger book. Each afternoon at 4:30 p.m., I arrived at the school and picked her up, and we went home.

I worked seven days a week until Christmas when Joy's brother Jesse returned home from the war where he had served for one year in the Navy after enlisting at age seventeen with his dad's permission. He moved in with us and slept on the living room sofa, relieving me of my daily rounds to the oil and gas wells on the weekends until he started to school the following September at the University of Texas in Austin. Mr. Heath paid him a small salary to help me with my work and thankfully, did not deduct it from my wages.

By February 20, 1946, the USAAF had released 734,715 service members in a process that was characterized as a demobilization. Brigadier General Leon W. Johnson, Chief of the Air Staff's Personnel Services Division, later noted, "We merely fell apart. We lost many records of all the groups and units that operated during the war because there was no one to take care of them, and they were destroyed."[13]

I continued my work, logging oil and gas production records for the next year. Then in October 1947, I received a letter from the newly formed Department of the Air Force informing me that I was eligible for enrollment in the U.S. Air Force reserves at my former rank of captain. If I joined, I would serve one weekend each month and two weeks in the summer. My monthly payment would be $23, and for the two weeks, I would be paid $160 for a total of $413 per year. The

knowing. On September 7, 1948, our daughter Penelope Corvin was born, and we decided to call her Penny. Two weeks after her birth, Joy returned to our house in Haskell with the new baby, and we decided that we needed to move to Austin, Texas, where I could complete my college education at the University of Texas (UT). So we moved into the veteran's students' housing section. Jesse had already enrolled in school there earlier that summer.

Cost of Living 1949

New House $7,450

Average Wages $2,950/year

Gallon of gas $.17 cents

Minimum Wage $.70/hour

Bread $.14 cents/loaf

Milk $.84 cents/gallon

Bacon/pound $.50 cents

Bananas/pound $.11cents

Coffee $.85 for two pounds

Fresh Chicken $.55/ pound

To accommodate some of the married students, UT had constructed the Brackenridge Apartments southwest of the campus near Lake Austin. WWII wooden barracks were moved from US Army bases in Louisiana to the complex, and they were divided into small two-bedroom one-bath apartments. Costing $27 per month, each had a kitchen and a living room and were approximately 400 square feet in size, about the size of a large motel room today.

Brackenridge Apartment building Austin, Texas

I qualified for the newly enacted G.I. Bill (established in 1944), which paid $500 per semester for tuition, fees, and books, so, in late September 1948, I began taking classes at UT. I also was paid a stipend of $20 per week but soon realized that after our savings ran out, it was not going to be enough money to support my family.

A next-door neighbor worked for the Austin police department and told me that with the growth of the city's population after the war, they needed an additional night radio dispatcher. I applied for the job and got it because I was familiar with radio equipment and military call procedures. A few days later, I began working the 7:00 p.m. to 3:00 a.m. graveyard shift five days a week and was able to study for my college classes at night. I was paid $0.70 per hour for a 40 hour week, so I was earning $28 each paycheck. Along with my weekly stipend, my total income per month was approximately $200, enough for us to live on.

Joy stayed home and took care of the kids and became friends with many of the women living in the adjacent apartments. For Christmas, her parents gave us a new Sylvania 16" black and white tabletop television set, which many years later I learned cost them $300. With long adjustable rabbit ears antenna on top, the kids and Joy were able to watch the Howdy Doody Show with Buffalo Bob and Clarabell the Clown (played by Bob Keeshan, who later became Captain Kangaroo). "Hollywood on Television," hosted by a young Betty White, and a new soap opera called "As The World Turns" were also favorites.

Although our daily schedule was hectic, we had many close friends who were WWII veterans. Occasionally we socialized with them at Scholz's Beer garden on San Jacinto Blvd. All the kids played together and ran around the outdoor patio picnic tables. We were a very happy family. I was working hard at my academics, carrying eighteen hours each semester in order to graduate as quickly as possible.

Transferring to the USAF Tactical Air Command reserve unit at Bergstrom Air Force Base, I began flying the P-51D Mustang again and was now being paid $33 monthly. For the next twenty-three months, we lived in Austin with Joy taking care of the two children while I was going to school and working nights at the downtown police headquarters. Frequently on the weekends, we took the kids to Lake Austin with our friends, where we set up campsites on the sandy beach shoreline and stayed overnight. Many times a young woman working at a nearby beer joint and wearing a cowboy hat, boots, and black bathing suit rode a horse with coolers strapped on each side of the saddle and sold ice-cold beer to the picnickers for fifty cents a bottle. Post-WWII life was good, and I looked forward to my college graduation. Then on June 25, 1950, the Korean War started, and everything changed!

CHAPTER 10

RECALLED INTO THE USAF

On June 15, 1950, I went for my two weeks of reserve training at the 81st Fighter-Interceptor Wing on Kirtland Air Force Base in Albuquerque, New Mexico. It was part of the Air Defense Command. Arriving there, I learned they had twenty-five P-51D Mustangs, about a half-dozen F-80 Shooting Star aircraft, and four F-86 Sabre jets. I hoped to eventually transition into the Sabre jets. Ten days later, on June 25th, North Korea invaded South Korea, and the armed conflict escalated dramatically.

Monday afternoon of the 26th while I was sitting in the operations building pilots' lounge drinking coffee, my commanding officer walked over to me carrying a thick manila envelope.

He grimly said, "Captian Corvin, I've just received word that you are to go to Nellis Air Force Base tomorrow for training in the F-84G Thunderjet. Then you'll transition into the transonic F-86A Sabre, after which you'll be transferred to Korea and assigned to a fighter-interceptor group. With your four years of flying fighters in World War II, you're one of the most experienced combat pilots I have, so you'll be in the first class of pilots at Nellis to fly the jets. I know this interrupts your college plans; however, you can resume your studies in a few months when the war is over." Then as he turned to walked away, he handed me the orders informing me that I was immediately being recalled back into the United States Air Force.

Stunned by the sudden change of plans, I went to the BOQ and reluctantly called Joy, telling her what had just happened.

"Can they do that?" she tearfully asked.

"Honey, I'm afraid they can because that's what the Air Force reserves are used for in case of war."

"I can't believe this is happening to us again like it did when you left for Iwo Jima six years ago, right after we were married."

"I know. It doesn't seem fair at all, but the Air Force is short of fighter pilots since the demobilization, and I'm about to start flying jets because of my extensive flight experience in P-51D Mustangs during the last war."

"Can I come out to Albuquerque with the kids and see you?"

"I'm afraid not right away because tomorrow morning I am being sent to Nellis Air Force Base in Las Vegas, Nevada, to learn to fly F-84G and F-86A jets. Maybe in a week or so after I get settled there, you can fly in, and we'll spend a weekend together. Besides, my commanding officer thinks we will be home from Korea by Christmas after we whip the Commie's butts."

But with my busy training schedule at the Nevada base, we never were able to spend any time together, and it was only in mid-October that I flew back to Austin to spend time with Joy and the kids before I left for Korea two weeks later. Also, my CO was very wrong about winning the war in a few months. Very wrong, indeed!

Nellis Air Force Base

On the morning of Tuesday, June 27, 1950, at 0700 hours, I boarded a C-54 Skymaster transport plane and flew five hundred-eighty miles from Kirtland Air Force Base to Nellis Air Force Base, arriving three hours later. Assigned to the 3595th combat crew training wing, I gave my orders to the duty officer at headquarters and was told to return after lunch and attend an orientation class. Then I boarded a blue Air Force bus, which took me to the BOQ, where I was assigned a room with twin beds, unpacked my B-4 suitcase and stored my flight equipment bag in the small closet.

After walking a few blocks to the officers' club, I ate lunch and then attended a two-hour preliminary briefing at the wing headquarters with about twenty other experienced fighter pilots. They all had served in World War II. Many were recalled into the USAF from schools and universities all around the country. I was excited to be in the first class of F-84 Thunderjet pilots and looked forward to flying in my first jet aircraft.

After the class, we were driven by bus back to the wood WWII barracks BOQ built next to the flight operations building and the main runway. When I walked in, I saw a short, stocky captain smoking a stogie and signing the register with his back to me. Recognizing him, I said, "Ed, what are you doing here?"

He quickly turned around and said, "Well, I'll be damned. I'm sure glad to see you, Stan. I've been assigned to the first class of F-84 Thunderjet and F-86 Sabre pilots. Is that why you're here?"

"Yes, it is. It's good to see you. You rascal! It's been nearly five years since we last saw each other after we returned to California from Iwo Jima."

Nellis AFB Runways

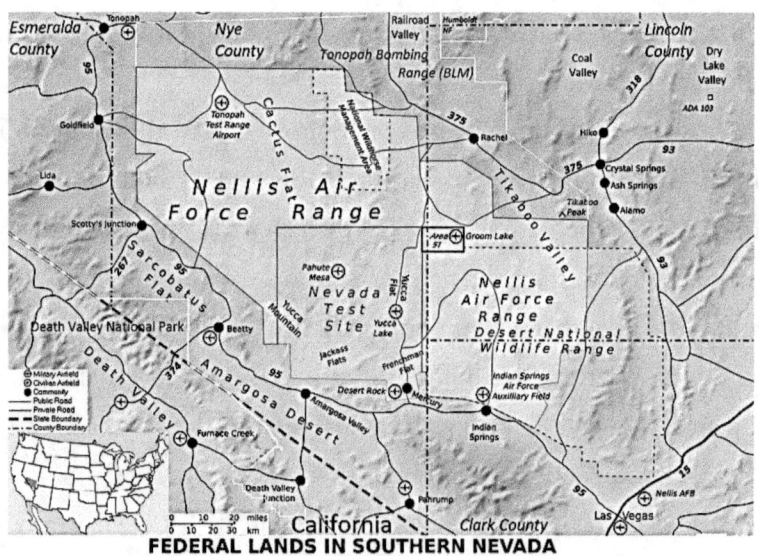

Nellis AFB Gunnery Ranges

Then we hugged like long-lost brothers and slapped each other on the back. Ed turned back to the enlisted clerk and said, "Please put me in the same room with Captain Corvin. My flight was late coming here today, and I missed the orientation; however, the XO said it was okay, and I could begin classes tomorrow morning with everyone."

Walking down the hall to our room, Ed told me about meeting his wife, Martha, at the University of Arkansas in Fayetteville, where he had just received his Master's Degree in mechanical engineering. He had a two-year-old son and a one-year-old daughter and joined the USAF reserves in January 1948 about the same time I did to help with his college expenses. Once he graduated, he was promoted to captain and sent to Nellis for jet flight training.

F-84G Thunderjet Training

After eating breakfast at 0700 hours with several other pilots at the officers' club, we boarded a bus that took us to a classroom near the flight line where we began our study of the Republic Aviation F-84G Dash-1 operating manual. At noon we broke for lunch and were again taken to the officers' club. Afterward, we returned to the air-conditioned classroom and continued learning about the operating systems of the jet from a ground school instructor until 1700 hours when we were dismissed. Ed and I went back to our room and studied for another two hours and then went to the officers' club where we had dinner. The next morning we started the same routine again and continued studying about the F-84G Thunderjet, including all day on Saturdays. Because of the urgent need for qualified jet pilots in Korea, we were on an accelerated training schedule for eight hours a day, six days a week. At the end of two weeks, we had ninety-six hours of ground school instruction and were ready to begin flying.

The Eagle Above

F-84 Thunderjet

F-84 Thunderjet Cockpit

Walking out to the flight line at 0700 hours with an instructor pilot who also was a USAF captain, Ed and I went to our assigned airplanes. There was a crew chief standing beside each of them and a ground crew member with a big fire extinguisher mounted on large rolling wheels. The temperature was already 85° and predicted to climb to 108° by late afternoon. The canopy was open, and a yellow metal platform with several steps was placed on the left side below the cockpit of the plane. The instructor told me to begin my pre-flight check, which I did while he watched.

I began by walking along the left side of the leading edge of the wing, then checked the front landing gear strut and tire, walked along the right side of the fuselage to the leading edge of the wing also checking on the condition of the right landing gear and tire. Walking around the tip tank, I checked the right aileron and trim tab, although I couldn't move them because they were hydraulically actuated after the engine started. Moving to the aft section, I carefully examined the leading edge of the right horizontal elevator and then walked around to the left elevator but also was unable to move it. Looking at the rudder, I saw that it was in the neutral position, then walked to the left elevator and again checked the leading edge of the left side of the tail. Because of occasional foreign object damage (FOD) while taking off and landing at approximately 120 miles per hour, the preflight check out was essential for safely flying the F-84G. Ingesting a rock or debris into the engine intake or blowing out a tire on takeoff could be fatal.

Completing my inspection, I climbed the several steps up to the metal platform where the instructor pilot was standing, then stepped into the tight cockpit and sat down. I removed the starting checklist from the left pocket of my flight suit and began going through the required steps to start the turbojet engine. With my right thumb, I turned on the master switch and heard the faint hum of the electric gyros as they began to spin up and checked the fuel gauges, which showed the tanks were full. Checking to make sure the parking brake was set and the throttle lever was to the rear, I pressed and held the ignition toggle switch to start the engine. Making a whining sound as it spooled up, I slowly moved the throttle control to the idle position and began to hear the deep-throated roar of the turbojet as it started. My heart rate also began to increase significantly.

It was an exciting moment for me to be flying a jet aircraft with tricycle landing gear after having flown tail dragger propeller planes for so many years. I laughed as I thought about the first airplane I had ever flown nine years earlier. It was a Fleet Finch IIB training biplane for the Royal Canadian Air Force in Ontario, Canada, which I crashed into tall pine trees on a tiny island in a remote lake. *"Boy, I have come a long way since 1941."* Then I thought about something funny my father-in-law Jesse Heath laughingly said when things were going very well, "Now we're cooking with gas for sure." *Indeed now, I was cooking with JP-4!*

Fastening my oxygen mask and securing the nylon strap to the right side of my helmet, I made sure the corrugated rubber hose was connected to the oxygen outlet, and the regulator was set to 100%. Then I inserted the two ¼ inch communication plugs into their jacks. Turning on the radios and navigational aids, I looked over and nodded at the instructor pilot who smiled and gave me a right thumbs up and then climbed off the metal platform, which was quickly moved away from my plane. While walking to the aircraft, we had been instructed to wait until both Ed and I had started our engines and then to carefully taxi the airplanes to the runway after calling the Nellis ground control and getting permission.

Releasing the parking brake, I tuned the VHF radio to 121.8 and pressed the radio transmission button on the throttle grip and said, "Nellis ground control, this is Thunderjet 5478 ready for taxi and takeoff, over."

"Roger, 5478, you are cleared to taxi to runway 21 right. Hold short and contact the tower on 132.55 before departure, over."

"Roger 132.55. Thank you, sir, out."

Then I released the parking brake and increased the throttle until the aircraft began to move forward slowly. Tapping both toe brakes, with my boots to made sure I was able to stop if I needed to, I heard Ed call ground control and get permission to taxi to the same runway. Leading the way, I taxied to the end of runway 21R then stopped to tune the VHF radio to 132.55.

"Nellis Tower, this is Thunderjet 4578 holding short of 21 right. Ready for takeoff, over."

"Roger, 4578. You are cleared for takeoff with a right departure. Winds are 240° at 8 knots, and the altimeter is 3006. Over"

"Roger 3006 and right departure. 4578. Out"

Slowly taxiing on to the asphalt runway and swinging the nose of the aircraft to the right to a heading of 210°, I closed the canopy, paused for a moment to set the Kollsman window barometric pressure setting to 30.06 and lowered the flaps for takeoff. Heatwaves rising from the black asphalt runway created a shimmering mirage in front of me. Then I saw Ed move into position behind me. He called the tower and said that he would be taking off immediately after I did. They gave him the same instructions as were given to me and then gripping the throttle lever I steadily pressed it fully forward with my left hand as I released the toe brakes. The acceleration of the F-84 pressed me back into the seat and was much more powerful than the P-51D Mustang I'd flown for so many years. Because there was no torque from a front-engine mounted propeller, I didn't need to compensate on the pedals for it, although I had trimmed the rudder slightly to the right as the Dash-1 instructed.

Watching the airspeed indicator, I quickly accelerated to 120 miles per hour, and slowly pulled the stick back, felt the nose wheel, and both the left and right landing gear lift off the 10,000-foot runway. With my left hand, I reached over and raised the flaps and landing gear lever on the left side of the instrument panel and soon felt the bump as the gear retracted into the wheel wells. Reaching the crosswind altitude of 2,400 ft. I banked right 90°, climbed to 2,900 feet, and departed the traffic pattern to the north, where I steeply increased my climb angle and flew straight ahead to 35,000 feet while accelerating to 500 miles per hour.

Within two minutes, Ed pulled up alongside my right-wing and gave me a right thumbs up and waggled his wings. I imagined him grinning in his oxygen mask as I was now doing in mine. *"Wow. This is fantastic! It is so much easier to fly a jet than the Mustang."* For a few minutes, we continued flying north until we reached the Nellis gunnery range known as the Desert National Wildlife Range. In our ground school classes, we had been warned not to overfly nearby Groom Lake where Area 51 was situated and the highly secret USAF base where Lockheed's clandestine Skunk Works flight testing facility was located.

Flying over the mountains north of the gunnery range, near Crystal Springs and Hico, I motioned to Ed that I was going to descend and slowly nosed the jet over in a dive and watched the machmeter rapidly climb to the red line at .81 Mach which was 622 mph. "Exhilaration" was the word that came to mind while my heart rapidly beat in my chest. As I slowed and leveled off at 20,000 feet, Ed rocketed past me in his inverted airplane, waving his hand vigorously. I rolled over and began to chase him, soon catching up to him 10,000 feet above the Sierra Nevada mountains below. For a few seconds, we flew side by side, upside down, over the rugged terrain tilting our heads back and looking at the fast-moving landscape below. Minute amounts of dust and dirt from the floorboard fell on the plexiglass canopy as did my small checklist and folded up sectional map. It had been a long time since I'd had this much fun flying. I rolled upright and indicated for Ed to follow me, and we headed over to the Indian Springs auxiliary field to shoot some touch and gos.

Fifty miles northeast of the airfield I called the tower on their VHF frequency of 118.30 and said, "Indian Springs Tower, this is Thunderjet 4578 I am leading a flight of two F-84s requesting permission to enter your traffic pattern and shoot some touch and go's. Over."

"4578, there is no traffic in the area, so you are cleared for a straight-in approach to runway 26. Winds are 270° at 10 knots. The altimeter is 3009. Sir, use a left traffic pattern, which will have you parallel to Highway 95. Over"

"Roger Indian Springs Tower, left pattern 3009. Out"

Turning west in the direction of the auxiliary airfield Ed and I started our descent. Thirteen miles to the east of the runway was Hayford Peak, which was a 9,912-foot mountain. Cruising at 500 mph meant that we were flying one mile every 7.2 seconds, so we were approximately six minutes away from the runway. Once we crossed over the mountain peak, Ed pulled in behind me, and I lowered my landing gear and 25° of flaps, slowed to 120 mph, and started the approach to the 9002-foot asphalt runway in a 500 foot per minute descent. One mile from the approach end, I called the tower.

"Indian Springs Tower, this is Thunderjet 4578 on short final for touch and go runway 26. Over."

"4578, you're cleared for touch and go. Over"

"Roger that. Out"

A few feet off the runway, I leveled the aircraft, flared slightly, touched down on the asphalt, then heard the tires squeak and applied full power. Near the end of the runway, the aircraft lifted off, and I raised the landing gear and flaps. Climbing to the pattern altitude of 4,200 feet, I made a left crosswind circling turn and watched the cars on Highway 95 as I paralleled it on the downwind leg of the traffic pattern. Once at 45° past the end of the runway, I made another left circling base leg to set me up on final approach back to runway 26. I saw Ed about a mile behind me.

Reducing power and slowing down I lowered the landing gear, and flaps then called the tower and said, "Indian Springs Tower, this is 4578 on short final for touch and go 26. Over."

"4578, you're cleared for touch and go. Out"

Touching down, I again applied full power, took off, raised the landing gear and flaps, and continued around the flight pattern. Ed and I made about a dozen landings and takeoffs then I called the tower and thanked them, and we departed the area and headed back to Nellis Air Force Base. After calling the tower and entering the traffic pattern, we landed on runway 21 right and taxied to the flight line with our canopies open and parked our aircraft. The outside air temperature (OAT) was already 95° and quickly getting hotter. The metal platform was brought to the aircraft, and I stepped out of the cockpit drenched in sweat from the stress of flying my first jet aircraft and because of the hot desert sun beating down on me.

Our instructor pilot walked over to us and asked, "How did everything go?"

In unison, Ed and I smiled and said, "No problem. It's a piece of cake to fly." Looking at each other, we laughed and walked into the operations building, where we removed our parachutes and helmets and hung them up in the ready room; then, each of us filled out our aircraft log, indicating there were no problems with the flight.

"Hold up, guys." The instructor said when he walked into the room. "Go ahead and take a break and drink plenty of water, then grab your gear and go out and fly another two hours. Because we are on an accelerated schedule, you will fly two times a day in the morning in addition to your ground school training in the afternoon after lunch."

Nodding at him, I said, "That's fine with me," as I walked over to a large window-mounted swamp cooler air-conditioning unit and stood in front of its blower fan with my arms outstretched and my K2-B flight suit partially unzipped to cool down.

Over the next four weeks with only four days off on Sundays, Ed and I accumulated slightly more than ninety-six hours of flying time in the F-84G and the same number of ground school training in its hydraulic, electrical, mechanical, and avionics systems. Then came the fun part—armament training and gunnery practice. Most Korean War fighter pilots will tell you the thrill of firing six .50 caliber heavy machine-guns while flying a jet aircraft is a kickass experience creating an adrenaline rush like nothing else does. The rocky hills in the vast unpopulated northern gunnery ranges afforded a natural backdrop for weapons practice.

For several days our ground school classes taught us how to use the F-84G's new factory-installed AN/APG-30 radar ranging unit coupled with the A-1CM gun, bomb, and rocket sight. Then it was time to go to the range and try it out. After briefing us about the tactics used while making gun runs firing at stationary targets on the ground, Ed and I, along with our instructor pilot, went out to the flight line and took off as a flight of three with the IP in the lead.

Arriving at our assigned range, he called the ground control officer and obtained permission for us to begin firing at several white painted cement block structures built into the side of a hill. Then while Ed and I watched, the IP began a steep dive, and we saw him fire a three-second burst of .50 caliber machine gun rounds at the target. Every fifth round in the metal linked ammunition belt was a tracer, so a cyclic rate of fire of 1250 rounds per minute (21 per second) meant that four tracers were visible each second and were easily seen by the pilot. All of the armor-piercing rounds hit the center of the target indicating the IP had lots of experience firing the machine guns from the F-84B.

He called me on the radio and said, "Corvin, it's your turn now."

"Roger that," I replied as I set up for my firing run, armed my guns, and proceeded to dive at the target. Pulling the trigger, the massive firepower coming from the weapons startled me as I watched the bullets miss the target by twenty feet above it. Coming out of the dive and banking to the left, I climbed back up to altitude and fell in behind the IP's airplane.

Then he said, "Okay, Skelton, it's your turn."

"Roger," Ed said as he began his dive. Then I saw smoke pour from his gun barrels and watched as all of his bullets hit the center of the target just as the IPs had.

"Good shooting, Skelton. I think you have the hang of it," he said. "Stan, steepen your dive, place your sight pipper on the base of the target, and that should be enough adjustment for you to hit the center of the target also."

Lining up with the target again, I waited to begin my dive so that it would be steeper, armed my guns, and placed the brightly glowing pipper on the base of the concrete blocks and pulled the trigger for two seconds. Almost instantly, the bullets hit the center of the target, and I was elated that it was so easy to use the new radar-ranging gun sight.

Making several more gun runs, we were all out of ammunition and returned to Nellis to rearm and refuel. After flying for another three hours, we finished our first gunnery practices and landed back at the base. Then for the next two weeks, we continued to utilize the ranges several times each day, including firing the twenty-four five-inch rockets we each carried; however, they were not very accurate at all.

Finally, after taking an extensive written exam covering the Dash-1 manual and the flight characteristics of the F-84G Thunderjet, we completed the course on August 15, 1950. It had been an exciting adventure to fly my first jet. Still, it was only a forerunner to what I was about to encounter flying the much faster and more agile Northrop American Aviation F-86A Sabre.

F-86A Sabre Jet Training

"Oh, my God, that's fast!" I yelled aloud into my oxygen mask. I had just leveled off the swept-wing transonic jet at 20,000 feet over the barren Nevada desert after diving from 48,000 feet. I was smiling broadly, having reached the F-86A's maximum operating VMO speed of 687 miles per hour, Mach .90, indicated airspeed (IAS), which nearly was the sound barrier. *(The speed of sound is 761.2 mph at sea level and an air temperature of 59° F.)*

F-86A Sabre

F-86A of the 4th FIW, 335th Squadron "Chiefs"

F-86A SABRE

General characteristics
- **Crew:** 1
- **Length:** 37 ft 1 in
- **Wingspan:** 37 ft
- **Empty weight:** 11,125 lb
- **Loaded weight:** 15,198 lb
- **Max takeoff weight:** 18,152 lb
- **Fuel provisions** Internal fuel load: 435 US gallons, Drop tanks: two 120 or 206 gallons, JP-4 fuel
- **Powerplant:** 1 - General Electric J47-GE-27 turbojet, 5,970 lb. thrust

Performance
- **Maximum speed:** 687 mph (Mach .89) at sea level
- **Range:** 785 miles to 1,525 miles with ferry tanks
- **Combat radius:** 414 mi with two 120 US gallons drop tanks
- **Service ceiling:** 49,600 ft at combat weight
- **Rate of climb:** 9,000 ft/min at sea level[14]

For four weeks, Ed and I had spent nearly two hundred hours of classroom work studying the Dash-1 flight manual and another twenty hours in an F-86A cockpit simulator. One thing the instructor pilots repeatedly emphasized was that the wing's solid leading edge and increased internal fuel capacity improved the aircraft's combat performance but worsened a dangerous and often fatal handling characteristic if the nose was raised prematurely from the runway upon takeoff. This over-rotation danger was a concern for newly transitioning F-86A pilots. Unlike modern zero-zero ejection seats, the F-86A had to be at a minimum airspeed and altitude for the pilots' ejection to be survivable. So, several fatalities occurred because the aircraft was too low and slow for the pilot to eject safely after they over-rotated.

Finally, in October 1950, Ed and I completed our F-86A flight check out and gunnery training at Nellis Air Force Base and received orders for transfer to the 4th Fighter-Interceptor Wing. It was made up of the 334th, 335th, and 336th squadrons temporarily based at Dover, Delaware. They were preparing to ferry their F-86A Sabres to the West Coast, where they and the unit personnel and equipment were to be loaded on an aircraft carrier then taken to Japan.

I was given two weeks' leave before reporting to my new unit and flew back to Bergstrom AFB in Austin, TX, after having been gone for four months. Joy and the kids picked me up, and we went to our apartment. Later that evening, we celebrated my return with several neighboring couples, including some of Joy's close friends. Although the war was going to last for only two or three months, my wife and the kids were required to move to another apartment because only military veteran students currently enrolled at the university could live in the Brackenridge apartment complex.

A few days after my return, we rented a small, inexpensive

two-bedroom garage apartment near the campus. With the help of several friends and some neighbors, we packed everything and moved into it. I intended to be home by Christmas or New Years Day at the latest and enroll in the university for the 1951 spring semester.

At the time, the population of Austin was 132,459, so it was a fairly large city with many parks and recreational facilities. One of our favorite places to go was Zilker Park in south Austin. It was located on three-hundred fifty-eight acres and had Barton Springs Pool, which measured three acres in size (208' x 624') and was fed from underground springs with an average water temperature of 68°- 70°. Even the Texas sun didn't heat that much water, so it was always a very cold swimming hole.

Several times in the two weeks before I left for Korea, Joy, the kids and I spent the warm Indian Summer fall days in the park where we placed quilts under huge oak trees. Usually, Stan Jr. was running around trying to fly his new kite or small balsa wood airplane, and Penny was playing with her dolls and baby toys. In the evening before going home, we always went to our favorite restaurant, Youngblood's Chicken Shack on South Lamar Boulevard, to eat their crispy fried chicken and freshly made soft rolls slathered with butter and honey. After the meal, the kids played on the hand-cranked toy cars built on a circular rail track located beside the restaurant.

Once my two weeks' leave was over, Joy, and the kids took me to Bergstrom AFB for my departure. Saying goodbye to my family was tough because I didn't want to leave them and knew how difficult it was going to be for my young wife to live alone. At only twenty-seven years old, she was caring for my five-year-old son and two-year-old daughter with no family nearby. After a tearful exchange of goodbyes with Joy and promises to write frequently to each other, I boarded a C-54D MATS Skymaster four-engine aircraft and flew to my new unit in Dover, Delaware. It was the gathering point for the 4th FIW before it deployed to Japan and Korea.

While en route, I remembered reading an *Austin-American Statesman* newspaper story about the disappearance of the same type USAF aircraft earlier that year with a crew of eight and thirty-six passengers during a flight between Elmendorf AFB, Alaska and Great Falls AFB, Montana. Thirty-four passengers were military personnel, and two were civilian tech reps. No trace of the aircraft or its occupants was ever found. Several other aircraft accidents and incidents I had heard about added to my uneasiness about flying on the big multiengine transport plane; however, the flight to Dover AFB was uneventful, and at dusk, we landed safely. Checking in at base operations, I saw that Ed Skelton had arrived earlier in the afternoon from Little Rock, Arkansas. A staff car took three other pilots and me to the BOQ, where we signed into our new temporary quarters and then went to the Officers' Club.

"Stan, come over here, and join me," Ed shouted while waving as we walked into the stag bar. He was sitting with two other pilots who we had gone through our jet training at Nellis Air Force Base. They were drinking beer, and he ordered another round for all of us.

"How are Joy and the kids?" he asked.

"They are doing fine, but Joy is worried about my going back into combat so soon after we got back from the Pacific. How are Martha and your kids doing?" I replied.

He said, "Martha and the kids are okay, but she's also anxious about my going to Korea and flying in combat. But I suppose that's the way it's got to be for now."

"Well, Ed, don't worry; everything's going to be okay once we come home by the end of the year."

Of course, I was wrong about the war ending so soon, and both Ed and I served in Korea until December 1951. We each flew slightly over one hundred total combat missions in the F-86A Sabre, which was the statutory maximum set by the planning standards board of the Far Eastern Air Force (FEAF) command.

For the next week, Ed and I and eight other pilots spent each day flying two and one-half hours, covering four hundred eighty-six miles, in a USAF C-54 Skymaster transport from Dover to Columbus, Ohio. There we picked up newly manufactured F-86As at the North American Aviation plant. The return flight only took fifty-four minutes because we were cruising at 540 miles per hour! Finally, there was an early morning briefing for the pilots, and the plan was announced to ferry forty-eight of the transonic jets to Coronado, California, two days later.

With four hundred thirty-five gallons of fuel in four self-sealing internal tanks and two two-hundred six-gallon in external auxiliary tanks, each aircraft had about a 1,600-mile ferry range. A total of 847 gallons meant the maximum time we could fly until "bingo" fuel was approximately two hours and thirty minutes since the jet was burning approximately three hundred gallons per hour. Our planned route would take us from Dover, Deleware to Tinker AFB in Oklahoma City, a distance of 1,400 miles where we would refuel after flying for two and one-half hours. From Tinker AFB, we were to fly another one hour and forty-five minutes to Williams AFB in Mesa, Arizona, which was a distance of 964 miles where we would stay overnight. Then the next morning, we were to fly to Coronado, California, a distance of 366 miles.

With our commanding officer, Lieutenant Colonel William

Drake planning to lead the first flight of four F-86As, Ed and I were selected to be flight leaders along with nine other experienced WWII fighter pilots. Two days later, after an extensive early morning briefing at 0400 hours, we all were taken to the flight line in a blue Air Force bus, and each of us was dropped off at our assigned aircraft. Each flight of four fighters was assigned a letter starting with "A" flight going through "L" flight, totaling twelve flights, which amounted to forty-eight F-86As. Over the next two days, we flew cross-country arriving in Southern California at Coronado NAS the first week of November 1950. Within a few days, all of the airplanes were loaded on board an aircraft carrier, and we departed for Japan and the Korean War.

While smoking a cigarette standing on the flight deck of the massive ship after we were underway and far out to sea, I thought, *How ironic that I'm now leaving on another aircraft carrier to go to another war in the Pacific ocean as I did six years ago in October of 1944 during World War II. Hopefully, this war will be over in a couple of months, and I can go home to my family in Austin and resume college.* But unfortunately, things didn't happen at all as I expected!

CHAPTER 11

THE KOREAN WAR

"The Air Force is on trial in Korea."
GEN. HOYT S. VANDENBERG, USAF CHIEF OF STAFF, 1950[15]

Living up to its famous motto "Fourth but First," the 4th Fighter-Interceptor Wing (FIW) arrived in Tokyo Bay on December 1, 1950, with the first F-86As Sabres, which were offloaded from the aircraft carrier at piers near Haneda Air Base, Japan. After the jets were washed down to remove the saltwater and prevent corrosion, we flew them a short distance to Johnson Air Force Base, which was only twenty-four miles northwest of Tokyo. From there, detachments began deploying in mid-December to bases in South Korea.

The majority of the pilots from the wing were experienced World War II veterans, and their combined combat victories during that war totaled slightly over one-thousand downed enemy aircraft. The wing's primary mission was to establish air superiority over the North Koreans, and the Sabre was undoubtedly capable of engaging the Soviet-built MiG-15 on equal terms. At least that's what the brass hoped would happen!

Ed and I accompanied the first advanced detachment of the 335th and 336th squadron's F-86As arriving at Kimpo airfield (K-14) west of Seoul on December 15, 1950, and we flew our first combat mission two days later on December 17th. It was an armed reconnaissance of the area just south of the Yalu River. Lieutenant Colonel Bruce H. Hinton, commander of the 336th Squadron, succeeded in shooting down one MiG-15 out of a flight of four to score first blood for the legendary Sabre. Neither Ed nor I engaged any enemy aircraft but were exhilarated to see the area was a target-rich environment even if they were located across the river, and we were forbidden to fly there.

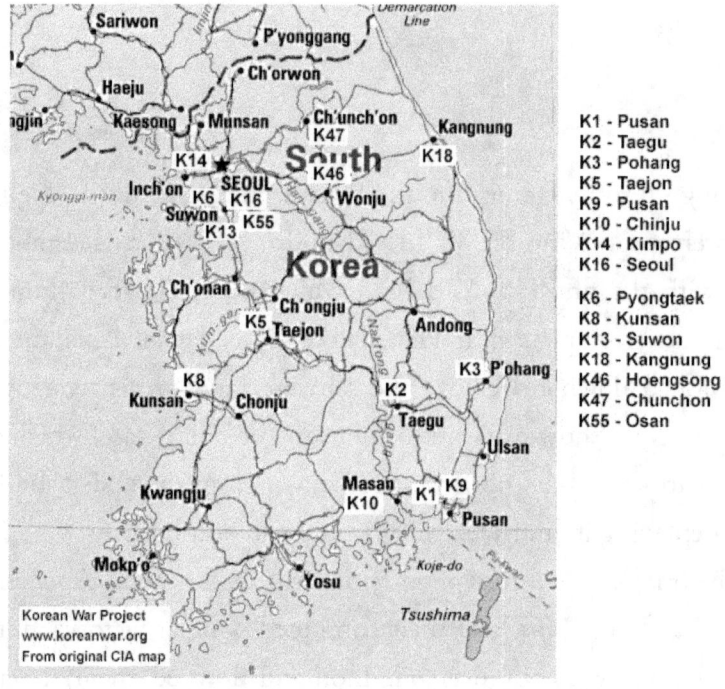

Korean Airfields With K Numbers

F-86As at Kimpo Air Base, Korea

Our combat operations center was located at the north end of the airstrip, as was our living quarters, mess hall, and small Officers' Club. According to 4th FIW command records, before the end of December 1950, we flew two hundred thirty-four combat missions, seventy-six of which involved air-to-air combat that resulted in eight MiG-15 victories and one F-86A loss. Again, neither Ed nor I shot down a communist aircraft. But we both engaged them at high altitudes, and our gun cameras confirmed we each hit some with our .50 caliber machine guns armor-piercing incendiary (API) bullets.

On January 2, 1950, Fifth Air Force hurriedly withdrew the forward-based F-86s, assigned to the 4th FIW, from North Korean threatened Kimpo airfield near Seoul, to the wing's home station at Johnson AFB, Japan. Then five weeks later, the entire group began operations from Suwon AB, South Korea, also known as K-13. The USAF had numerous air bases in Korea, and many of these were former Japanese airfields. The spelling of Korean locations on maps varied greatly, and many times villages had a Korean and a Japanese name. Thus a "K" number identified individual air bases in both northern and southern Korea to prevent confusion among locations.

North American Aviation F-86A Sabres of the 4th Fighter Interceptor Wing, Suwon, South Korea, circa June 1951. (U.S. Air Force photo)

A major part of life on the base throughout the Korean War was dealing with the dust in summer and mud and snow in winter. USAF pilots and crew members lived in large eight-man squad sized tents with wooden or concrete floors, and we stored our clothing and flight gear in primitive furniture made from scrap wood or crates. Even though each had an oil-fired potbelly stove, our tents were freezing cold in the winter when the temperature was frequently twenty-five below zero.

Four-foot deep dirt slit trenches were dug between them and served as an emergency bunker in the event of enemy mortar or artillery attack. Several two-hole outhouse style latrines were placed in our tent area, which emitted a horrible stench in the summertime and were bitterly cold in the frigid winter. They were only used as a last resort, and no one lingered very long inside the wretched toilet facility.

Because our tents were placed next to the flight line, the noise level was very loud since flight operations took place twenty-four hours a day, with various aircraft continually taking off and landing on the nearby runway. Sandbags were stacked around the tents outside to a height of about five feet to protect us from any shrapnel from "Bed Check Charlie," a North Korean pilot who flew over Suwon every night and dropped a small bomb on the concrete and pierced steel plank (PSP) runway or our housing area.

Communist AN-2 Bi-Plane

Soviet & Chinese Antonov AN-2 (Bed check Charlie's Favorite Aircraft)
(Photo Licensed under the Creative Commons)

COMMUNIST AN-2 BI-PLANE

General characteristics
- **Crew:** 1–2
- **Gross weight** 11,993 lb.
- **Fuel capacity:** 320 US gal.
- **Powerplant:** 1 - Shvetsov 9-cylinder air-cooled supercharge radial piston engine, 1,010 hp.
- **Propellers:** 4-bladed constant-speed propeller
- **Maximum speed:** 160 mph
- **Cruise speed:** 120 mph
- **Stall speed:** 31 mph
- **Range:** 525 miles
- **Service ceiling:** 14,800 ft.
- **Rate of climb:** 690 ft. /min.
- **Fuel consumption:** 51 gal. /hr.

Under typical conditions, the AN-2 could take-off in 560 ft. while the landing run was 705 ft. The AN-2 had no stall speed, a fact which is quoted in its operating manual. A note from the Soviet pilot's handbook reads: *"If the engine quits in instrument conditions or at night, the pilot should pull the control column full aft and keep the wings level. The leading-edge slats will snap out at about 40 mph, and when the airplane slows to a forward speed of about 25 mph, the airplane will sink at about a parachute descent rate until the aircraft hits the ground."*[16]

Pilots of the AN-2 have stated that they are capable of flying the aircraft in full control at thirty mph; as a contrast, a modern Cessna four-seater light aircraft has a stall speed of around fifty mph. This slow stall speed actually makes it possible for the aircraft to fly backward relative to the ground. If the airplane is pointed into a headwind of roughly thirty-five mph, it will travel backward at five mph while under full control at thirty mph.

USAF F-80s and F-84s were used for close air support of ground troops, and our F-86s were used primarily for combat air patrol (CAP) operations to maintain air superiority once the MiG-15 began to be used by the North Koreans. A combat air patrol was a mission provided over a specific area for the purpose of intercepting and destroying the North Korean aircraft before they could attack their targets, which were the slower American F-80s and F-84s.

It typically involved our fighters flying a high altitude (49,000 feet) tactical pattern around a particular target, while looking for incoming enemy attackers. Capping operations differed from fighter escorts in that the CAP force was not tied to the group it was protecting. It also was not limited in altitudes and speeds it flew and had tactical flexibility to engage an enemy threat. On the other hand, fighter escorts typically stayed with the bomber group they were supporting and at their slower speed. The fighters were a final reactive force against a close-in enemy threat.

The 4th FIW pilots mainly conducted counter-air patrols and attacked and destroyed enemy aircraft whenever possible. During April 1951, we attacked five hundred-forty MiG-15s and destroyed twenty. Besides combat air patrol and bomber escort missions, our Sabres attacked targets spread across the northwestern Korean terrain from airfields on the Yalu River at Sinuiju and Uiju to rail yards further south at Kunu-Ri. We also flew armed reconnaissance sorties and occasionally provided close support for ground forces. The 4th FIW was the deadliest interceptor wing of the Korean War. It accounted for five hundred and sixteen air-to-air victories, representing more than half of all the enemy aircraft forces destroyed.

MiG-15

Mikoyan-Gurevich 15 (MiG-15) also called the Fagot

MIG-15

General Characteristics
- **Crew:** 1
- **Length:** 33 ft 2 in.
- **Wingspan:** 33 ft 1 in.
- **Empty weight:** 8,115 lb.
- **Gross weight:** 11,120 lb.
- **Max takeoff weight:** 13,461 lb. with two 160 US gal. drop-tanks
- **Fuel capacity:** 380 US gal. internal tanks
- **Powerplant:** 1 - Klimov VK-1 centrifugal-flow turbojet, 5,950 lb. thrust

Performance
- **Maximum speed:** 669 mph (Mach .87) at sea level
- **Cruise speed:** 530 mph (Mach 0.69)
- **Range:** 1,570 mi. with two drop-tanks
- **Service ceiling:** 50,900 ft.
- **Rate of climb:** 10,080 ft/min.

MiG-15 Original Cockpit

A North Korean Peoples' Air Force Mikoyan-Gurevich MiG 15 in a hangar at Kimpo Air Base. Pilot defected.

ignition chamber and finally exited out the tailpipe of the MiG-15's engine creating the thrust.

The F-86A was powered by the GE J-47, axial-flow engine. The engine sucked in air through a series of fans placed together, pumping air in and increasing compression. The compressed air then entered a large front chamber, which ignited the fuel, and then passed through turbine wheels on the rear end, providing the forward thrust. This was known as the axial flow engine and came to be used worldwide in all jet aircraft.

The MiG-15 was one of the first jet fighters to incorporate swept wings to achieve high transonic speeds—generally considered to be between Mach .72 and 1.0. In combat over Korea, it outperformed straight-winged jet fighters, which were largely relegated to ground-attack roles, but was soon quickly countered by the similarly equipped American swept-wing North American F-86A Sabre.[17]

In December 1945, at the end of WWII, the Soviet aviation minister Mikhail Khrunichev and aircraft designer A. S. Yakovlev suggested to Premier Joseph Stalin that the USSR buy the conservative but fully developed "Nene" engines from Rolls-Royce, for the purpose of copying them in a minimum of time. Stalin is said to have replied, "What fool will sell us his secrets?" However, he gave his consent to the proposal, and aircraft designer Artem Mikoyan, engine designer Vladimir Klimov, and others traveled to the United Kingdom in 1946 to purchase the engines. To Stalin's amazement, the British Labour government and its Minister of Trade, Sir Stafford Cripps, were perfectly willing to sell the engines and to provide technical information and a license to the Russians to manufacture the Rolls-Royce "Nene."

Sample engines were purchased and delivered with blueprints. Following evaluation and adaptation to Russian conditions, the windfall technology was reversed engineered and then tooled for mass-production as the Klimov RD-45 to be incorporated into the MiG-15. The first production example flew on December 31, 1948. It entered Soviet Air Force service in 1949, and subsequently received the NATO reporting name Fagot."[18]

The British designed "Nene" jet engines the Russians bought worked on a centrifugal compressor principal. It had a muti-blade centrifugal impeller near the front intake, which spun around and compressed the air that was sucked in and then went through an

CHAPTER 12

MIG ALLEY

One morning in early May, after our .50 caliber machine guns were charged in the armament area, we took off from Suwon Air Base (K-13), climbed to forty thousand feet in about ten minutes, and leveled off at 600 mph. Spreading out slightly, we all briefly test-fired our guns, as I led my flight of four F-86A Sabres on a northwesterly heading that would take us to the south side of the Yalu River and the infamous MiG Alley.

USAF photo of the Torii Gate leading to the Sabre flight line at Kimpo Air Base

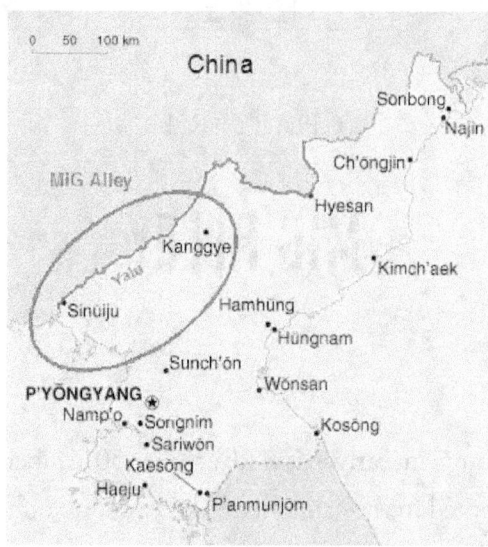

Infamous MiG Alley

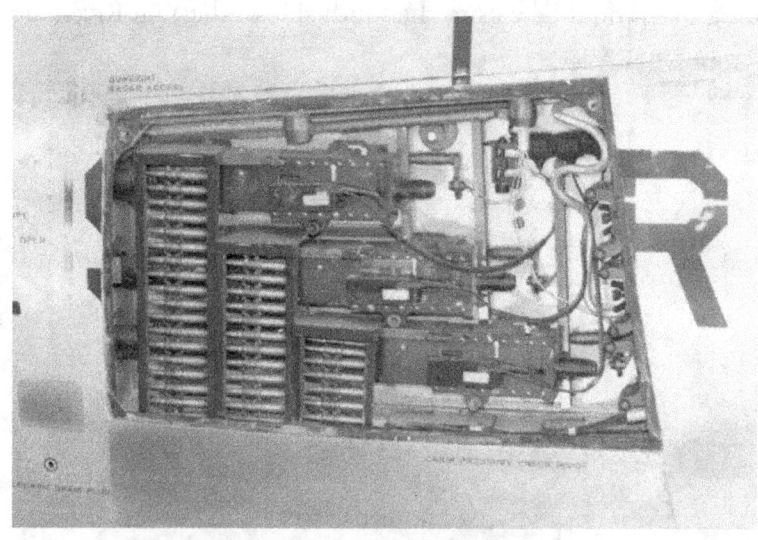

Three M-3 machine guns mounted on each side of an F-86 Sabre.

An F-86 Sabre having its nose-mounted heavy-machine guns harmonized.

We were part of a larger sixteen aircraft group flying a counter-air patrol to lure enemy aircraft to engage us in dogfights. We provided top air cover against the North Korean MiG-15s for the American F-84s and F-80s who were attacking enemy held roads, bridges, and railroads. Our group was made up of four flights named; green, white, blue, and red. I was leading the green flight, with call sign Green 1. Captain Ed Skelton was leading the blue flight with the call sign Blue 1.

At our 0400 hour flight briefing, we were instructed not to attack nor destroy the Chinese hydroelectric plant and the Sup'ung Dam on the Yalu River originally built by the Japanese in 1943. Threatened with expulsion from the 4th FIW, we also were warned not to cross the river under any circumstances, except while in hot pursuit of a specific enemy aircraft. Finally, we were told to expect large groups of enemy planes to launch from Antung Airfield, located on the northern side of the river in China across from the North Korean city of Sinuiju. Earlier reconnaissance photos showed a 6,000 feet concrete runway had replaced their previous two gravel airstrips with hard-surfaced taxiways and rudimentary revetments protecting numerous aircraft including seventy-five MiG-15s.

Leaving the early morning briefing, Ed and I were elated at the prospect of attacking a large group of MiG-15s with our F-86As, which we knew were superior aircraft. Ed said, "Stan, let's keep our flights within sight of each other once we arrive at the Yalu so that we can join forces if we encounter the MiGs. Maybe you can shoot down a couple of enemy planes like you did those Japanese Zeros at Osaka five years ago."

Yalu River Hydroelectric Plant Built By Japanese
From 1937 to 1943 at the Sup'ung Gravity Dam (Photo in Public Domain)

targets near the mouth of the river. We had maintained radio silence during the short flight to our objective because the North Koreans and Chinese monitored our frequencies. We continued that practice while flying over the F-80s and F-84s we were protecting.

Suddenly, my wingman urgently said on the radio, "Green 1, bogeys 5 o'clock high." When I swiveled my head around to look over my right shoulder, I saw a dozen MiGs diving down at us from 50,000 feet. I quickly checked my gyros on the gunsight in preparation for an imminent dogfight.

I knew the Soviet-built MiG-15 had a better turning radius than my F-86A and more powerful weapons—two 23 mm Nudelman-Rikhter NR-23 autocannon in the lower-left fuselage with eighty rounds per gun, and one hundred sixty rounds total. It was a single-barrel, short recoil-operated cannon capable of firing approximately seven hundred fifty rounds per minute but had only 6.4 seconds of total firing time. Additionally, they had one 37 mm Nudelman N-37 autocannon in the lower right fuselage and a total of 40 rounds. With a cyclic rate of fire of four hundred rounds per minute, it had only ten seconds of firing time before the ammo ran out.

While the MiG-15's weapons were more deadly than our six .50-caliber machine guns, I was confident that with my four years of flying fighters and dogfighting over Europe, North Africa, and Iwo Jima during World War II, I was more than a match for any "Russkie" or North Korean "Gook" pilot flying against me. (Early in the war, General Douglas MacArthur issued a written order banning the term "Gook" from being used when referring to any person of Asian descent. He feared its use by the NATO forces would offend the South Korean allies.)

After breaking up into our two-ship elements, I indicated with

Yalu River frozen over in winter.
(Photo use with permission of Creative Commons)

"Sure, we'll do that, and hopefully we'll catch them by surprise before they can attack. You know most of their pilots are Russians who were flying in the last war and are very experienced in tactical combat flight operations, so be careful," I said as I slapped him on the back.

It was about 200 miles to MiG Alley from Suwon. Fuel limitations allowed our F-86As to remain in MiG Alley for about twenty minutes and less if we engaged in combat. We staggered the missions, so the next flight of F-86s arrived before the previous patrol had to depart. Time was not a factor for the MiG pilots, who waited until the F-86s approached before launching from Antung and other Manchurian bases across the river.

Arriving at our destination along the south side of the Yalu River, we spread out, and I took my green flight east towards the Yellow Sea to provide cover for several USAF fighter groups attacking ground

my right hand for my wingman to make a hard right turn, rolled my fighter, and started a climb up to the flight of MiGs. I had learned in the previous war, the best attack maneuver, at least for me, was to fly directly at the lead aircraft and scatter their flight—basically a high speed chicken maneuver. However, with our combined rate of closure speed of nearly 1,400 miles per hour, we were covering approximately 2,000 feet per second, and within three seconds, we passed each other. I made a tight 180° right turn and dove after the MiGs and saw several of my flight, including my wingman, do the same as they tried to keep up with me.

Our aircraft had been retrofitted with the new A-1B GBR sight, and AN/APG-5C ranging radar equipment. This combination was designed to automatically measure the range and calculate the appropriate lead before the guns were fired, relieving me of the task of having to manually adjust an optical sight to determine the range to the target. When activated, the system automatically locked onto and tracked the target. The sight image was projected onto the armored glass of the canopy, and the illumination of a radar target indicator light on the sight indicated the time to track the target continuously for one second before firing.

While the gunsight and radar ranging equipment was very helpful in acquiring and firing at a swiftly moving enemy target, I quite frankly had not anticipated the problem of dogfighting at near-supersonic speeds until my first encounter with the MiGs on December 17th. One second, I saw an approaching bogey, and the next second, it was gone. In order to survive Korean combat flying, I had to increase my reaction time in acquiring and engaging the MiG-15s. I also learned that for all practical purposes, we were equally matched.

K-14 gyro computing gun sight

F-86 Showing K-14 Gyro Gun Sight

As I rapidly approached the enemy planes from above, I could see them attacking a group of four F-84s who were providing tactical air support for a large group of American ground troops. Suddenly, after seeing us diving to them, the MiGs dispersed and headed back to the

Yalu River and the safety of their Chinese base. Rolling into an almost inverted attitude, I made a long deflection shot at the trailing MiG. However, the distance was too far for the gunsight and ranging radar to calculate the lead accurately, and I shot behind the enemy target.

My wingman and I descended to five thousand feet and flew along the south side of the river, hoping the MiGs would try to attack us. But it didn't happen. Finally, someone said, "Bingo fuel" on the radio, and we all turned to fly back to Suwon. Then coming from behind me, several large bright orange basketball-size enemy projectiles passed by the right side of my fuselage a few feet from the wing root and cockpit where I sat. They were from a MiG-15's 37 mm cannon. I instantly made a hard left turn pulling four to five Gs and saw the enemy aircraft about a thousand yards away, turning back to the Yalu River. Straightening my wings, so they were level, I placed the glowing pipper on the retreating enemy jet for a split-second, pulled the trigger, and watched the .50 caliber bullets strike its exhaust tailpipe and horizontal stabilizer.

Immediately black smoke began to pour out of the MiG, and it made a steep dive to treetop level. I followed it down and fired another short burst of my machineguns but saw the bullets were too low to hit it. Then we crossed the river, and I was now flying in the forbidden zone. But I remembered that it was permissible to enter Chinese airspace as long as I was in hot pursuit, and so I continued to chase the smoking enemy plane. The pilot was jinking his jet left then right between the hilltops to avoid being hit anymore by my guns. Following his every wild move, we suddenly passed over an airfield at low-level, and several antiaircraft gun emplacements began firing at both of us. Then the MiG turned due north to continue flying further into China. I broke off contact, not wanting to risk flying deeper into forbidden territory. Staying just above the trees and hilltops, I soon crossed the river and began a steep climb to thirty-five thousand feet on a heading that would take me back to Suwon. Once at a safe altitude, I looked around but didn't see any of my flight or other aircraft.

I checked my RT-82/APX-6 transponder to make sure it was still on the correct frequency, so the base radar would not think I was a lone MiG about to attack the base. The device was not a radio; it was used for IFF (Identification, Friend, or Foe). The unit was used to automatically identify the aircraft as friendly whenever it approached an American airforce base or NATO installation. The power output was one kilowatt, and its frequency range was 800-1300 MHz. The transponder also contained explosives for the destruction of the tuning heads (the cavitrons) in the event the unit was about to fall into enemy hands. There were three cartridge activated devices (CADs) about the size of a .45 caliber round mounted on the front of the unit controlled by a battery bus. Flipping a red guarded switch on the IFF panel manually activated them, and the pilot could quickly destroy it if needed. There also was a built-in impact switch to automatically destroy the transponder upon a crash landing. This was done to keep the North Koreans from determining the operating frequency, which, at that time, was changed every day.

By now, I was low on fuel and needed to land soon. Nearing the airfield, I called the tower and told them I was low on fuel and got clearance for a straight-in approach and landing. Once on the ground, I taxied to the F-86 revetment area and shut the engine down. All of my green flight was parked, so I was relieved they had made it home with no problems. Then I unstrapped my shoulder harness and climbed out of the cockpit.

Ed came running up to me and excitedly said, "Your wingman

by USAF F-86As and the NATO rules of engagement requirement not to cross the Yalu River prevented us from completely decimating the North Korean air force. However, over the three years while in Korea, the 4th FIW did inflict considerable damage to it and was the deadliest interceptor wing of the Korean War. It accounted for five hundred sixteen air-to-air victories, representing more than half of the enemy aircraft destroyed.[19]

On Thanksgiving day of 1951, Ed and I boarded a USAF C-54D MATS Skymaster cargo plane at Suwon and flew to Tokyo, Japan, where a few days later, we embarked on a ship that took us to San Francisco. Arriving there nearly two weeks later, I called Joy and told her I was back in the states and would soon be in Austin. We took a shuttle bus to Travis AFB, forty-three miles away, and said our good-byes at the MATS departure terminal, and he flew home to Arkansas, and I flew to Bergstrom Air Force Base in Austin, Texas.

The Korean War continued until July 27, 1953, when the armistice was signed. During my assignment there, I flew one hundred and two combat missions in F-86As but never shot down any MiG-15s. However, several of my fellow pilots did become Aces, and overall, the forty-one 5th Air Force Aces shot down forty percent of all the MiG-15s that were destroyed in combat. The kill ratio of F-86 Sabres to Mig-15s has often been debated and initially ranged from 14:1 to 10:1. However, it has now been confirmed to be 7:1 as the official USAF figure.

While I was in Korea, there were five F-86 Sabre pilots from my unit shot down, but only three were killed. One was rescued, and one was captured by the North Koreans and held as a POW until the end of the war, when he was repatriated in a prisoner exchange called "Operation Big Switch," which took place August 5 to December 23,

said he thought you had been shot down or crashed north of the Yalu River because he saw you disappear at treetop level chasing a MiG. What happened?"

Looking a little sheepish, I said, "Well, I definitely hit him when I fired my machine guns because his engine started smoking, and I could see the bullets hit his T-tail horizontal stabilizer and elevators, but he didn't go down. Instead, he dove down to just above the treetops and tried to lose me by jinking in wild left and right turns in between the hills. Those MiGs are tough birds and can fly with substantial damage. I know because I just witnessed one that got away, dammit."

Ed and I walked into the operations Quonset hut, and I filled out a report about shooting and hitting the MiG-15 and my incursion into the Chinese airspace in hot pursuit of the enemy plane.

Later that evening, while eating in the mess hall, my CO come over to the table where Ed and I were sitting and told me to be more careful about entering Chinese airspace north of the Yalu River even while chasing a North Korean MiG. The higher echelon USAF commanders were catching diplomatic flak from NATO because of the frequency of USAF incursions into the forbidden territory. It was a very sensitive subject with the commanders and the pilots.

Wars End For Me

Ed and I continued to fly our CAP missions, and occasional fighter sweeps throughout the summer and fall until our departure date in late November. Although there were several other times, I fired at MiGs when they flew into our area of operations; I never shot one down. Their tactic of fleeing into Chinese airspace when confronted

1953. I had survived another major war resulting in 36,574 American deaths and felt sure there would be no more global conflicts while I was serving in the United States Air Force. Of course, I was wrong because the Vietnam War started eight years later in Southeast Asia on February 28, 1961.

Descending the short metal stairs of the C-47 "Skytrain" carrying my B-4 bag, I saw Joy and my kids standing by the fence vigorously waving to me. They rushed up to me as I walked through the gate, and frankly, I got choked up, holding my wife and children for the first time in nearly a year. It was really good to be home finally, and I vowed not to leave my family again for another overseas unaccompanied assignment. But the United States Air Force had other plans for me, and two years later, I broke my vow to participate in a unique mission I never thought would happen in my lifetime.

CHAPTER 13

CRAIG AIR FORCE BASE

On January 5, 1952, Joy, the kids and I arrived at the main gate of Craig Air Force Base located south of Selma, Alabama. I showed my ID card to the MP and was given directions to base headquarters where I signed in. I had been on leave since arriving in the United States on December 12th from Korea. Joy and I had several heated discussions about my transferring from the Tactical Air Command (TAC) to Air Training Command (ATC) so that I could stabilize my family life and prevent unexpected overseas deployments when there was a major world conflict. I finally relented and requested the transfer from the Air Force Personnel office and received permanent change of station (PCS) orders relocating me to the training base and transferring me to the Air Training Command (ATC). We drove to Selma, Alabama, from Austin, Texas, where Joy and the kids had been living while I was overseas.

After going to the base housing office, I was assigned a two-bedroom two-story duplex, we picked out some furniture in their warehouse, drove to the officers' housing area and found our new home in a Wherry housing complex. Although only two years old, the structure was already showing signs of neglect with peeling paint on the outside and screen doors needing replacement. The construction quality was very shoddy and looked as if it had been hastily built—as cheaply as possible.

Joy walked through the interior rooms with the kids, then came to me and sadly said, "This is awful, Stan. The only bathroom is upstairs near the bedrooms, and the commode doesn't work. The kitchen stove is filthy, and the sink doesn't look like its ever been cleaned. Do we have to live here?"

"I'm afraid so," I replied. Explaining that I needed to be near my unit's briefing and classrooms and the flight line behind them.

Looking a little miffed, she said, "Okay, but we need to go to the commissary and get some cleaning supplies so I can scrub everything down before we move in."

After leaving the housing area, we drove to the commissary, and Joy bought the supplies she needed to make our new home livable. She did a great job, and we moved into the duplex after our personal belongings arrived.

Stan Jr. started the spring semester of second grade in an elementary school in Selma. He, along with several other military personnel kids, rode yellow school buses from our housing area to and from the school. Joy stayed at home looking after Penny, occasionally leaving her at the base daycare center when she went to an officers' wives club event at the "O" club.

Craig AFB was an undergraduate pilot training facility, and I was assigned to a flight squadron in the 3615th Pilot Training Wing as an instructor pilot (IP) flying the T-28B Trojan single-engine airplane. In early January 1952, ATC began a four-phase pilot training program consisting of pre-flight, primary, basic, and advanced. Pre-flight, lasting twelve weeks, weeded out unfit applicants and sorted candidates

T-28A Trojan Two-Seat Trainer (USAF photo)

T-28A Trojan Cockpit (Public Domain Photo)

into pilot, navigator, and other aircrew categories. Primary training pilots who were accepted flew the T-6 Texans for eighteen weeks at Randolph Field in San Antonio, Texas. Basic training pilots spent sixteen weeks flying the T-28B Trojans for one hundred-thirty hours at Craig AFB and several other locations. Advanced training pilots destined for fighter aircraft flying jet trainers as the T-33 Shooting Star flew for seventy-five hours. After about two hundred-ten hours of flight instruction, those students who didn't wash out graduated from training and were commissioned as second lieutenants in the United States Air Force.

About a week after arriving at Craig AFB, I met my three student pilots in our squadron briefing room when the new class began their training. I had been flying for eleven years and, at first, was uncomfortable explaining the mechanics of flying an airplane to the fledgling pilots. But soon, their youthful enthusiasm rubbed off on me, and I decided to help them become the best pilots they could be. They continually plagued me with questions about what it was like flying in combat during World War II and the Korean War. I didn't want to talk about it with them because I wasn't accustomed to talking to anyone that had not been in either war. Additionally, our commanding officer had warned the instructor pilots not to get distracted from the training mission by telling war stories to the students.

But I soon realized they were just curious young men in their early twenties, so occasionally, I shared some of my experiences with them. They were especially fascinated with the story about me crashing a Fleet Finch bi-plane in 1941 on a small Canadian island in the middle of a remote lake. Of course, I told them the engine quit because of carburetor icing instead of my foolishly buzzing a flock of geese floating on the water.

First T-28 Flight Class with Nine Instructor Pilots Standing Twenty-Six Students Sitting (USAF Photo)

My family life fell into a pleasant routine consisting of my flying with the three students each day for five days a week, then going home in the evening to be with Joy and the kids. On the weekends, Joy and I frequently went to the Officers' Club and met friends for cocktails and dinner. We occasionally took the kids to the Paul M. Grist State Park seventeen miles northeast of Selma. There we picnicked under huge pine trees and using long cane poles fished for bluegills and catfish on the small one hundred acre lake.

My instruction with the pupils in the T-28 usually consisted of a few takeoffs and landings (typically touch and gos) in the traffic pattern to get them warmed up. Then climbing to an altitude of about 12,000 feet, we practiced inverted flight (not to exceed 10 seconds), loops, Immelmanns, Split-Ss, aileron rolls, wing-overs, chandelles, spins (inverted spins were not permitted), barrel rolls, and one-half Cuban eights. The students were enthusiastic and highly motivated, so they quickly learned how to perform these basic aerobatic maneuvers.

Late one afternoon, after completing a normal training session, I told the student who was flying the airplane to head back to the airfield. We were twenty miles north of the base over the Talledega National Forest at 5,000 feet when unexpectedly, the engine started sputtering, and then the two-bladed propeller stopped turning. The silence was very unsettling!

I immediately said, "I've got the aircraft," and took over the controls, made sure the fuel selector switch was on the fullest tank and attempted to restart the engine as we began descending to the dense pine forest below.

After gliding through 2,000 feet and unable to start the engine, I told my student pilot that we were going to have to bail out of the aircraft.

I got on the radio and said, "Mayday! Mayday! Mayday! Craig tower, this is Trojan 785. Our engine has quit, and we are bailing out approximately twenty miles north of Craig Air Force Base over the Talladega National Forest."

On the intercom, I told the student, "I want you to unplug your oxygen hose and microphone cord, unbuckle your shoulder harness and seatbelt, and when I say 'Now,' I'm going to roll the aircraft inverted, and you'll fall out. Immediately pull the rip-cord and open your parachute. Do you understand me, lieutenant?"

"Yes, sir, I do," he half-heartedly answered.

I quickly unbuckled my shoulder harness and seatbelt, opened the canopy, then said, "I'll see you on the ground in a few minutes—Now!"

Craig AFB Control Tower

*Talladega National Forest where
Dad and Student bailed out of a T-28.*

Waiting a couple of seconds, I rolled the aircraft to the right after unplugging my oxygen hose and mic cord and saw the student fall out of his back seat at the same time I did. I immediately pulled my rip-cord, and the parachute popped out, billowed open and filled with air. Not far away, I saw the student floating down in his parachute. I waved to him and gave a thumbs up. He vigorously waved back and gave me a thumbs up indicating that he was okay. He had a huge grin on his face. I also saw the inverted T-28 begin to spin and then crash into the forest about one-half mile away. While floating down, I thought, *"How ironic. I spent five years flying dangerous combat missions in two wars and never had to bail out, and yet here I am about to land in the pine trees in Alabama."*

As the tops of the trees slowly approached, I closed my eyes, covered my face with my arms, clamped my knees tightly together just about the time I hit them. For what seemed like an interminable amount of time, I bounced and fell through the limbs scraping my face, arms, and legs on the rough pine bark branches, grateful that I was wearing my flight helmet. Then suddenly, my descent stopped as the parachute canopy caught in the top of the tall pine tree.

Looking down, I realized I was only three feet above the pine needle covered forest floor. Hanging there for a minute, and breathing a sigh of relief, I reached into the right pocket of my flight jacket, took out my Day-Glo orange parachute cord cutter with its razor-sharp hook-shaped blade, and pressed the switchblade button opening it. Carefully cutting the cords, I fell to the ground after the last one was severed.

Standing up, I wondered where the student had landed and shouted, "Lieutenant, can you hear me!" He didn't answer. Then shouting louder, "Lieutenant, where are you!"

I heard him say, "Captain Corvin, I'm over here. Sir, I'm caught in some tree branches."

Walking in the direction of his voice within a few minutes, I saw him hanging in his parachute harness five feet off the ground with a big smile on his face. "Sir, that was fun! Boy, will I have something to tell the other students when we get back to the base."

I tossed him the parachute cord cutter, and soon he fell next to me. "Are you okay, lieutenant?" I asked.

"Yes, sir, I'm fine," he answered excitedly while jumping to his feet.

Looking around at the darkening forest, I said, "Before I landed in the trees, I saw a paved road a short distance north of here, so let's go in that direction."

Removing our harnesses and gathering up our parachutes, we

walked for approximately thirty minutes then came to an asphalt road. By now, the sun was setting, and it was beginning to get dark. Walking along the tree-lined pavement, we soon came to a Highway 183 road sign and another one beside it with Adler, Alabama printed on it.

A short distance down the road, I saw an old log cabin with crumbling gray chinking sitting back under the towering pine trees with a thin column of gray smoke coming from its rock chimney. A dimly shining coal-oil light was hanging from a porch rafter hook, and an elderly woman with a frayed homespun gray shawl around her shoulders was sitting in a rocking chair knitting and smoking a short corn cob pipe. Standing beside her was a big white-haired, old man wearing a dusty sweat-stained wide-brimmed hat, faded blue bib overalls, brogans, and a dingy threadbare denim shirt. Cradled in his arms was an ancient muzzle-loading double-barreled shotgun pointed in our general direction.

Slowly approaching the cabin, we stopped, and I waved, saying, "Excuse me, folks, we had a problem with our airplane and had to bail out of it. Can I use your telephone to call the base and have somebody come pick us up?"

Squinting at me, the old man spit a thin stream of brown tobacco juice off the porch, and in a slow southern drawl, said, "Son, I ain't got no phone. But, I'll drive you to the base in my truck if'n you want me to."

"Are you sure that won't be too much trouble?" I asked.

"No, son, it ain't. I need to go to town anyway, and besides, watching the airplane crash into the woods not far away is the most exciting thing that's happened to me and Ma since 'ole Boomer' was kilt by a black bear in '49. I want to tell this to some of the old-timey fellers sittin on the park benches outside the courthouse."

Chuckling to myself, I thought, *"'49? This place is very old, but I doubt that he meant 1849 because they both aren't that old. Although I'm not entirely sure."*

After setting the shotgun inside the front door, he motioned us over to his rusty old brown Ford™ pickup, where we put our helmets and parachutes in back then climbed in the cab. Before getting in, the old man took out a small cloth bag from his bib pocket and, after opening the drawstring top, bit off a large plug of chewing tobacco with his few remaining snaggled, stained teeth. Loudly masticating it for a minute, he moved the wad into the back recesses of his jaw with his grimy right index finger, causing a bulky lump to be visible in his jawline.

Driving to town with the windows rolled up, and the truck heater turned on full blast, soon the combined stench of the old man's chew, which sporadically dribbled down his tobacco-stained yellow chin whiskers and his strong, foul-smelling body odor made the lieutenant sitting next to him gag and cover his nose with his hand. Because I didn't want to offend the old man, it took all my self-control not to laugh at the student and our predicament.

Forty-five minutes later, he dropped us off at the main gate of Craig AFB, where I thanked him profusely for helping us get home. The MPs called my squadron commander, and in a few minutes, he and the executive officer arrived in a blue Air Force staff car, which we saluted as it drove up. They took us to the base infirmary where a flight surgeon checked us over, declared that we were fit for flying duty, and a nurse cleaned the scratches and abrasions on our faces and arms with alcohol, which stung. Then with a small glass tube with a bulbous end attached to its cap, she swabbed liberal amounts of Merthiolate commonly referred to as "tincture of hellfire" on our facial cuts and arm scrapes. It lived up to its reputation and burned like hell.

Later, we walked outside laughing; both of us looking like painted Indians with the carmine red-brownish antiseptic streaking our faces! My CO told me to take the next day off from flying but wanted me to come in and file an accident report. Then he drove me to my quarters after dropping off the lieutenant at the student barracks.

It was nearly 8:00 p.m. when I opened the squeaking wooden front door and walked into our small living room. Stan Jr. and Penny came running out of the kitchen, yelling, "Daddy's home! Daddy's home!" and abruptly stopped, looking horrified when they saw my Merthiolate painted face, which they thought was streaked with blood.

Then Joy came out, drying her hands on a towel, looked at me and in a quivering voice, asked, "Are you okay? Your XO came by late this afternoon and said you had bailed out of your airplane with your student, and search parties were looking for you in the Talladega National Forest."

I hugged her and the kids and assured them that I was okay, just a little scratched up from landing in the pine trees.

After I mixed a cocktail, we sat on the sofa, and I told them the story about the engine quitting and my student and me bailing out of the airplane. We put the kids to bed, and Joy and I sat in the living room talking until my adrenaline high was gone after I consumed the third scotch and water highball.

The next morning I went to my squadron operations office and filled out an accident report indicating the T-28's engine quit in mid-flight, and my efforts to restart it failed. Nothing more came from the accident investigation, and the airplane was never recovered because it crashed too far in the densely wooded national forest where there were no roads or logging trails. I resumed my duties as an instructor pilot with my three students; they completed the course and left the base for the next phase of their training. A new class arrived, and I was assigned three more students and began the training process all over again.

After Labor Day, Stan Jr. started third grade in the Selma public school system. Throughout the summer, there had been numerous racially motivated incidents in town involving Air Force personnel and civilian townspeople known as locals. Although not as pervasive, the attitude of discrimination carried over to the military dependent children attending public schools. Finally, in December 1952, the base commander issued an emergency directive placing the town of Selma off-limits. He did that in order to ensure the safety and welfare of military personnel shopping in town. He also ordered all military dependent children to immediately withdraw from the Selma Independent School District and be taught in makeshift classrooms on the base. The existing student pilot classrooms were used by the school children, ranging from first grade to high school.

Along with several other officers' wives, Joy volunteered to teach fifth grade in one of the temporary classrooms while our three-year-old daughter Penny stayed at the base daycare facility. Stan Jr. thought it was the most exciting thing he had ever done, attending school in what looked like a pilot briefing room with aeronautical charts covering the walls and a giant silver aluminum painted E-6B flight calculator sitting on an easel beside the blackboards. The student pilots had built several model airplanes and hung them from the ceilings with fishing line. Every morning he hurriedly dressed, finished eating his breakfast, and was standing outside waiting for the blue Air Force bus to pick him up and take him to his new classroom. Many years later, he and I talked about it, and he said it was the most fun he ever had in school. Three years later, in 1955, a multi-grade school was built on base exclusively for the use of military dependents.

The student pilots were all moved into two large flightline hangers, separated into their different classes, and arranged around the perimeter of the buildings. It wasn't the best way to teach the young novice pilots. Still, everyone understood the need to ensure the military personnel and children's safety, and it created a strong feeling of camaraderie and of being one big family on the ATC base.

My family and I remained at Craig AFB until the summer of 1953 when I received orders transferring me to the 3525th Training Squadron (Advanced Single-Engine) at Williams Air Force Base in Mesa, Arizona, a suburb of Phoenix. There, I was to be assigned as an instructor pilot (IP) in the Lockheed T-33A Shooting Star.

Joy packed our household goods, personal belongings, and clothes, and the movers picked them up and shipped everything, except Stan Jr.'s massive rock collection, to our new home. We drove to her parents' house in Levelland, Texas, and stayed about a week. One afternoon, before we traveled on to Arizona, her dad and I went to Lubbock, and I traded in our 1946 Jeep station wagon for a new 1953 Buick four-door sedan. It seemed very luxurious compared to what we had been driving for seven years, and although it had no air-conditioning, with all four windows rolled down, it was bearable out on the highway with the wind blowing.

CHAPTER 14

WILLIAMS AFB

Pulling up to the base operations building, I told Joy and the kids that I would only be a few minutes there, and then we would go to the housing office. Walking into the building adjacent to the tall orange and white control tower, I went over to the duty officer and told him that I needed to report to the 3525th Training Squadron. He gave me driving instructions to their headquarters. Before leaving, I went into the pilots' lounge to see if I knew any of the people there. But I didn't, so I left and went back to the car. After signing in at the training squadron headquarters, I was told to report back in three days when I would be assigned to a specific flight group.

3525th Training Squadron Williams AFB

After driving over to the housing office, Joy and I went in and were pleased to learn that new ranch-style one-level houses had been built by the Wheery Corporation, and we were being assigned to a three-bedroom one bath unit. Going to our assigned quarters, we pulled into the carport attached to the side and went inside. Although hot from the desert air, the interior was freshly painted, and everything smelled new. Joy was thrilled the house was much cleaner and nicer than our house at Craig Air Force Base. She went from room to room, deciding where our furniture was going to be placed. There was a large evaporative air conditioner, called a swamp cooler, mounted on the roof that was operated by a switch in the hallway outside the bedrooms. Turning it on, soon, cool, moist air began to blow out of ceiling vents in the bedrooms, kitchen, breakfast room, and living room. After a while, we left and went to a hotel in Mesa, where we stayed about a week until our furniture and personal effects arrived on the moving van. Joy and the kids were amazed at the number of orange trees lining the streets, and Stan Jr. frequently rode his bicycle around the neighborhood, gathered up the fallen fruit on the ground, and brought it home in his wire handlebar basket.

I checked in with my squadron and was assigned to a flight class that had about thirty students and ten instructors. The flight line day started with a morning briefing attended by all students and IPs. The flight commander ran the briefing and covered such topics as weather, landing pattern information, and general knowledge questions. Following the briefing, the flight class began its routine schedule. If a student was not scheduled to fly an aircraft, they were expected to sit in the flight room and study until their flight time came up.

Walking out to the flight line with my student, we arrived at our assigned T-33, and I showed him how to perform the pre-flight of the aircraft. Having already been trained in the T-28 propeller-driven airplane, he quickly learned the sequence of the inspections. Climbing a ladder, attached to the fuselage, we each took our seat in the tandem cockpit. I sat in back, and the student was in front. The crew chief had already opened the canopy, so the interior was cooling down. But it still was hot.

Dad with a T-33 "T-Bird"

After starting the engine, I called ground control on its VHF frequency and asked for permission to taxi to the active runway, 12R. Getting approval, I released the brakes, increased power, and began to taxi to the north end of the 10,401-foot runway with our canopy open to provide some air circulation. Williams AFB had two other parallel runways; 12C at 10,201-feet, and 12L at 9301-feet. Arriving at the end of the runway, I changed to the VHF tower frequency and told them I was holding short of 12R ready for take-off. They told me I was cleared for take-off on 12R and to make a right departure from the traffic pattern. He also gave me the direction of the wind and barometric pressure.

As required, I repeated the instructions back to the tower operator, closed the canopy, applied power, and taxied to the center of the long runway and turned right to a heading of 120 degrees. Making a final check of the instruments, and adjusting the Kollsman window to the correct barometric pressure, I lowered the flaps to 32 degrees, ran the engine up to 90-percent rpm to check the oil pressure, and was ready for takeoff. I slowly applied full power and heard the engine spool-up to its maximum exhaust gas temperature (EGT) as we began to roll down the runway. The rudder became effective at fifty knots, and at ninety knots, I applied slight back pressure on the control stick to establish a seven-degree nose-high attitude. Holding this, we took off at about one hundred and ten knots.

Once clear of the runway, I raised the landing gear and saw the green gear up light come on. Retracting the flaps during climb out at one hundred-forty knots, I applied slight back pressure on the stick to prevent the nose from pitching down. Reaching pattern altitude, I changed power to the normal climb speed of two hundred twenty knots and departed the area. We flew southwest toward the Sonoran Desert National Monument and climbed to 30,000 feet, reaching that altitude in six or seven minutes. Then after adjusting the power setting to hold a three hundred ninety-six knots cruise speed, I told the student to take the controls and instructed him in various aerobatic maneuvers while making sure we did not fly past the United States/Mexico border and invade their airspace. After an hour, I took over the controls we returned to Willie AFB.

I called the tower, entered the traffic pattern on the downwind leg at one hundred eighty-five knots, pressed the dive-brake switch on the throttle, extended the landing gear and flaps, and turned on to the base leg. Then slowing to one hundred twenty-five knots on the final approach, I crossed the end of the runway at one hundred ten knots and touched down at about ninety knots. It had been a routine flight and was the first of many with my students.

I was happy to be in Air Training Command, where I was able to fly and teach during the day and return home to Joy and the kids after work. Many times on the weekend, we drove eighty miles northeast to Theodore Roosevelt Lake and fished from the rocky banks of the reservoir. Using live bait, which was large salamanders called water dogs, Stan Jr. once caught a largemouth bass that was one of the biggest I had ever seen. He was proud of his catch and posed for a picture with it beside the lake.

Stan Jr. with a bass he caught.

Other times on Saturdays, we drove east into the Superstition Mountain Wilderness Area. We set up camp in a recreation park beside a slow-moving shallow stream with a rocky bottom where the kids played in the water, while Joy and I relaxed in cloth-backed reclining chairs drinking beer. I was truly happy with my job and family life and enjoyed the rugged desert environment of Arizona.

One day after I been stationed at Wille for about six months, several other pilots and I were ordered to come to the base commander's office for a meeting. Arriving there, we learned that against base regulations, our kids had built several forts out of large cardboard paper boxes in the green zone common area behind our homes in the officers' housing area. Apparently, the MPs patrolling the base had discovered the forts and reported the infraction to base headquarters.

Officers' Housing Area Williams AFB

With a stern warning from the base commander to remove the paper forts, immediately we left the headquarters building. I drove home and saw Stan Jr. and Penny in the grassy common area with a bunch of other kids. They had built a massive structure out of large cardboard boxes used to ship refrigerators, washers, and dryers and were scrambling around inside them like a bunch of wild gerbils whooping and yelling and having a great time. Several of my pilot buddies arrived, and we got all the kids out of their forts and dismantled everything. We admonished the kids never to build any more cardboard forts.

Stan Sr. in Flight Gear

Stan Jr., Future Pilot

After living a year at Willie, I received orders assigning me to Tsuiki Air Force Base on the island of Kyūshū, Japan, for an unaccompanied tour. That meant Joy and the kids could not go with me to the new assignment. It also was the strangest assignment I ever received that did not include wartime flying.

CHAPTER 15

TSUIKI, AFB JAPAN

Shortly after receiving my orders to Japan, I was released from the 3525th Training Squadron, and we prepared for the movers to pick up our household furniture and store everything until I returned home in eighteen months. Joy and the kids were going to live with her parents, in Levelland, Texas, while I was overseas. Although not happy with the prospect of another lengthy separation; for the time being, she was resigned to the way the Air Force moved personnel every year or so and made the best of living with her parents again. Fortunately, they had a large house that comfortably accommodated everyone, and soon after moving in, she got a job as a fourth-grade elementary school teacher.

After my leave was over, Joy, the kids, and my in-laws drove me to Reece Air Force Base west of Lubbock, Texas. There I boarded a MATS C-118 Liftmaster, which was a four-engine Douglas DC-6 capable of carrying fifty-three to sixty-eight passengers. With 2,400 hp engines, it cruised at three hundred fifteen mph and had a range of nearly 3,000 nautical miles.

We flew non-stop to Travis AFB near San Francisco, California. Changing planes, we went on to Elmendorf AFB in Alaska, then after a brief stop, continued to Johnson AFB northeast of Tokyo, Japan. From there, I caught a C-47 "Gooney Bird" to Tsuiki Air Force Base on the southwestern island of Kyūshū, arriving late in the afternoon. Disembarking on the asphalt ramp, I checked in at base ops, and an airman drove me to the headquarters building where in his office, I met my commanding officer Lieutenant Colonel Bennet P. Browder, who was from Dallas, Texas.

Tsuiki AFB Main Gate 1954

*Col. Bennet P. Browder CO Tsuiki AFB 1954–1955
with New Japanese graduates of T-33 Flight Training
Japanese Air Self-Defense Force (JASDF) photo*

Sitting down, he warmly welcomed me, and after a cordial conversation about my family and the flight, he told me that I was one of two American fighter pilots who were chosen to teach former WWII Japanese fighter pilots how to fly the T-33 "Shooting Star" jet aircraft. I sat there, flabbergasted! My written orders only said to report to Tsuiki Air Force Base as an instructor pilot but didn't say anything about the students I was going to be teaching. Nine years earlier, in August 1945, while flying from Iwo Jima, I had strafed Japanese bases on their mainland, destroying parked Mitsubishi A6M Zeroes, and killing many enemy soldiers as they shot at me from anti-aircraft gun emplacements and ground slit trenches. Just before Japan surrendered, I had even shot down two Zeroes over Yokohama and one over Osaka, making me an Ace. I thought, *"This is absolutely insane! Why are we teaching our former enemies how to fly jet aircraft after the bastards shot down so many of our bombers and fighters?"*

Lieutenant Colonel Browder explained that since the end of WWII, Japan had renounced all military aggression and had recently formed the Japanese Air Self-Defense Force (JASDF). But they needed their pilots to fly the jet aircraft to protect the country from North Korea, which was only one hundred thirty-six miles away. Additionally, the Chinese Communists who were only four hundred nine-three miles away were threatening Japan, especially after they learned about the murderous killings and sexual assault during WWII of 300,000 Chinese civilians over six weeks during the infamous Rape of Nanking by hordes of drunken Japanese soldiers.

"Stan, these Japanese pilots are all around forty years old, like Lieutenant Colonel Kenshi Ishikawa, your first student and Major General Minoru Genda whose fifty. All of them have thousands of hours of combat flying time in fighters because of how long Japan was at war. So, they will quickly learn how to fly the T-Bird. I guarantee it. Besides, they all know how to speak English."

Taking a deep breath, I leaned back in my chair and said, "Okay, sir. I'll make the best of it and not let my attitude get in the way of teaching these guys."

Standing up, Lieutenant Colonel Browder said, "That's the spirit, Stan, I know that you can do it because you came highly recommended for this assignment." Then he said, "My duty officer will assign you to one of the squad tents near the flight line, so plan on meeting at the operations center tomorrow morning at 0700 hours, and we'll discuss the first group of students who are going to arrive here in a few days."

"Yes, sir, I'll be there first thing in the morning," as I saluted him and then walked out of the building, wondering, *"Who was the bastard that recommended me?"*

Officer quarters and base personnel

The first lieutenant and I went outside, got in a jeep, and we drove to a large group of new tents built on raised planked foundations with wood sides extending up about four feet all around the walls. The latrine and showers were located several tents down the gravel road leading to the flight line. Before dropping me off, he said, "Captain Corvin, a Japanese house boy, will be assigned to your quarters in a few days, and each day he will wash your clothes and clean your living area. They have all been carefully screened, so you don't have to worry about them."

Unloading my B-4 bag and duffel bag with my flight suits and gear near a metal bed at the back of the tent, I sat down on it and thought, *"Will I ever reach a time in my career where I don't have to sleep in a stinking, oil smelling tent?"* Only one other bed was being used, so it looked like I was going to have just one roommate. The duty officer also told me a newly built wooden building located at the other end of the row of tents was the Officers' Club stag bar where pilots wearing flight suits could go after flying. So, once unpacked and after stowing my flight gear in a wall locker next to my bed, I went down there and walked inside.

There were a half-dozen tables and chairs and a bar at the far end with liquor bottles lining wooden shelves in front of a large mirror. A pool table was in the middle of the room, and a long shuffleboard table was against one wall. The bartender was a very pretty young Japanese woman wearing a dark blue dress and white apron.

As I sat on one of the tall barstools, she smiled at me and asked, "Sir, may I mix you a cocktail, or would you prefer a beer?"

I said, "I'll have a beer, please."

Surprised at her flawless English, she was the first Japanese person I had ever spoken with or even met. When she brought me an ice-cold Schlitz™ in a can, she said, "My name is o-jo-san Akiko. It means Miss Sparkle Bright in English." Then she smiled, happily showing her brilliant white teeth.

She told me that she was born in 1934 and was now twenty years old. She had learned to speak and write English while attending local Catholic schools, which I learned was very unusual for Japanese girls because ninety-nine percent of the population are Buddhists or Shintos. Finishing my beer, I went back to my tent and rested from the long journey.

Tsuiki Air Force Base was built in 1942 by the Imperial Japanese Navy and the Fujita Corporation. Three years later, the last remaining Kamikaze unit departed on its final suicide mission from this base to attack a U.S. naval fleet patrolling off the eastern coast of Kyūshū. Flown by young, very inexperienced teenage boys, who were not trained to land their airplanes, all of the barely flyable Japanese aircraft were quickly shot down before damaging any U.S. naval ships. On August 7, 1945, the base, including its only runway, was heavily bombed by one hundred USAAF B-29 Superfortresses, destroying it for further operational use.

Tsuki's runway was 7,870 feet long and 150 feet wide. Built of concrete, runway heading 257° extended several hundred feet into the bay and had a ten feet high approach end that was a sheer drop off into the water. The reciprocal runway heading was 077°. Landing on the 257° runway at night or during rain and fog was going to be very dangerous. If you touched down short or landed only a few feet lower than its fifty-five foot mean sea level, MSL, runway height, you would crash headlong into the massive concrete extension. The shallow water surrounding the coastal approach was littered with destroyed airplane fragments whose pilots had made a fatal miscalculation in their landing altitude on short final.

While dozing on my bunk, just before dark, I heard the wooden door open and saw a tall, lanky pilot sporting a big mustache walk in wearing a flight suit and captain bars on his service cap. Getting up, I walked over to him and said, "Hello. I'm Stan Corvin."

Tsuiki AFB Runway

Tsuiki AFB, Kyushu, Japan 1954 USAF Official Photo

Shaking hands, he said, "Glad to meet you. I'm Walt Tanner." Sitting down across from each other, I learned he was from Oakland, California.

"Where are you from, Stan?"

Hesitating a moment, I said, "Well, my wife and kids are living with her parents in West, Texas, but I'm originally from Southern, Ohio."

We chatted for a while, then went to the Officers' Mess Hall for dinner, where we sat with Lt. Col. Browder and his executive officer (XO), Major Bill Taylor. We learned that Walt and I were the only instructor pilots assigned to teach the Japanese pilots how to fly the T-33 jets. We each were initially going to have three students, so the first class contained only six people.

We stayed for a while after eating, drinking beer then just before leaving Lieutenant Colonel Browder asked, "Do you guys play bridge?"

Walt said that he didn't, but I said, "Yes, sir. I do. Several of my Canadian RCAF buddies taught me to play while we were traveling from Nova Scotia to Southampton, England, in 1941, after I graduated from their flight training."

"Great, Stan, then we'll play some in the evenings after dinner. There isn't much entertainment here on base. The movie theater is pretty dilapidated and plays the same movie five or six days in a row. There are a couple of sleazy bars outside of the main gate, but I recently placed them off-limits because of fights that kept occurring."

Early next morning, Walt and I shaved and showered, put on our flight suits and went to the mess hall, and ate breakfast. Getting a metal divided tray, I opened two biscuits, and then a young KP airman poured a ladle full of "SOS" on top of them. The thick white cream gravy and chopped sausage pieces smelled great, and I realized I was hungry. Sitting down with Walt, I looked around the room and saw a few officers, but none were wearing flight suits, and they didn't have wings on their left breast pocket. *They're probably weather guys or aircraft communication people,* I thought as I spooned the food into my mouth.

At 0645 hours, we walked to the quonset hut operations center next to the flight line for our first briefing. Lieutenant Colonel Browder, Major Taylor, and a weather officer were already there drinking coffee. After saluting our CO, and pouring ourselves a cup of coffee, we sat down, and he began to explain what our role would be in teaching the Japanese pilots.

"All of the students will become the senior leaders and commanders of the newly formed Japanese Air Self-Defense Force, and they have ranks ranging from Lieutenant Colonel to a two-star Major General. Although we whipped them in World War II, now they are our allies, and we must treat them with respect. So, be sure to salute them when it is appropriate and always address them using their rank and last name. They are all highly respected by the Japanese people because of their Bushido code of conduct, which essentially is 'always be prepared to die.' They are regarded as modern-day Samurai warriors.

"All of them were involved in attacks on American forces during the war, including Pearl Harbor, Wake Island, Midway, and the Battle of the Philippine Sea. Many of them shot down United States Army Air Force bombers and fighters attacking their territories, air force bases, and military installations around the world."

Hesitating a second, he took a deep breath and said, "Stan and Walt, you must put aside any personal animosity you hold against them and just do your job. I've met all six of them, and they are excited to learn to fly jets; they speak passable English and hold no grudge against Americans for winning the war. Also, you can take solace in knowing that their average monthly salary is the equivalent of ninety dollars, which is about one-fourth of what you guys are making as captains."

Then he looked at me and said, "Stan, your first student is going to be Lieutenant Colonel Kenshi Ishikawa. I've put you two together because, during the war, he was the group commander in the Osaka area when you shot down two Zeros at his airfield on June 6, 1945. Several weeks earlier, Ishikawa had shot down seven B-29 Super Fortress bombers that were bombing his airfield. So, he killed seventy American pilots and crewmembers. I know it's going to be hard to overlook that fact, but you absolutely must! Do you think you can do it?"

Dumbfounded at the irony, I said, "Yes, sir. I can. The war has been over for nine years now, and I've already moved on with my life, so no problem."

But then I remembered the Japanese wolves attack on the pilots' tent area at Iwo Jima, where Ed Skelton and I killed seven of them in hand-to-hand fighting. Taking a deep breath, I slowly let it out and thought, *"I've got to let go of my hatred for them."* What I didn't know at the time of our morning briefing was that without telling his commanding officer, my younger brother, Walter Corvin, a U.S Army buck sergeant stationed near Tokyo had just married a young Japanese woman. So, I had a Japanese sister-in-law!

Then Lieutenant Colonel Broward turned to Walt and said, "Walt, your first student is going to be the famous Japanese carrier pilot and multiple Ace Lieutenant Colonel Masanobu Ibusuki. He shot down twenty-five American planes over Pearl Harbor and Midway, and later five British ones when he participated in the raid on Port Darwin, Australia. He's probably the most experienced fighter pilot in the class and is anxious to learn how to fly T-33s. Once he graduates, he will be a commander in the Japanese tactical air force, which will have armed F-86s. By the way, ten years ago, in July 1944, he took part in the Battle of the Philippine Sea, which was the largest carrier-to-carrier battle of the war where he flew Zeros in the Great Marianas Turkey

Daily Flying

The first six Japanese students arrived in a few days, and Walt and I met them at Lieutenant Colonel Broward's office. They were very polite with a lot of bowing but no shaking of hands, which was more of an American custom than Japanese. A flight briefing room had been set up next to base operations, and after the initial meeting and greetings, we all were driven there. The room was furnished with multiple desks and chairs and was similar to what I had seen at American bases worldwide.

Lieutenant Colonel Kenshi Ishikawa and the other two Japanese pilots sat down at one of the tables, and I began to tell them about the training they could expect in the T-33. After a while, one of the other students asked, "Captain Corvin, is it true you are from Texas?"

Surprised at his question, which implied he knew more about me than I thought, I said, "My wife and children are living there right now with her parents. So I guess you can say I am a Texan."

Hesitatingly, he asked, "Is it true there are cowboys and Indians in Texas?"

Leaning back in my chair and clasping my hands behind my head, I laughed and said, "There are a lot of cowboys, but most of the Indians are on the movie screens in theaters."

Everyone laughed at that, and the Japanese student, somewhat chagrined, had no more comments. However, it caused everyone to relax and begin to bond as a flight group.

Over the next several weeks, we met each morning at the flight room for a weather briefing and to receive any specific information concerning our training schedule or our flight area. I was nervous about flying with Lieutenant Colonel Ishikawa for the first time, but

Shoot. During that aerial battle, the Japanese lost over 600 aircraft while only 123 American planes were shot down."

Continuing, he said, "After the weather briefing, go ahead, and each of you take a T-33 parked outside and familiarize yourselves with the airfield, its landing patterns, and the surrounding area where you'll be flying with your students. It's probably a good idea to practice landing on runway 257° so you can get an idea of what the approach is like over the water and the sheer concrete drop off at its end. There's a GCA approach available, so try several of those landings and give the controllers a chance to practice with you when the weather isn't at or below minimums, which it frequently is this time of year. Remember, at night, isn't the time to practice a GCA approach when you are low on fuel and must land in zero, zero weather conditions."

After the briefing, we gathered our parachutes, helmets, and gear and walked out to the ramp where five new T-33s were parked. Walt and I decided to stay together in our exploring of the area where we were going to be flying with our students. Taking off from runway 077, we climbed out straight ahead to 30,000 feet over the water then turned southeast. The view was breathtaking in the clear air with few clouds. Because Kyūshū is an island, in the summertime, its maritime climate generally includes thick clouds and rain. However, today it was CAVU (ceiling and visibility unlimited). We flew for an hour looking at the mountains, volcanic landscapes, and marked terrain features on our aeronautical charts to help with our instruction of the Japanese pilots. Returning to base, we practiced a couple of GCA landings, then taxied to a large hanger near base ops and shut the engines down. The maintenance crews towed them inside to protect them from storms that were supposed to move into the area overnight.

he had meticulously been studying the Dash-1 and was very familiar with all of its contents, including the emergency procedures.

After taking off on runway 077, I climbed us out through dense clouds, leveled off at 30,000 feet, adjusted our speed to five hundred miles per hour, and told him, "Okay, sir. You take the controls now."

After making several steep high-G left and right turns, getting the feel of the jet, he suddenly did a snap roll to the right, leveled the aircraft, and then immediately did a slower one to the left. Then he began a sharp climb resulting in an Immelmann reversing our course 180°. My first thought was, *"Oh, my God! I'm glad I never got in a dogfight with this guy, or I might have been shot down."* Although he had never flown the T-Bird before, he clearly was the best pilot that I had ever seen and instinctively knew how to control the jet. I showed him several other maneuvers, which he performed flawlessly. Returning to the base after an hour, I asked for a GCA approach and let him take us down through the heavy cloud cover but took over the controls as we approached short final and landed.

Climbing out of the airplane, we went back to the flight room, where we discussed the training flight. Then individually, I took the other two Japanese students for their flights. While they were proficient in executing all of the maneuvers, they were not as good as Lieutenant Colonel Kenshi Ishikawa. Later that evening, Walt and I discussed our students, and he said the same thing about Lieutenant Colonel Masanobu Ibusuki, that he was an excellent pilot and far superior to any other student that Walt had ever taught. We both decided that we were glad we hadn't encountered these pilots during the war.

Over the next four months, the Japanese students were involved in what was called a 100/100 flight instruction program. Because they were all very experienced fighter pilots, with thousands of hours of flying time, they received one hundred hours of ground school instruction and one hundred hours of actual flight time in the T-33.

One evening after eating dinner at the officers' club, I was playing bridge with Lieutenant Colonel Browder, Major Taylor, and a new guy, Capt. Don Kidwell, the new weather section commander.

Lieutenant Colonel Browder turned to me and said, "Stan, a former war correspondent, Peter Kalischer, is arriving the day after tomorrow and is going to interview us about our flight program teaching the Japanese students to fly the T-33. The story angle will be former enemies now coming together to create the new Japanese Air Self-Defence Force. He'll want to interview you, Walt, and the Japanese students."

Continuing on, he said, "At the end of World War II, after serving with the Army's counterintelligence corps under General MacArthur's command in the Philippines, he became a reporter with United Press International (UPI). Two years ago, he joined *Collier's Magazine* in Tokyo and is their Far East correspondent and Tokyo bureau chief. He'll be with us for a few days while he gathers information about our program and writes an article about the rearming of Japan. It will be published in *Collier's Magazine* sometime in the near future. He'll stay with you and Walt in your quarters while he's here. Show him around and give him access to the flight training room and the Japanese students."

"Yes, sir. I will," I said while thinking, *"Oh, great! That's all I need, a nosey reporter that's going to do a hatchet job on us."*

But I was wrong, and Pete turned out to be a good guy that was a very competent reporter and writer. "You Step Out Of Time," the article he wrote is published in the March 2, 1956 issue of *Collier's Magazine* with Grace Kelley and Prince Ranier on the cover.

Collier Magazine *with Capt. Corvin's Story*

The Eagle Above

"If anybody told me twelve years ago, when I was flying against these boys out of New Guinea, that I'd be running a training base in Japan to teach them how to fly jets—well, I'd have had his head examined," said Tsuiki's base commander, Lieutenant Colonel Bennett P. Browder, of Dallas, Texas.

Browder has nothing on Captain Stanley Corvin, a jet pilot instructor from Levelland, Texas. Corvin flew P-51 fighter escort for B-29s and shot down two Japanese interceptors over Osaka and one over Yokohama. His star pupil, Lieutenant Colonel Kenshi Ishikawa, was the group commander in the Osaka area and shot down seven B-29s.

Corvin and Ishikawa—slated to be senior squadron leader in the Japanese air force—share the respect of two professionals in a pretty exclusive profession. The years have erased everything but a fascination for flying, with the Japanese satisfying a 10-year frustration. There are 30 applications for every opening in the new Air Self-Defense Force. The entire training program is taught in English, a real skull-cracker for many who have to learn the language from scratch. The first crop of pilots are all old men of nearly forty and include World War II aces like carrier pilot Lieutenant Colonel Masanobu Ibusuki, who took part in the attack on Pearl Harbor and the Battle of Midway. Ibusuki shot down 25 American and five British planes. As a flying lieutenant colonel with a family he gets a take-home pay of $90 a month.

Collier Magazine *story about Japanese pilot's flying.*

Once again, the Japanese are building military strength —somewhat reluctantly, but at the strong urging of the United States government

T33s in Formation. Capt. Corvin flying Peter Kalischer.

Major General Minoru Genda

After the Japanese students graduated at the end of their training cycle, Lieutenant Colonel Browder came up to me at their celebration party at the Officers' Club and said, "Stan, please come to my office in the morning at 0800 hours, and I'll brief you on a very special student I'm assigning you, two-star Major General Minoru Genda."

Lieutenant General Minoru Genda

I answered, "Yes, sir. I'll be there," thinking, *"I wonder what that's going to be like having an enemy general as a student? He's got to be a tough son-of-a-bitch to survive the war and the criminal investigations that resulted in so many of those commanders being hung as war criminals."*

Arriving at headquarters the next morning, Lieutenant Colonel Browder opened a dossier folder marked CONFIDENTIAL, and said, "Stan, I'm assigning Major General Minoru Genda to you for this training cycle. He'll be your only student, and you'll be on an accelerated schedule of six weeks because he's going to be the Chief of Staff of the JASDF. He's the guy who planned and helped carry out the Japanese attack on Pearl Harbor on December 7, 1941. Here is his file, so go ahead and read it here in headquarters, but leave it on my desk when you are finished. Also, please be sensitive to the fact that he had several family members that were killed by the atomic bomb dropped on Hiroshima on August 6, 1945."

I stood up, took the file, saluted my CO, and went outside to a vacant desk and began to read about my newest student Major General Minoru Genda. He was born in 1904 in Kaké, a suburb of Hiroshima, fifty years ago. I thought, *"Hmm, that's pretty old for a fighter pilot to put his body through all the G-forces of jet training."*

Reading on, I learned he graduated from Japan's Imperial Naval Academy in 1924, and at the time of Pearl Harbor, he was a staff officer with the Japanese Imperial Air Fleet and flew a torpedo bomber; although, he claims he never hit an American Naval ship. After he graduated from the Naval Academy and became a fighter pilot, he organized the bi-plane acrobatic Genda Circus that toured Japan for a year. He later was a flight instructor and also an assistant naval attaché. Genda was personally selected by Admiral Isoroku Yamamoto to create the aviation forces for the Japanese Navy. Between July and September of 1942, he served as an air officer aboard the Japanese carrier Zuikaku. After two months as a staff officer of the 11th Air Fleet, he was attached to the Imperial General Headquarters in Tokyo until January 1945. Between January 1945 and the end of the war, Captain Genda, with 3,000 hours of flight time, was assigned as the commanding officer of the elite 343rd Air Group.

They operated out of Matsuyama, Kanoya, Kokubu, and Omura,

airfields, and flew the N1K2-J Shiden-Kai aircraft. Then-Captain Genda, was in charge of using the 343rd Air Group to gain air superiority, clearing the way for kamikaze pilots attacking Allied ships, particularly during the Okinawa campaign between April and June 1945. Genda and his combat-hardened pilots also fought several air battles over Kyūshū toward the end of the war.

N1K2-Ja Shiden Kai Airplane (Allies called it "George.")

Major General Genda's preferred World War II fighter aircraft was the N1K2 – Ja Shiden Kai *(Japanese: "Violet Lightning-Improved")*. It was the newest fighter used in significant numbers by the Japanese Navy during the last days of World War II. Known by the Allies as the "George," this highly maneuverable, heavily-armed fighter was a formidable opponent in the closing months of the war. The Shiden Kai was considerably better than the Japanese Navy's most famous fighter aircraft, the A6M Zero. With a top speed of three hundred sixty-nine miles per hour, the George was about twenty mph faster than the A6M Zero. It also had surprisingly good maneuverability due to a mercury switch that automatically extended the flaps during turns. These combat flaps created more lift, thereby allowing significantly tighter turns.

Additionally, its four 20 mm automatic cannon provided significantly more firepower than earlier Japanese weapon designs. Unlike the A6M Zero, the Shiden Kai could compete against the best late-war U.S. Navy and U.S. Army Air Forces fighters.[20] After reading Major General Genda's dossier, I returned it to Lieutenant Colonel Broward and left the headquarters building.

At a 437 miles per hour top speed, the P-51D Mustang was 68 miles per hour faster than the George aircraft Major General Genda had flown at the end of World War II. I expected he was going to be very impressed with the T-Bird's six hundred three miles per hour top speed and its five hundred miles per hour cruise speed. Also, the T-33's maximum ceiling of 47,500 was more than twice the altitude limit of the George at 21,500 AGL. So, we were going to be flying higher than he'd ever flown during the war.

Two days later, Major General Genda and his two aides, a lieutenant colonel and a captain, arrived at Tsuiki Air Force Base in a new blue staff car that had been given to him by the United States Air Force. A day earlier, Lieutenant Colonel Browder received a telephone call, telling him that his VIP guest would arrive the next morning by 1000 hours.

When he drove up to the headquarters building and walked inside with his aides, Lieutenant Colonel Browder, Major Taylor, and I came to attention and saluted him. Smiling broadly, he returned our salute and walked over to us, shook our hands vigorously, and said, "Bennett, how have you been?"

"Sir, I'm doing well, and your pilots have been exceptional students learning to fly the T-bird."

"That is good, indeed," Major General Genda said.

Then Lieutenant Colonel Browder said to Major General Genda,

"Sir, this is Captain Stan Corvin, and he's going to be your instructor pilot while you are here. He is a fighter pilot trained by the Royal Canadian Air Force in 1941 then flew Spitfires for the British before joining the USAAF and flying for them until the end of the war. He became an American Ace while flying P-51 Mustangs from Iwo Jima."

Looking surprised, Major General Genda said, "Captain Corvin, you must be a very good fighter pilot to have flown against my pilots and shot down five of them. I'm looking forward to flying with you." Then he stuck his hand out and shook mine, which was very uncommon for a Japanese general to do with anyone, much less a subordinate officer.

I thought, *"Maybe this guy is going to be okay after all."*

Major General Genda and his two aides moved into the nearby town of Fukuoka, where the Japanese government had rented him a beautiful house with multiple gardens and koi ponds. It was staffed with a cook and several house servants to clean everything. Daily, at 0700 hours, he and his aides arrived at the flight briefing room, where he quietly sat and listened to the information regarding weather, flight activity, etc. Then he attended ground school training with Walt's three students for four hours before changing from his uniform into a flight suit in the ready room next door at base ops. On Friday afternoons a Japanese Air Force C-47 with orange "Rising Sun" markings landed at Tsuiki and took Major General Genda to Tokyo, where his wife and three children lived. He returned on Monday mornings at 0600 hours in time for his ground school classes.

Flying with Major General Genda for the first time, I quickly learned that he was marginally proficient in operating the T-Bird, probably because he had not flown much in the years since the end of the war. We repeatedly shot touch-and-gos at Tsuiki and practiced aerobatic maneuvers over the waters of the nearby Suo Gulf. Finally, I was convinced it was safe for him to solo, and he flew alone for the first time, as Lieutenant Colonel Browder and I watched along with the general's two aides.

After about thirty minutes, Genda landed and taxied to the ramp by base ops. With his oxygen mask off, he had a huge smile on his craggy face and clasped his hands together over his head before climbing down the ladder placed beside his jet. As he walked over to us, we came to attention and saluted him. He grabbed our hands, and vigorously shook them, thanking us for his training. Then he said, "Bennett, I want you and Stan to come to my house this evening for dinner and sake."

Lieutenant Colonel Browder said, "Yes, sir, what time would you like us to come over?"

"Plan on arriving at 1900 hours."

Later, after changing into our blue class "A" uniforms, Lieutenant Colonel Browder and I were driven to Major General Genda's house in a staff car. The trip to his home in Fukuoka was an eye-opening experience for me. The streets were very narrow and not paved, and most of the dwellings were made of surplus wood with tar-paper covered roofs. I now understood why General Curtis LeMay had decided to use incendiary devices to fire-bomb the Japanese cities at the end of the war. Unable to escape, more civilians were killed by the raging firestorms than by the atomic bombs dropped on Hiroshima and Nagasaki.

Arriving at Major General Genda's house, we drove into a wood gated courtyard. Met by his senior aide, we went into a large traditional-style Japanese home built with a carved wooden roof and paper walls. Beautiful stone walkways were weaving between koi ponds,

and began carrying trays of medium cooked Wagyu beef steaks and sauteed vegetables into the room and served each of us. The aroma was fantastic! Wagyu beef *(Japanese: "wa" means Japanese-style, and "gyu" cattle)* originated in Kobe, Japan, where the cattle were brought in to help cultivate rice during the second century AD. Major General Genda told us the beef had been cooked on a hibachi grill, which is called a shichirin in Japanese and has a charcoal flame with an open grate design. Basically, an oriental barbeque grill!

The steak was very tender and easily cut by the razor-sharp Damascus layered steel knives placed beside our plates. With chopsticks, called hashi in Japanese, I clumsily put a bite in my mouth and was astounded by the succulent taste of the best steak I had ever eaten! *"Oh, my God, that's good!"* I murmured under my breath while chewing.

Major General Genda laughingly said, "So, Stan, do you like it?"

"Yes, sir. That steak is incredible," I said as I cut more pieces of it into manageable bites I could handle with the chopsticks. The conversation around the table was congenial and friendly as we discussed flying the T-33 jets; however, there was no mention of the war that had ended nine years earlier. Finishing dinner, the table was cleared, and more sake was poured. Then the two young ladies brought in a tray of round translucent Moshi rice cakes, which were lightly laced with powdered sugar and honey. More sake was poured until General Genda looked at his watch, laughed, and said, "Gentlemen, I usually go to bed by 2000 hours and get up every morning at 0400, so it is past my bedtime." I admired his straight-forward means of communication and candor.

After thanking our host for his generous hospitality, at 2200 hours, Lieutenant Colonel Browder and I excused ourselves and returned to

large rocks, lighted Japanese lanterns, and lush green plants. Dozens of pots containing beautiful miniature bonsai trees were suspended by curved metal hooks placed strategically around the ponds. As we approached a side room off the central kitchen, a large paper door slid open, and the general was standing there wearing light-colored slacks, a navy blue wool turtle-neck sweater, and heavy dark "Tabi" socks with the traditional split-toe design.

He was relaxed and happy to see us. Then he said, "Gentlemen, please remove your shoes and place them beside the door."

Awkwardly, we untied our shoes, put them by the door, and stepped into the room. There was a short table about eighteen inches high sitting in the center with four thick cushions placed around it. After we sat down, two beautiful young women dressed as Geishas wearing colorful floral silk Kimonos slid open a side door and walked in. They were carrying bamboo trays holding small cups called sakazukis and ornately painted sake bottles on them. Placing cups on the table in front of us, they poured the cold sake into it then left.

Sake is an alcoholic beverage made by fermenting rice that has had the bran removed. Unlike wine, in which alcohol is produced by fermenting sugar that is present in fruit, sake is produced by a brewing process more like that of beer, where starch is converted into sugars, which ferment into alcohol.

Raising his cup, Major General Genda nodded to Lieutenant Colonel Browder and then to me, saying, "Kanpai." *(Japanese: "Cheers.")* We both said, "Kanpai," in unison, and drank the cold beer. It had a sweeter taste than American beer and was more like wine, but it was delicious, and I liked it. We talked about flight training for a while, and then I smelled meat sizzling and heard it cooking in the adjoining kitchen. Soon the two young ladies slid the door open

the base. Dropped off at my tent, the stark contrast of my current living conditions versus the general's lovely house made me homesick for my wife Joy and the kids. I was ready to go home but had nearly twelve more months before I could leave Tsuiki Air Force Base and be reunited with my family.

Over the next few weeks, Major General Genda improved in his flying skills and ultimately finished the jet training course and returned to Tokyo, where he became the Chief of Staff of the Joint Air Self-Defence Force. He also transitioned into the F-86 Sabre jet, which became Japan's first line of defense against Chinese and North Korean aggression should they attack.

I continued teaching new classes of Japanese students and looked forward to returning home. Before Christmas in 1955, Walt and I took a T-33 and flew to Tokyo, where I bought an expensive strand of cultured pearls for Joy, a pair of six power Nikon binoculars for Stan Jr., and several sets of Japanese wooden dolls for Penny. I shipped them to Levelland, Texas, where my family was living with Mr. and Mrs. Heath. I also bought a black Nikon S2 rangefinder camera with a Nikkor 50 mm f/1.4 lens for myself and shot dozens of rolls of color film with it while in Japan before going home.

Finally, I reached the end of my unaccompanied tour and received orders to report to Webb Air Force Base in Big Spring, Texas, as an instructor pilot.

(Author's Note: Minoru Genda was promoted to a four-star general and was instrumental in getting Lockheed F-104 Starfighters added to the Joint Air Self-Defence Force's fleet of supersonic jets. In 1962 he was awarded the "Legion of Merit" medal by President John F. Kennedy, a WWII Navy veteran, for his contributions to peace and as an ally of the United States

of America. It is the highest military award given to a foreigner. In 1969 he traveled to America as a guest of the U.S. Navy and spoke to the graduating class of midshipmen at Annapolis. Several Pearl Harbor veterans' groups opposed his trip.

On Aug. 17, 1989, when General Genga died at the age of eighty-five, The New York Times obituary, written by Peter B. Flint, said that once when he was asked about his ties with Americans, he replied, "Of course, I get along fine with them. The American pilots especially are a wonderful, congenial bunch of men." Questioned about the scars of combat, he said, "Wars are fought, and then they end, and when they end, we don't look back—only forward."[21]

CHAPTER 16

WEBB AFB

Joy, her parents, and the kids all stood by the fence at Reece Air Force Base's flight terminal when I landed in July. Stepping down the ladder, I was surprised at how hot the weather was. Then Stan Jr. and Penny ran to me, and I grabbed them in a bear hug. They both had grown a lot, but my son had shot up in height and was much taller, now coming up to my shoulder. Joy ran to me, and she hugged us tightly, then reached up and kissed me, saying, "Welcome home, stranger. You going our way?"

"Yes, ma'am, if you'll have me." We kissed again and held hands as we walked over to Mr. and Mrs. Heath, who were smiling at us.

Maude hugged me, and Jesse shook my hand. "Welcome home, Stan. How was your flight?" he asked.

"It was fine, sir. A little long and cramped, but I'm here now and glad to be able to stretch my legs."

After a few days, Joy, the kids and I drove one hundred eleven miles to Big Spring, Texas, and Webb Air Force Base located on the west side of town. I was assigned to the 3560th Pilot Training Wing equipped with T-33 jets. Several training squadrons were in the final phase of instruction, and their students would graduate in about two weeks.

Webb Main Gate

Pamphlet cover about Webb AFB

Joy and I took some time to look for a new home. She had taught elementary school for one and one-half years, saving most of her salary, and I had been living overseas, also saving mine. So we decided to buy our first home. We found a vacant one that was only five years old with three bedrooms and two baths and a small inground swimming pool in the backyard. It was located on the eastern side of town near Howard County Junior College. A local bank provided the financing, and the real estate company allowed us to move into the house early while all the paperwork was being processed. Our furniture finally arrived, and we moved into the new home. The kids were thrilled to have a swimming pool in the backyard, and I have to say that Joy and I were too. We bought patio furniture and a BBQ grill, and in the summertime evenings, when I came home, we usually stayed outside until it was time to go to bed.

Joy's sister Sallie lived with her husband Mac McEntire on their ranch about forty miles south of town near Sterling City, Texas, and we had recently driven down there to visit. One day after being assigned to my training squadron, I took a T-33 and flew alone south towards their ranch, familiarizing myself with the area where I would be teaching students. Flying at five hundred miles per hour, it only took me five minutes to reach their ranch house after takeoff. I saw Mac's black Ford pickup truck parked in the caliche drive next to their house. Descending down to 2,500 feet, I flew over them and circled around. Within a few minutes, Sallie and Mac came out of the house and watched me fly overhead. I waggled my wings, letting them know that I had seen them, and they began to wave at me too.

Mac had been a staff sergeant in the US Army during World War II, and he and I had talked about our combat experiences in the Pacific when we had visited them a few weeks earlier. Part of the attack force on Okinawa, he was in the Tenth Army, a cross-branch force consisting of the 7th, 27th, 77th, and 96th infantry divisions of the US Army along with the 1st, 2nd, and 6th divisions of the Marines. The eighty-two-day battle was one of the bloodiest in the Pacific, with approximately 160,000 casualties on both sides. At least 75,000 soldiers and Marines and 117,000 Japanese, including many involuntarily conscripted Okinawans wearing Japanese uniforms, died. There were 149,425 civilians killed, including some that committed suicide with their children by jumping off high cliffs.

Near the end of the battle, and from a concealed cave position, a small group of Japanese soldiers attacked Mac's unit in a banzai raid, and suddenly he was in a desperate hand-to-hand fight with a Japanese officer. Killing him, Mac took his Samurai Katana-style sword as a trophy, eventually bringing it home. It had a beautifully engraved 29-inch curved blade and came with a very ornate scabbard. Kept in a gun closet, he occasionally took it out in the summertime to cut watermelons; however, its razor-sharp blade was very dangerous, and he carefully used it when his two children Pamela and Mackey were nearby.

One morning at our usual flight briefing, our wing commander came in and told us that General Curtis LeMay was going to be visiting later that afternoon. Our current training class of students flying the T-33 was one of the first to fly the new "Shooting Star" introduced into the Air Training Command in 1956. But there had been a few accidents in which students and instructors had to eject quickly through the canopy in order to escape a disabled or flamed-out jet. Several of them were severely injured, and some killed when going through the hard Plexiglas. Basically, its sharp edges shredded them.

Lockheed scientists and engineers had developed a new type of plastic canopy that was resistant to impact, such as bird strikes from the outside, but could easily be punched through on the inside. It was a significant manufacturing accomplishment that would save many lives in the future. Since Webb Air Force Base was a major Air Training Command facility, it was selected as the demonstration site of the new plastic canopy for the T-33.

I went home and changed into my class "A" blue uniform. As I was leaving, Joy drove up with Stan Jr. and Penny. I told her that I was going back out to the base to watch the demonstration.

Stan Jr., who was twelve years old, asked, "Dad, can I come with you?"

Pausing a moment, I said, "Sure. We'll go see how the new canopy operates and then stop by the Wagon Wheel restaurant and bring barbecue sandwiches home for dinner."

Parking near the flight line next to a large hanger, he and I walked over to the area where the demonstration was going to be held. Two seven-foot elongated T-33 canopies were tightly strapped down on sawhorses. Then hearing a large multi-engine airplane approach the base, we saw General LeMay's customized Douglas DC-7 on short final as he landed on runway 17 and taxied over to the hangar where a large group of Air Force officers, pilots, and local dignitaries had assembled. Followed by his aides and chief of staff, he climbed down the stairs and saluted a group of senior officers standing at the bottom. After talking for a few minutes, they all walked over to where the canopies and sawhorses were set up.

Stan Jr. and I were standing in front of about forty people. The civilian tech rep introduced himself to General LeMay and explained that he was going to hit the canopy with a sledgehammer to demonstrate its bird strike capability. Picking it up, he struck the plastic top sharply but did not break or even crack it. Doing it twice more, he had the same results. Then placing a gray cushioned rolling office chair under the canopy, he started to sit down when he saw Stan Jr. standing next to me.

Coming over to us, he said, "Captain, would you mind if I borrow your boy for the demonstration?"

Looking over at me, I saw that Stan Jr. was grinning and nodding his head enthusiastically.

"Sure. I guess that will be okay," I said.

Then the tech rep said, "Son, follow me and sit down in the chair under the canopy."

Going over to the side table, he picked up a pilot's survival knife with a 4-inch blade. Handing it to Stan Jr., he said, "Okay, son. Take the knife and see if you can punch a hole through the plastic above your head."

Gripping its handle tightly with his right hand, Stan Jr. placed the tip near the surface and then quickly thrust it. With virtually no resistance, the knife penetrated the plastic up to the hilt. The tech rep told him to do it several more times in rapid succession; he easily poked three more holes through the canopy then handed the knife to the Lockheed representative as the crowd began to clap their hands.

As my son was standing up, General Curtis LeMay, smoking a cigar, walked over to him and motioned for me to join them. He proceeded to ruffle Stan Jr.'s short burr haircut and said, "Son, are you going to be a pilot like your dad when you grow up?"

"Yes, sir, after I graduate from college."

Smiling, General LeMay removed his cigar and said, "How would you like to go to the newly formed Air Force Academy?"

Enthusiastically, Stan Jr. said, "Oh, yes, sir! I would like that if I can get in."

"I'll see what I can do to help with that when you're ready." He said, ruffling my son's hair one more time. But when the time came, Stan Jr. decided to attend Texas Tech and not go to The Air Force Academy.

After visiting with the dignitaries, commanders, and senior pilots, General LeMay walked over to a nearby T-33, which had a pilot sitting in the rear cockpit. Lighting another stogie, he leaned forward and looked into the dark exhaust outlet of the aircraft whose pilot was getting ready to start its jet engine. Suddenly, a Chief Master Sergeant ran over to the general, and firmly taking his arm, quickly pulled him away, saying, "Sir, you will be severely burned if you stand there and the engine starts."

Clinching down on the cigar with his teeth, General LeMay gruffly said, "It wouldn't dare!"

General Curtis LeMay – Times Cover

I continued to teach students to fly the T-33 for about a year then was promoted to major in 1958 and moved into squadron flight operations. While assigned there, I was responsible for updating the pilot training curriculum and student assessment program. These new responsibilities required attending numerous aviation conferences at Randolph Air Force Base in San Antonio, Texas, and occasionally some at Lowry Air Force Base in Denver, Colorado.

Joy was not happy with my being gone so much of the time, and we began to have serious marital problems because of my frequent trips away from home. In fourteen years of marriage, I had been gone for fourteen months at the end of WWII, sixteen months during the Korean War, and twenty months while I was assigned to Tsuiki, Japan; a total of fifty months or a little over four years.

We had occasional conversations about divorcing, but both of us were reluctant to make the final decision. The unaccompanied tours overseas, TDY assignments, frequent PCS transfers, and uprooting of the kids from school every year had taken a severe toll on Joy, and she was becoming sad, depressed, and stressed out because of the chaos of Air Force life. We had moved nine times since we were married in July 1944.

Then one day, in June 1959, I received a message to report to the wing commander. Arriving at his office, he told me that I had been selected as one of three Air Force pilots who were going to be sent in about a month to Edwards Air Force Base in Southern California after the current training cycle was finished. There I was to be assigned first to the Air Force Test Pilot School for thirty-two weeks and then for nine months attached to the 6512th Test Pilot Training Squadron, part of the Air Force Test Center (AFTC). Once all the training was completed, it was the equivalent of earning a two-year engineering degree. Then, along with the two other pilots, I would begin operational flight testing of the new Northrop Corporation's T-38 Talon supersonic trainer that was scheduled to replace the T-33s.

There was no available housing for Joy and the kids to live on base, and the surrounding desert communities didn't have much to offer either, so that was all it took for Joy to decide she wanted a divorce. It was not an easy decision for us to make; however, she was tired of living alone with our two kids while I was traveling all over the world. We sold the house to an Air Force lieutenant colonel assigned to Webb Air Force Base, and who had just moved to Big Spring. Joy arranged for the movers to pick up the furniture and deliver it to Levelland, where she and the kids were going to live with her parents until she could rent a house. On the day the movers came to load the furniture, I was already in California at Edwards Air Force Base.

I was very sad my marriage ended. But understood the stress the constant moves and my long absences placed on my family, and didn't blame Joy for wanting to get off the roller coaster our lives had become. However, the only way I could change our circumstances was to leave the US Air Force and start a new career as a civilian. Ever since flying in the WWI Jenny at the county fair when I was ten years old, all I ever wanted to do was to fly airplanes and frankly wasn't equipped to do much else.

Although the pay was not great, I was making nearly $800.00 per month and had agreed to pay Joy $150.00 from that for child support. Her teachers pay of about $375.00 per month, plus the money she received from me would allow her to be okay financially. She took the Buick as a means of transportation for her and the kids. I vowed to stay in touch with her and to call Stan Jr. and Penny by long-distance telephone frequently. My contact with the kids and Joy continued to be an important part of my life.

CHAPTER 17

EDWARDS AFB, TEST PILOT

Before going to Edwards AFB, I bought a 1959 Ford Thunderbird in Ohio when I went there to see my dad, sister Sue and her husband, John. After visiting with my family, I drove 2,130 miles in four days to Barstow, California, spent the night at a motel, then continued west through the Mojave desert a few miles to the north entrance of the base. The terrain around the base was barren and completely devoid of any vegetation. Crossing the north end of Rogers Dry Lake, formerly known as Muroc Dry Lake, I was impressed seeing a huge runway. With headings of 170° and 350°, I learned it was 39,097 feet long, having an extra 9,000 ft of hard-packed dry lakebed, making it capable of landing all known aircraft. At over seven and one half miles long, it was the longest runway in the world.

Checking in at the headquarters of the Air Force Test Pilot School, I briefly met Lieutenant Colonel Herbert V. Leonhardt, the commandant of the school who had graduated from it in 1956. He was highly educated with a B.S degree in aeronautical engineering from Virginia Polytech Institute and an M.S. degree in aeronautical engineering from Princeton University. He told me that a new advanced training class with ten students, including me, would begin in three days on Monday at 0800 hours and to report to the newly built training facility near the flight line.

Edwards AFB at Rogers Dry Lake (source: Public Domain)

I got a room at the BOQ, left my B-4 bag and flight gear there, and then drove to the Officers' Club on Doolittle Drive, where I had dinner. There were quite a few people there, but I didn't recognize any of the pilots, so after eating, I went back to the room and went to bed. The next morning I drove to the base library intent on learning about the test pilot school.

Sitting at a table with the course syllabus, I began to read about the different subjects we were going to study. Immediately, I saw there was going to be substantial calculus, physics, and aerothermodynamics involved in several of the entry-level refresher courses. Then the real classroom test pilot courses began with aircraft performance, calibration, and specific case studies examined. They also comprised airspeed system theory, including a review of Euler's and Bernoulli's equations.

Leaning back in the hard wooden chair, I breathed in deeply, exhaled, and thought, *"I don't know if I'm smart enough to be a test pilot. I've studied some of this over the years but have no idea who Euler was or what his equation solved."* Continuing on, I realized that I knew more than I first thought because of my eighteen years of studying Technical Order Dash-1's of numerous aircraft with increasingly complex operating systems. Finally, I decided. *"I probably can get help with some of the advanced mathematic problems if I need to, so I think I'll be okay."* And, indeed, I was. There were after hour study groups of electrical and aeronautical engineers that helped all of us understand the importance of the math calculations as they related to aircraft flight testing.

Our test pilot training was rigorous and consisted of three phases:

1. Phase one was a refresher course to prepare us for the engineering work ahead. It included algebra, trigonometry, calculus, physics to include mechanics and dynamics of bodies, aerodynamics, performance, stability, and control applications.

2. Phase two involved the theory and practice of the performance flight test. This included calibration testing of airspeed, altimeter, free air temperature, level flight-power required speed points, and range determinations. The climb tests required mastery of sawtooth climbs, check climbs, and cooling saws.

3. Phase three included stability and control of flight testing. That phase included longitudinal testing of stalls, static

dynamics, accelerated trim changes, landing analysis, and lateral directional test—static, dynamic, asymmetric power, aileron roll, and adverse yaw.[22]

Each of us flew our own tests, recorded the data gathered on the flight, and analyzed the results. Then we submitted the report of all the data, the analysis, and observations to our headquarters.

At the end of the thirty-two-week course, we took a final exam, and everyone passed, including me. Then the next day, I was transferred to the 6512th Test Pilot Training Squadron, part of the Air Force Test Center (AFTC).

T-38 Talon

T-38 Talon Super Sonic Trainer (USAF photo)

T-38 TALON

- Crew: Two—student and instructor
- Length: 46 ft 4.5 in
- Wingspan: 25 ft 3 in
- Height: 12 ft 10.5 in
- Empty weight: 7,200 lb
- Loaded weight: 11,820 lb
- Max. takeoff weight: 12,093 lb
- Powerplant: 2 × General Electric J85-5A afterburning turbojets
- Dry thrust: 2,050 lb
- Thrust with afterburner: 2,900 lb
- Maximum speed: Mach 1.3 (858 mph)
- Range: 1,140 mi
- Service ceiling: 50,000 ft

T-38A Talon Cockpit (USAF Photo)

*Test Flying Prototype YT-38 Talon at Edwards AFB 1959
(USAF Photo)*

Flying the White Rocket

"Oh, my God!" were the only words that came to mind as I recovered from the head-spinning 720° aileron roll. *"I've never flown anything this fast before in my entire career or anything that has a roll rate of two complete turns in one second."* It was my first day of flight testing the prototype YT-38 Talon at Edwards Air Force Base. I had taken off at 0700 hours while the dry desert air was still cool and climbed to 30,000 feet to familiarize myself with the single-seat twin-engine jet airplane. Flying northwest towards Bakersfield and then over the Sequoia National Forest and the Sierra Nevada mountains surrounding it, I was far enough from the other testing areas not to worry about encountering any aircraft during my aerobatic maneuvers.

Everything about the white, sleek, swept-wing aircraft was different than anything I had flown in the past. Simply starting the jet had been an unusual experience because there was no auxiliary power unit (APU) used. Instead, the crew chief attached a huffer unit, or palouste, large air hose to a manifold opening on the bottom of the airplane, near the left engine. After I pressed the left start button, it slowly spooled up, ignited, and as the RPM increased to fourteen percent, I moved the throttle to the idle position. The ground crewman manually moved the large air hose to the right engine, and I started it. I had spent two weeks and nearly eighty hours in ground school learning all of the Dash-1 procedures of the T-38 twin-engine, supersonic jet trainer. After passing a rigorous written exam, I was permitted to take it up for my first solo flight.

The previous day I had returned from Williams Air Force Base, where three other pilots and I flew in to be checked out on the new Martin-Baker Mk-4 ejection seat hooked up to a tall fixed tower stand. Once tightly strapped in, the instructor gave me a thumbs up, indicating I could pull the ejection seat handle between my legs with both hands. Hesitating a moment, I reached down and pulled the red handle. Instantly a loud explosive charge propelled me up the rails to a height of 45 feet at a force of ten Gs, which was somewhat painful on my back. The ejection seat was operational to 50,000 ft. and could be used at ground level provided the aircraft was traveling at ninety knots indicated airspeed (KIAS). The maximum operating speed was six hundred KIAS. Ejecting faster than that would shred the parachute (and pilot) when it opened. After the ejection seat ordeal, we had to undergo a hypobaric high altitude pressure chamber test, including removing our oxygen masks at twenty thousand feet and performing simple math problems as the altitude increased. Passing both phases was a mandatory requirement of the test flight squadron.

The sky was clear as I was flying over Mt. Whitney, the tallest mountain in the contiguous United States, with an elevation of 14,505 feet. Then I climbed to 40,000 feet and began my testing of the T-38. *"And to think, I get paid to do this job!"* I thought while I maneuvered the jet through the various phases of my planned maneuvers.

After an hour of adrenaline-charged flight testing, I returned to Edwards Air Force Base, and twenty-five miles out, I slowed my airspeed down to three hundred knots and called approach control for landing instructions. I was told to call the tower upon entering downwind for runway 23L, which was 15,024 feet in length and had VOR, ILS, TACAN, and DME instrument approaches. It only took a few minutes to reach the base, and as I switched to the tower frequency, I began my descent to the landing pattern altitude of 3,800 feet, which was approximately 1,500 feet above the field elevation of 2,303 feet.

At midfield, I rolled into a 65° left bank, losing seventy knots of airspeed and arrived on the downwind leg one half-mile away from the runway. At a right angle from the touchdown point, I lowered the landing gear and flaps, then increased the power to maintain two hundred knots airspeed. At 45° past the runway threshold, I rolled into a left turn, slightly lowered the nose, and continued circling the airplane around. Once lined up on final approach, I reduced my speed to one hundred seventy knots. Crossing the runway threshold, I shifted my visual focus down the runway, smoothly brought the throttles back to idle, slightly flared, and touched down. At one hundred knots, I lowered the nosewheel to the runway and slowed the aircraft to a fast taxi speed. Slowly exiting the runway, I switched frequencies to ground control and was given instructions to taxi to my initial departure point and park near the hanger. Shutting down the engines, I removed my helmet and sat in the cockpit for a few minutes enjoying the dry fresh air after the thrill of flying the "White Rocket."

Over the next eight months, I continued performing the aerial flight tests of the T-38 and finally completed my evaluation of it. Flying the 858 miles per hour "Talon" was great fun and set me on a course leading up to me flying the 1,473 miles per hour F-4 Phantom II. I was humbled to think that twenty years earlier, I started flying a Fleet Finch 16B bi-plane, which had a top speed of 104 miles per hour. My oh my, how things had changed in the field of aviation.

Once finished, I was given orders to report to Randolph Air Force Base in San Antonio, Texas, where I was going to set up the first pilot instructor training (PIT) flight squadron to use the T-38A Talon in training new undergraduate pilots student in their advanced phase of training. My time spent at Edwards Air Force Base was especially useful because it allowed me to see the need for better training of instructor pilots and gave me the skills to evaluate their ability to fly and teach in the new supersonic jets.

I now firmly believed in the mission statement summarizing the graduate level educational objective I achieved at Edwards Air Force Base.

"The mission of the USAF TPS is to produce highly adaptive, critical-thinking flight test professionals to lead and conduct full-spectrum test and evaluation of aircraft and aerospace weapon systems. Performing this mission allows the school to fulfill the vision of being the world's premier educational and training center of excellence for theoretical and applied flight test engineering."[23]

CHAPTER 18

RANDOLPH AFB

I had only been at my new assignment two days in San Antonio, Texas, and was staying at the BOQ when Joy called me late one night and said that her mother had died earlier that day while taking a nap at home. We had frequently talked by telephone because we were considering remarrying after I assured her that I would not accept any more long-term TDY assignments or unaccompanied tours of duty.

Tearfully she said, "Can you come to Levelland for the funeral? We are all having a rough time because Mother died so unexpectedly."

I said, "Let me make some telephone calls, and I'll call you back."

I called the duty officer and told him what happened. He gave me the emergency number of my commanding officer. When I called him, he permitted me to take two weeks of leave to be with my family. I immediately called Joy and told her that I would be at her house in about eight hours and quickly packed for the four hundred twenty-five-mile trip.

Arriving at the Heaths' house at 8:00 a.m., I hugged and kissed Joy and Penny when they came out to greet me. I didn't see Mr. Heath because he was at the funeral home, making the arrangements for Maude's burial two days later. Stan Jr., who got his driver's license two years earlier when he was fourteen years old, was driving up from the ranch, where he had been working for the summer as a cowboy. About two hours later, he, Sallie, Mac, and their kids drove up in two cars, and we all went out to meet them. I was surprised to see how much my son had grown. Very tanned, lean, and muscular from the hard ranch work, Stan Jr. was as tall as I was at 5'11!

Later, when we drove in my car to pick up some donuts for breakfast, I told him that his mother and I were going to remarry and that they were going to move to San Antonio. He wasn't surprised and actually thought it was a good idea. I was relieved because he and I had been somewhat estranged since the divorce. Returning to the house, everyone was gone to the funeral home except Joy and Penny. While sitting at the kitchen table eating donuts, Stan Jr. said that he didn't think his grandfather should be left alone after everyone went home. He also said that he wanted to move in with him to finish his last two years of high school at Levelland. Although his demeanor was sad and serious, what he proposed made a lot of sense, so his mother and I agreed.

The day after the funeral, which took place in Caddo, Oklahoma, Joy and I went to the Levelland City Hall and were married by a county judge. I helped Joy pack up her house, and after a few days, a moving company from Lubbock loaded everything. They took it to a home we rented over the telephone in Universal City near Randolph AFB. Stan Jr. moved his clothes and guns into Mr. Heath's house, and a month later started his junior year of high school.

After moving to Randolph Air Force Base, one Saturday evening, driving down the long two-lane boulevard, we went past the "Taj Mahal" administration building. Joy and Penny were impressed with the beautifully illuminated 170-foot tall white building and were surprised when I told them the towering structure concealed a large water tank behind the ornate façade. We had recently moved into our house near the base and were going home after eating at the elegant officers' club's main dining room for dinner.

Randolph AFB Building 100 "Taj Mahal"

Randolph AFB was often called the "Showplace of the Air Force" because of its concentric circular street design and its beautiful Spanish Colonial Revival style architecture. Its humid subtropical climate with hot summers and warm to cool winters resulted in vast amounts of lush green vegetation growing everywhere. Stunning landscapes containing flowers, shrubs, and multi-colored bushes were planted everywhere around the main buildings. The lawns were immaculately manicured and edged.

Designed to be a flight training base, Randolph was built during the Great Depression with 500-plus buildings and thirty miles of roadways. Construction started in 1928, and it became operational as a primary flight school on November 2, 1931. The base was unique with its circular street layout housing the various facilities bordered by two 8,352 foot parallel runways. Separate control towers were built for each runway, and aircraft hangers were next to them. The Officers'

Club was located in the center of the circle, and extending out from that was the officers' housing. Enlisted barracks and base services lined the area between the circles and the hanger rows.

Randolph AFB with parallel runways 17/35

3510th Flying Training Wing

Later designated as the 12th Flying Training Wing (12 FTW), I was assigned to the 3510th FTW and tasked with setting up a new flight squadron, which was going to train instructor pilots using the T-38 Talon; the aircraft I had just been testing at Edwards AFB. It was part of the USAF's Air Training Command Pilot Instructor Training

(PIT) program, which consolidated nine training squadrons from four different bases. The purpose was to standardize the way instructor pilots were trained. Once their training was completed, they were then assigned to an undergraduate pilot training (UPT) base and ultimately took their novice student pilots into the jet age.

Before the students arrived, I spent several weeks developing a written PIT curriculum and syllabus. It was similar to the program that undergraduate pilot training (UPT) students completed but focused mainly on instructor pilot techniques and specific methodology involving flight maneuvers and safety. All of the PIT enrolled students were already skilled pilots who had served at least one assignment as an instructor. The new program took four months to complete, including one-hundred flying hours in the T-38 Talon.

Each day began at 0700, with four students and me sitting in a briefing room, where we learned about the current weather, any flight schedule changes, and other information for the day's activities. Afterward, I had one-on-one meetings with my students before each of their flights to discuss the flight maneuvers and procedures we would perform during the training. Throughout the day, classroom instruction and other needed program matters took place in the newly constructed flight training building. I was very familiar with this format since I had participated in hundreds of similar sessions since first attending the RCAF's fighter pilot training in 1941, twenty years earlier.

One morning after the briefing, I walked out to the parked T-38 Talon, with my student, a young captain from Sheppard AFB, and we began to preflight the sleek new airplane. Next to the cockpit, a ladder was attached to the edge of the canopy. Standing on it, I reached in and turned on the battery, checked the fuel and oxygen levels, landing gear lights, and looked for any cockpit warning lights. Turning the battery switch off, we reviewed the aircraft's maintenance forms to ensure the plane was ready to fly and not red X'd *(a written notation meaning the aircraft was not to be flown under any circumstances until a serious maintenance issue was corrected.)*

Continuing clockwise, we began at the left engine inlet, looking for any evidence of foreign object damage (FOD), then checked the leading edges of the thin wing, and slowly walking along, looked closely at the honeycomb-composite flight control surfaces and wingtips. Then we inspected the right engine inlet, the landing gear doors, and speed brakes. Removing the landing gear pins and pitot tube cover, the student placed them in the fueling access panel below the left engine inlet and unplugged the ground wire from the nose and moved it away from the airplane. We put on our parachutes, and with the help of the chief crew, climbed into the aircraft. The student sat up front, and I sat in back on a seat ten inches higher than the front.

The crew chief helped us strap in our seats as we connected our oxygen tubes and communication jacks. Then he attached the forced air huffer hose to the left manifold, and I started the engine. Once it was idling, he moved the hose to the right manifold, and I started it. After it was idling, he removed the large diameter hose and pulled away the chocks around the landing gear. I ran through a series of flight control checks making sure the control surfaces moved the way they were supposed to, the main landing gear doors were set properly, and the horizontal stabilator was in its usual takeoff position.

After saluting, the enlisted crew chief backed away from the aircraft, and I pressed the nose wheel control button on the stick, increased power, and the T-38 Talon began to turn to the right. Then I called ground control.

to accelerate to two hundred fifty knots then pulled the throttles back out of afterburner. Making a right turn, out of the traffic pattern, I continued to climb, increasing, and holding my airspeed at three hundred knots. Contacting departure control, I told them we would be leaving the area to the west and flying a training mission. With the nose at 12°, I was climbing at 12,000 feet per minute and reached 48,000 feet in four minutes. (Note: Full afterburner climb at the same speed results in a 30,000-feet per minute rate of climb.)

Leveling off, I turned to a westerly heading and accelerated to .86 Mach which was 642 knots (739 mph). Crossing Medina Lake and Bandera, Texas, I said to the student, "You have the aircraft," letting him take control of the stick.

We practiced 180-degree turns and acceleration to a maximum supersonic airspeed of Mach 1.3, which was 746 knots (858 mph). Then taking the controls, I demonstrated several supersonic barrel rolls and descending rolling turns, producing about four Gs. Retracting the throttles out of afterburner, I slowed the jet to cruise speed, and after warning the student to hold on, demonstrated a one second 720° right-hand full aileron roll. Steadily leveling the wings after rolling past horizontal by 20°, I heard him yell, "Wow! That's amazing."

Laughing, I said, "How about them cookies, Captain?"

We descended to 30,000 feet and practiced loops, slow-rolls, and precision four-point rolls hesitating at 90°, 180°, and 270°. We also performed clean stalls, power-approach stalls with landing gear, and flaps down. Finally, returning to Randolph, we shot three touch and go landings and then taxied back to the parking area by the hanger, and I shut the engines down. We had flown for a little over one hour. Climbing down the ladder, I saw my student grinning like a Cheshire cat, although his flight suit was completely sweated out.

"Hangover, ground control, this is Talon 287 requesting taxi to runway 15 Romeo."

"Talon 287 proceed to runway 15 Romeo and hold short; then contact hangover tower on frequency 120.5."

After a few minutes, we reached the end of runway 15R, where I held short and switched to the tower frequency.

"Hangover tower, this is Talon 287 holding short of runway 15 Romeo ready for takeoff."

"Talon 287, you're cleared for takeoff on runway 15 Romeo with a right departure. Winds out of the south 180° at 3 knots and barometric pressure is 2914. Have a good day, sir."

"Roger 2914, Talon 287 is taking the runway and will make a right departure, out."

Reaching up with my left hand, I pulled the canopy down tight against the fuselage and locked it with the mechanism on the right and saw the student do the same thing. Immediately, I heard air blowing as the cockpit was pressurized. Making sure the IFF Mk-10 was turned on, I increased the engine's power, and the airplane slowly began to roll to the middle of the two hundred foot wide runway, where I made a 90° turn to the right lining up on the centerline of the 8,352-foot runway and stopped. I checked the instruments one final time and pressing down on both brakes; I held them tightly in position. Then I eased the throttles up to the military power setting, checked the gauges, and released the brakes. Beginning to roll down the runway, I pushed the throttles forward into the afterburner position. The aircraft accelerated quickly, and at one hundred thirty-five knots, I applied slight back pressure on the stick. At one hundred sixty knots, the airplane became airborne.

After takeoff, I raised the landing gear and flaps and continued

Coming up to me, the student said, "Major Corvin, that's the most fun I've ever had flying an airplane. After work, please let me buy you a beer in the stag bar at the Officers' Club."

Smiling, I said, "Sure thing, I'll meet you there." Later after flying with my other students, I finished the paperwork and drove to the Officers' Club and drank a beer with him before going home.

Over the next three years, we enjoyed living near San Antonio, and frequently Joy and I went to the downtown restaurants near the river. Most served Mexican food, which was our overall favorite. However, there was an exclusive restaurant called La Louisianne located on Broadway across from the Brackenridge golf course that served New Orleans style French-Creole cuisine and was rated in the top five restaurants in the nation by *Holiday Magazine*. George Dareos and his wife Olive were the owners, and we became friends after meeting them at the Randolph AFB Officers' Club at a reception welcoming a new base commander.

One evening while eating at their restaurant, George introduced us to Henry B. Gonzales, a member of the U.S House of Representatives recently elected in 1961 and a very powerful local politician who was the first Hispanic American to represent Texas. He and his wife Bertha frequented the restaurant, and many times Joy and I saw him there with his large extended family, including eight children. Anytime he saw us in the restaurant, he stopped by and visited with us at our table. Upstairs, where we usually were seated, there was a dance floor with a Latin combo band playing dinner music. Occasionally when the musicians played something slow, Henry B. came over to our table and asked Joy to dance, knowing that she had studied dance and music in college. She always graciously accepted, knowing that he was a masterful dancer.

A couple of years later, on November 22, 1963, Henry B. Gonzales was in the motorcade behind President John F. Kennedy and

Jacqueline when Lee Harvey Oswald fired the fatal shots from Dallas's Texas School Book Depository. We never saw Henri B. and his entourage at La Louisiannes' again because of his numerous legislative commitments helping with the preparation of the Warren Commission's report of President Kennedy's assassination.

Because there were many beautiful lakes around Central Texas, I bought a 1950 fully-restored 22-foot solid mahogany hulled Chris Craft ski boat with a 106 horsepower four-cylinder inboard engine. Its classic powerboat design and white outlined forward deck brought many admiring looks and comments from people at the docks where we launched it. Forty miles west of the base, Medina Lake was one of our favorite places to go. For $5.00 per day, I rented a 15' by 15' floating wooden platform mounted on empty oil drums and anchored in the middle of the lake. From there, we picnicked, skied, fished, and camped overnight. The clear blue water's shoreline was mostly surrounded by tall limestone bluffs, which prevented any muddy runoff from entering the lake during rains.

Although Joy could not swim, at all, she loved to water ski, so I strapped two orange-colored cork-filled cloth ski belts to her waist, and she floated high in the water before being pulled up on the skis. In the evenings, we frequently ate a supper of pan-fried fish cooked on a two-burner camp stove served with pork and beans, sliced tomatoes, onions, and potato chips. Then when it was dark, I lit our green Coleman two-mantle gas lantern. With 20-foot long cane poles and using live nightcrawler worms as bait, we fished for yellow catfish and crappie from the sides of the platform. After the holidays each January, the Texas Parks and Wildlife staff took Christmas trees and sank them around each platform to create underwater cover for the crappie.

Later at night, we lay on Army surplus air mattresses, which we inflated during the day to float on in the water. Lulled to sleep by the gentle rocking of the platform and the cool Texas breeze, I sometimes dreamed about crashing on the Canadian island and sleeping next to the water's edge, hearing the occasional splash of a jumping fish. Although I had severely cut my scalp in the crash landing, I survived, and that was a fond memory of a bygone time.

It was a very good phase in my life, and I was happy as I instructed pilots in T-38s during the day and was home with my family each evening. However, after three years at Randolph AFB, I knew that I would soon receive orders sending me to another assignment. Then one day, they came in, transferring me to Bitburg, West Germany, and the 36th Tactical Fighter Wing. But first, I was being sent to Davis-Monthan AFB in Tuscon, Arizona, for eleven weeks TDY to get checked out in the McDonnell F-4C Phantom II.

Walking into our home after work, I hugged Joy and cheerfully said, "How would you and Penny like to move to West Germany with me?"

Excitedly, she said, "We would love that. Can we go to Paris, tour castles, and explore the Alps?"

"Sure, we'll travel all over Europe as my work schedule allows. We'll even go to Amsterdam in the spring during the Tulip Festival and see all the flowers."

Laughing happily, she hugged me and said, "Another adventure with my handsome pilot."

Frowning, I said, "But first I'm being sent to Davis-Monthan Air Force Base in Tuscon, Arizona for three months to get checked out in a new supersonic jet called the F-4 Phantom. While I'm gone, Penny can finish out the school year, and then we will leave for Europe. Is that okay with you?"

Hesitating, Joy said, "Well, I don't like the separation, but if you promise to take me to Paris to see the Eiffel Tower and the Louvre museum then I guess it's going to be okay." Then she smiled broadly, and I knew everything was going to be okay between us.

F-4D Phantom II

F-4D Phantom II (source: Public Domain)

MCDONNELL F-4D PHANTOM II

- **Wingspan:** 38 ft. 4-7/8 in.
- **Length:** 63 ft.
- **Height:** 16 ft. 6 in.
- **Empty Weight:** 29,535 lbs.
- **Gross Weight:** 61,651 lbs.
- **Top Speed:** 1,485 mph
- **Service Ceiling:** 62,650 ft.
- **Range:** 1,885 miles
- **Engine/Thrust:** Two General Electric J79s @ 17,900 lbs. each
- **Crew:** 2
- **Armament:** One M61A1 20 mm cannon; various combinations of AIM-7 Sparrow and AIM-9 Sidewinder missiles
- **Ordnance:** Up to 12,980 lbs. of bombs/ordnance on four wing pylons

A few weeks after I received my new orders, I flew to Davis-Monthan Air Force Base and checked in with my headquarters, the 4453rd Combat Crew Training Wing. DOUBLE UGLY IS ITS NAME, SHOOTING DOWN ENEMY AIRCRAFT IS ITS GAME was a sign I saw next to the flight line, where approximately fifty of the supersonic fighters were parked.

During the eleven-week course, the pilots completed thirty flying hours in the Phantom. After two familiarization rides, the class was divided into twelve two-man crews who practiced instruments, low-level and high-level navigation, radio and radar navigation, air to air intercepts, dive-bombing, rocketry, low-level bombing, close ground support, nuclear delivery, in-flight refueling, and formation flying.

We learned to work as part of a two-man team. The front seat pilot is the aircraft commander (AC) who makes the landings and take-offs, flies the aircraft, and handles the armament. The rear seat pilot, the pilot systems operator, also flies the aircraft but additionally must operate the Phantom's sophisticated radar and navigation equipment. Besides the standard ground school, pilot systems operators got an additional two hundred fifty hours of classroom work in radar systems and navigation techniques. Since I wasn't going to be the backseater pilot systems operator, I finished the course in the eleven-week allotted time frame then returned to Randolph.

Taking thirty days leave, Joy, Penny, and I drove to the ranch in Sterling City, where we visited with Sallie and Mac and left Pug, our little black Pekingese dog, with them until we returned to the states in three years. Stan Jr., who was a sophomore at Texas Technological College in Lubbock, drove down to the ranch for a couple of days, and we visited with him before returning to San Antonio. He had grown another inch and was now six feet tall and was going to school full time while working two jobs to pay for everything.

Back home, I sold our ski boat and two cars while Joy packed the house before the movers came to pick up our furniture. On an accompanied tour (meaning the family was with me), I expected that we would live in Bitburg for about three years. The Air Force had begun to lengthen assignments to stabilize tours since many officers, pilots, and enlisted personnel were leaving the service because of divorces, marital problems, and family issues. The new change resulted in a significant decline in the Air Force's attrition rate, which reinforced the old adage, "If mama ain't happy, ain't nobody happy."

Back home, I sold our ski boat and two cars while Joy packed the house before the movers came to pick up our furniture. On an accompanied tour (meaning the family was with me), I expected that we would live in Bitburg for about three years. The Air Force had begun to lengthen assignments to stabilize tours since many officers, pilots, and enlisted personnel were leaving the service because of divorces, marital problems, and family issues. The new change resulted in a significant decline in the Air Force's attrition rate, which reinforced the old adage, "If mama ain't happy, ain't nobody happy."

A few weeks after I received my new orders, I flew to Davis-Monthan Air Force Base and checked in with my headquarters, the 4453rd Combat Crew Training Wing. Double Ugly is its name, shooting down enemy aircraft is its game was a sign I saw next to the flight line, where approximately fifty of the supersonic fighters were parked.

During the eleven-week course, the pilots completed thirty flying hours in the Phantom. After two familiarization rides, the class was divided into twelve two-man crews who practiced instruments, low-level and high-level navigation, radio and radar navigation, air to air intercepts, dive-bombing, rocketry, low-level bombing, close ground support, nuclear delivery, in-flight refueling, and formation flying.

We learned to work as part of a two-man team. The front seat pilot is the aircraft commander (AC) who makes the landings and take-offs, flies the aircraft, and handles the armament. The rear seat pilot, the pilot systems operator, also flies the aircraft but additionally must operate the Phantom's sophisticated radar and navigation equipment. Besides the standard ground school, pilot systems operators got an additional two hundred fifty hours of classroom work in radar systems and navigation techniques. Since I wasn't going to be the backseater pilot systems operator, I finished the course in the eleven-week allotted time frame then returned to Randolph.

Taking thirty days leave, Joy, Penny, and I drove to the ranch in Sterling City, where we visited with Sallie and Mac and left Pug, our little black Pekingese dog, with them until we returned to the states in three years. Stan Jr., who was a sophomore at Texas Technological College in Lubbock, drove down to the ranch for a couple of days, and we visited with him before returning to San Antonio. He had grown another inch and was now six feet tall and was going to school full time while working two jobs to pay for everything.

CHAPTER 19

BITBURG, AFB

Joy, Penny, and I took off from McGuire AFB near Trenton, New Jersey, and after an eight-hour flight, arrived at the Rhine-Main terminal in Frankfurt, Germany, where we were met by our sponsors, Major Baxter "Buck" Rogers, and his wife, Tillie. They lived at Bitburg, and Buck was the assistant operations officer with the 53rd Fighter Squadron, which was part of the 36th Tactical Fighter Wing commanded by Colonel Benjamin B. Cassiday, Jr.

Driving one hundred twenty-eight miles to Bitburg in Buck's light blue Mercedes-Benz 190D sedan, we arrived late in the afternoon at a small downtown hotel called a gasthaus. It had an elaborate mural called a Lüftlmalerei, painted on the large front wall depicting 17th-century workers gathering wheat in a field. Joy was fascinated by its multi-color styling and thought it was the first indication we truly were in a foreign country. We stayed there for approximately two weeks until our furniture and personal effects arrived, and we were assigned on-base quarters consisting of a two-bedroom, one-bath apartment.

I was attached to the 53rd Fighter Squadron and met its commanding officer, Lieutenant Colonel Alex McDonald. He was surprised to learn that I had spent the last three years setting up and running the pilot instructor training program at Randolph Air Force Base. When I explained to him that I had been given that assignment because I was one of the three test pilots at Edwards Air Force Base in California, who certified the airworthiness flight capabilities for the T-38 Talon, he was impressed.

We visited for a while, talking about family and football. He was a graduate of the University of Michigan and a big fan of the Wolverines football team. Since I had attended Ohio State University, I was a supporter of their football team, The Buckeyes. Of course, this set us up for some good-natured rivalry because they played each other during the fall season.

During our conversation, he paused, then said, "You know, Stan, what I really need is someone like you to be sort of an ad hoc standardization and evaluation guy. You'll report directly to me and let me know when you see any problems or issues in flight training, safety, and operations that need to be addressed. I'll put you in the operations section, but you'll have carte blanche authority to fly sorties with the different flights as we train for close air support (CAS) of American and NATO forces. You will attend all the morning flight briefings, and fly on some of the sorties as a flight leader. You'll also go to Wheelus Air Force Base in Libya for gunnery training. Do you think you can handle that?"

Nodding my head, in approval, I said, "Yes, sir. That sounds good to me. I'd like the freedom to look at everything and see if there are areas where I can suggest improvements."

Lieutenant Colonel McDonald stood up, shook my hand, and said, "You're hired! Plan on starting next Monday morning. Oh, by the way, the Michigan Wolverines are going to beat the Ohio State Buckeyes for sure this fall." Then he laughed uproariously.

However, in the last minute of the game in Ann Arbor, Michigan, on Nov. 20, 1965, a late 28-yard field goal increased the Buckeyes lead 9 to 7 over the Wolverines. Coach Woody Hayes was carried off the field on the shoulders of his Ohio players, and I won $20 bucks from my commanding officer. Imagine that!

Cruising at five hundred eighty miles per hour, it took less than three hours to fly the 1,500-miles to the gunnery range at Wheelus AFB. The trips were great fun, and I enjoyed the camaraderie of the F-4D Phantom pilots as we trained in close air support tactics as if there were American troops on the ground. The "Double Ugly" was a fantastic supersonic airplane to fly. Its sheer size was impressive. After flying the supersonic T-38 Talon for three years, I was used to everything being at eye level when performing the preflight of the small, sleek aircraft. But the F-4D Phantom was gigantic having a verticle stabilizer reaching sixteen and one-half feet off the ground.

Bitburg AFB (USAF photo)

The Phantom had a top speed of over Mach 2.2, nearly twice the speed of a T-38A Talon. Carrying more than eighteen thousand pounds of weapons on nine external hardpoints, it had air-to-air missiles, air-to-ground missiles, and various bombs and napalm capability. The F-4D also had a centerline mounted M61A1 "Vulcan" rotary cannon firing six thousand rounds per minute of 20 mm armor-piercing incendiary (API) or high-explosive incendiary (HEI) projectiles. However, because of weight constraints, it carried only six thousand rounds of ammunition weighing two thousand seven hundred pounds, allowing for a total of one-minute shooting.

To avoid using all the rounds at once, a burst controller was installed to limit the number of rounds fired with each trigger pull. Bursts of from two or three up to forty or fifty could be selected by the aircraft commander. Firing the Vulcan cannon at stationary targets, usually shot-up World War II-era tanks, in the Libyan desert gunnery ranges, produced awe-inspiring moments for the flight crew when the projectiles struck the tanks and exploded. After our daily gunnery range exercises, we returned to the base, had a debriefing, showered, and changed uniforms at the BOQ, then went to the beautiful Officers' Club for dinner and cocktails. Returning to Bitburg a week later, we resumed our normal daily routine of morning briefings and training flights in the F-4D Phantom II.

Paris, France

Driving on the autobahn at one hundred miles per hour, we were traveling to Paris two hundred seventy-four miles from Bitburg. Joy was enjoying driving her new white two-door Porsche 912 coupé with its four-speed manual transmission. Before leaving the United States, we sold both of our cars, and after arriving in Bitburg, Germany, I bought a five-year-old VW beetle for $400.00 to drive to and from my work. Once settled into our apartment on the base, we drove the "bug" two hundred eleven miles to Stuttgart to the Porsche factory and bought the new sports car for $4,200.00. With its black leather interior and sliding sunroof, Joy thought it was beautiful and loved its low slung rear-engine design. Although small, the rear seat was big enough for Penny to sit in because she was a young teenager.

We were driving to La Ville-Lumière (The City of Light) as the French people called Paris. Before leaving for ninety days TDY in Arizona, I had promised Joy we would go there sometime after arriving in Germany. Armed with a thick copy of Fodor's Travel Guide and a large foldout map of the European continent, containing all of the autobahns and paved roads, we were able to easily navigate our trip to the renowned city and find street-cafes, restaurants, museums and local places of interest.

Arriving at our small boutique hotel on the Boulevard Saint-Michel in La Rive Gauche *(French: Left Bank)* south of the River Seine, we checked in and took our luggage to the small cramped room, which had only a double bed and a sofa in it. Joy and Penny weren't happy to learn that the communal toilets, baths, and showers were down the hall a few yards away from our room. But "C'est la Vie" *(French: That's life)* as the French say. However, I was pleased to learn that Ernest Hemingway, who wrote *The Sun Also Rises* and William Faulkner, who wrote *The Great Gatsby* had stayed at this hotel in the 1920s and were some of the expatriated American writers, and artists known as "The Lost Generation."

After strolling around the area, we ate a light dinner of grilled fish, green beans, and Pommes Frites *(French: French Fries)* at a nearby sidewalk café. Joy and I each sipped a glass of Cabernet Sauvignon while Penny tried an Orangina™ (a lightly carbonated orange juice), and we watched the people along the Boul Mich as it was colloquially known. There were many young couples holding hands as they walked on the wide sidewalk of the tree-lined boulevard, and Penny giggled when they passed by.

Before leaving San Antonio, Joy went to our bank and got ten rolls of Kennedy half-dollars, which were first minted in 1964. Ever since his famous West Berlin "Ich bin ein Berliner" speech in June 1963, Europeans loved him, and after his assassination, in November of the same year, he was revered as a free world martyr. It was in Paris that Joy began collecting menus from restaurants; generally being given one in exchange for the coveted fifty-cent piece.

The next morning while I stood watch at the communal bathroom door, Joy and Penny took showers, and then I did after they returned to the room to get dressed. In casual clothes, we ate a continental breakfast in the hotel's downstairs restaurant before leaving for a tour of the Eiffel Tower. Parking near the famous landmark, I bought tickets for the top observation deck for all three of us. After reaching the top by elevator (a height of 1,063 feet), we spent two hours wandering around, viewing the vast landscape through the myriad of one franc coin-operated telescopes mounted along the edges and taking photos of the sprawling city below. Several American tourists we met took pictures of Joy, Penny, and me with my new Minolta SLR camera with a 50 mm f1.7 lens, which I had bought at the Bitburg Base Exchange.

After a while, we went to the champagne bar on the observation deck, where Joy and I drank two glasses of Moet Chandon™. Penny tried a sip of mine, but wrinkled her nose in disgust at its taste and decided her Coke® was more to her liking. Having heard from several people that the observation deck restaurants were very expensive, we left the Eiffel Tower and ate lunch at another sidewalk café near our hotel.

Finishing our meal, and after consulting our Fodor's travel guide, we walked a few blocks to a River Seine dock for a ride on a "Bateau Mouche" open excursion boat that cruised the waterway. From its open upper deck, we saw the Eiffel Tower, Notre-Dame Cathedral, the Alexander III Bridge, the Pont Neuf, the Orsay Museum, and the Louvre Museum. We also saw Napoleon's burial site, Les Invalides. Returning to the dock an hour later, we went to our room and rested.

Even though it was small, the hotel had a concierge who made reservations for the three of us at 8:00 p.m. at La Tour D'Argent *(French: The Silver Tower)* restaurant. Buck and Tillie Rogers had told us about it and said the food was excellent, and the view of Notre Dame Cathedral when it was illuminated with lights was breathtakingly beautiful at night. Joy and Penny wore light summer dresses, and I wore my charcoal gray suit with a white shirt and dark tie. We'd been told the restaurant was very expensive and to expect to pay at least $100 for all three of us.

Arriving at the restaurant by taxi, not wanting to drive the Porsche after dark on unfamiliar Parisian streets, we were greeted by a uniformed doorman who escorted us to the elevator, which took us to the seventh-floor restaurant. The maître d' wearing a tuxedo led us to our table sitting in the corner next to a tall glass window overlooking the lighted Notre Dame Cathedral. It was indeed a beautiful sight. Joy and I were served cocktails, and Penny drank a Coke™ while we waited for our menus. A sommelier, also wearing a tuxedo, with a flat silver cup hanging on a heavy chain around his neck, came over with a heavy thick 400-page wine list and handed it to me. Thumbing through the book, I saw several expensive wines, including a 1959 Château Lafite Rothschild, which cost $400 per bottle, and a 1950 Château Latour costing $580. But several local vintners had listed their Beaujolais wines that cost only $20 per bottle, and that's what I ordered for us. Another waiter, again wearing a tuxedo, delivered a basket of bread and several different patties of butter.

Finally, our main waiter came over and took our order. Buck had told us that the restaurant's famous signature dish was pressed duck, and the restaurant owned a farm that raised the birds. Joy and I ordered the *"Canard à la Presse,"* but Penny repulsed at the thought of eating a cute duck didn't want to try it and only wanted a hamburger with Pomme Frites. Asking the waiter if they could bring her one, he smiled and said, *"Certainement,"* as if they served burgers to everyone. I decided then that this was a pretty classy joint.

I also ordered escargot for Joy and me as an appetizer. Neither of us had eaten snails before, but Buck had said they were especially good at the restaurant, so we tried them. Served hot in special dishes with garlic butter, we used the stainless steel tong holders to grasp the shells and then took a tiny fork to pull the snails out. They were fantastic, and we quickly devoured them!

In a few minutes, a different waiter brought Joy and me postcards with our bird's serial numbers, stamped on it, and a separate piece of paper explaining in English the cooking process. First, a plump young duck is strangled to retain its blood. Then after plucking, and removing its entrails, it's partially roasted, and the liver is removed, ground up, and seasoned, then the legs and breast are removed. The remaining carcass, including the other meat, bones, and skin, is put in a specially-designed screw-down device, similar to a wine press.

Immense pressure is applied to extract the duck blood and other juices from the carcass. The extract is thickened and flavored with the duck's liver, butter, and cognac, and then combined with the breast to finish cooking. The result is a wonderful dish called *canard à la rouennaise* or duck in blood sauce. Served with mashed potatoes and steamed spinach, the thinly sliced duck is a delicious and exotic meal—known the world over.

Three waiters delivered the food to us while one used a long silver knife to scrape the breadcrumbs off the white linen tablecloth, especially around Penny's plate, and on to a saucer. The main waiter finally said, *"Bon Appétit!"* And then with crossed arms positioned himself with three other waiters at each corner of the table and watched us eat.

Joy looked at me and raised her eyebrows as if to say, *"Are they going to stay here the whole time we eat?"*

Shrugging my shoulders, I began to eat the succulent duck and was amazed at how delicious it tasted—including the congealed blood sauce. Throughout the meal, the waiters periodically would softly say something to each other in French and nod their heads or frown, which Joy and I found a little disconcerting. But the meal was delicious, and Penny enjoyed her hamburger, so we finished off our dinner with a Grand Marnier souffle.

After the two-hour meal, I was handed the check and saw that it was $140. With a 20% tip, the total bill came to $168.00, which was more than Joy usually spent on food for us for an entire month. But again, as they say, *"C'est La Vie."* When in Paris do as the Parisians do. It had been a wonderful meal and a beautiful experience sitting by the tall glass windows overlooking illuminated Notre Dame Cathedral.

Before leaving the table, Joy motioned for the waiters, the sommelier, and maître d' to come over and gave each person a shiny newly minted Kennedy half-dollar. Very surprised, they each thanked her profusely. The maître d' asked in English if there was anything he could do to make our visit more memorable, and that's when Joy inquired if she could buy a menu. Immediately, he snapped his fingers and summoned a waiter, took a menu from him and gave it to her, saying it was a gift from *La Tour D'argent*. Thanking him, we walked to the front entrance elevator, now followed by an entourage of waiters, sommeliers, and the maître d' all thanking us for coming to their restaurant and graciously giving out the coins. Downstairs, the doorman hailed a taxi for us, and Joy gave him a glistening half-dollar.

Astonished, he began to bow repeatedly to Joy, saying, *"Merci beaucoup, madam,"* over and over until we escaped into the interior of the taxi, and it drove away. Laughing, we decided it really had been a memorable evening.

The next morning we showered, ate a light breakfast at the hotel, and drove to the Louvre Museum. After paying for the tickets at the entrance, we walked into the massive building with its multiple galleries of world-famous art. We saw the Winged Victory, Mona Lisa, numerous huge paintings, and then came to the Sleeping Hermaphroditus sculpture by the master sculptor Bernini. It is a massive work of intricately carved marble art depicting a hermaphrodite woman-man laying nude on what looks like a softly cushioned bed.

Penny walked around it, then abruptly stopped, pointed and loudly, said, "Look, Mom, that lady has a man's pee-pee. Is that even possible?"

Of course, several of the bystanders started laughing while Joy's face turned a deep shade of red, as she rushed over to pull Penny away from the reclining sculpture and hushed her. They quickly walked further down the hall and came to the statue of the Venus de Milo.

Standing beside each other, I heard Penny say in a loud whisper, "Mom, why doesn't she have on a bra covering her boobs?" Looking around, she loudly continued on, saying, "Why are there so many pictures and sculptures here that show nekkid people?" Joy whispered something to her, then grabbed her hand and dragged her down the hall with several people staring at them.

For the next two hours, we walked the halls and galleries of the Louvre Museum and admired the stunningly beautiful artwork that was displayed there. Finally, after buying several souvenirs in the gift shop, we drove back to the hotel and spent the afternoon walking on the Boulevard Saint-Michel and window-shopping at quaint shops and bookstores. The next morning we loaded the Porsche and drove back to Bitburg Air Force Base. The easterly drive through France into Germany was fun as Joy drove through the small villages and finally to our home on base. Our trip to Paris had been a memorable one that we frequently recalled with laughter, mainly because of Penny's hilarious antics at the Louvre Museum.

After living at Bitburg AFB for two and one-half years and becoming the operations officer at the 53rd Fighter Squadron, I was promoted to Lieutenant Colonel in December 1967. I also received orders assigning me to the 366th Fighter Wing in Danang, South Vietnam, a few days before my son, Stan Jr., received his orders to fly helicopters there for the U.S. Army. He had been drafted a year earlier. But because he had a private pilot's license and instrument rating, which he received at Reese Air Force Base in Lubbock while attending Texas Technological College, he was accepted in the U.S. Army's helicopter pilot training program.

Just before his graduation, I called him at Hunter Army Airfield in Savannah, Georgia, to tell him both of us would be serving in the same theater of war. Stan Jr., knowing that I already had served in the USAF for twenty-six years, thought that I should put in for retirement and not go to South Vietnam, which is exactly what Joy wanted me to do.

She was extremely upset when she learned that he was going to a war zone in an extraordinarily dangerous capacity as a helicopter pilot. Then, when I received my orders to go to Danang, she was beside herself with anxiety, bursting into tears whenever we tried to talk about the situation. Another issue we had to resolve was the "sole surviving son" problem of both my son and me serving in the same war zone at the same time. However, a solution to the problem soon presented itself, although in an unexpected way.

Early one morning, a week after talking to my son, and while walking to my headquarters building, from the parking lot, I suddenly became sick at my stomach, began to sweat profusely, and had a major pain radiating from my left arm up to my neck. Sitting down on a bench next to the sidewalk and lighting a cigarette, I began to feel very short of breath as I inhaled the smoke. Thinking it was a result of my drinking too much at the Officers' Club the night before, I tried to dismiss the symptoms as the effects of a slight hangover.

A chief master sergeant walked by me and said, "Sir, are you okay?" Before I could answer, suddenly, my vision began to blur, I blacked out and collapsed on the ground.

Awakening on a gurney in the back of a blue Air Force ambulance, I was confused and unsure of what had happened. The emergency medical technician sitting beside me was holding an oxygen mask over my mouth and said, "Sir, you're having a heart attack, but we will be at the hospital in just a minute. So try to relax as much as you can."

Shallowly breathing and feeling significant pain in my chest, all I

The Eagle Above

same theater of war. Stan Jr., knowing that I already had served in the USAF for twenty-six years, thought that I should put in for retirement and not go to South Vietnam, which is exactly what Joy wanted me to do.

She was extremely upset when she learned that he was going to a war zone in an extraordinarily dangerous capacity as a helicopter pilot. Then, when I received my orders to go to Danang, she was beside herself with anxiety, bursting into tears whenever we tried to talk about the situation. Another issue we had to resolve was the "sole surviving son" problem of both my son and me serving in the same war zone at the same time. However, a solution to the problem soon presented itself, although in an unexpected way.

Early one morning, a week after talking to my son, and while walking to my headquarters building, from the parking lot, I suddenly became sick at my stomach, began to sweat profusely, and had a major pain radiating from my left arm up to my neck. Sitting down on a bench next to the sidewalk and lighting a cigarette, I began to feel very short of breath as I inhaled the smoke. Thinking it was a result of my drinking too much at the Officers' Club the night before, I tried to dismiss the symptoms as the effects of a slight hangover.

A chief master sergeant walked by me and said, "Sir, are you okay?" Before I could answer, suddenly, my vision began to blur, I blacked out and collapsed on the ground.

Awakening on a gurney in the back of a blue Air Force ambulance, I was confused and unsure of what had happened. The emergency medical technician sitting beside me was holding an oxygen mask over my mouth and said, "Sir, you're having a heart attack, but we will be at the hospital in just a minute. So try to relax as much as you can."

Shallowly breathing and feeling significant pain in my chest, all I

Standing beside each other, I heard Penny say in a loud whisper, "Mom, why doesn't she have on a bra covering her boobs?" Looking around, she loudly continued on, saying, "Why are there so many pictures and sculptures here that show nekkid people?" Joy whispered something to her, then grabbed her hand and dragged her down the hall with several people staring at them.

For the next two hours, we walked the halls and galleries of the Louvre Museum and admired the stunningly beautiful artwork that was displayed there. Finally, after buying several souvenirs in the gift shop, we drove back to the hotel and spent the afternoon walking on the Boulevard Saint-Michel and window-shopping at quaint shops and bookstores. The next morning we loaded the Porsche and drove back to Bitburg Air Force Base. The easterly drive through France into Germany was fun as Joy drove through the small villages and finally to our home on base. Our trip to Paris had been a memorable one that we frequently recalled with laughter, mainly because of Penny's hilarious antics at the Louvre Museum.

After living at Bitburg AFB for two and one-half years and becoming the operations officer at the 53rd Fighter Squadron, I was promoted to Lieutenant Colonel in December 1967. I also received orders assigning me to the 366th Fighter Wing in Danang, South Vietnam, a few days before my son, Stan Jr., received his orders to fly helicopters there for the U.S. Army. He had been drafted a year earlier. But because he had a private pilot's license and instrument rating, which he received at Reese Air Force Base in Lubbock while attending Texas Technological College, he was accepted in the U.S. Army's helicopter pilot training program.

Just before his graduation, I called him at Hunter Army Airfield in Savannah, Georgia, to tell him both of us would be serving in the

could think about was, "Well, shit! This will stop me from ever flying again." At forty-seven years of age, I did not want my Air Force career to end this way.

When we arrived at the emergency entrance to the hospital, I was rushed inside, and a gray-haired doctor began to listen to my heart with his stethoscope. "Lieutenant Colonel Corvin, you are having a heart attack called a myocardial infarction. I have started an IV to replenish your electrolytes, and I've given you some morphine to ease the pain. We will move you to an intensive care unit room after you are stabilized here. There isn't much more we can do for you here in Bitburg; however, in a couple of days, we are going to transfer you to the Wiesbaden Air Force Base hospital, where they are better equipped to handle cardiac patients." Then he left.

A few minutes later, Joy and Buck Rogers walked into the small room. Coming over to my bedside, Joy gently stroked my hair, smiled, and said, "How's my handsome flyboy doing?"

Sighing deeply, I said, "Well, I think this has ended my career as a pilot, and I doubt that I will ever be flying again."

And I was right.

Wiesbaden AFB

Front Gate Lindsay Air Station, Wiesbaden, Germany

While the nurse was tucking in the sheets around me in the hospital bed, my wife and daughter walked into the room and waved at me. It was midmorning, and I had arrived at the Wiesbaden hospital after the one hundred-mile ride in an Air Force ambulance. Joy picked Penny up from school, and they followed us in the Porsche.

A cardiology doctor came in a few minutes later, and after reviewing my chart containing an electrocardiogram (ECG) and electroencephalogram (EEG), said, "Stan, you are very lucky. Both the ECG and EKG show that you have had a mild myocardial infarction, and you will ultimately recover. However, your blood pressure is too high, and your kidneys are not functioning as well as they need to be, so we will keep you here for about two weeks and monitor everything. After that, we'll need to see you once a week, probably for a year. I see that you're stationed at Bitburg. You may need to move here so that we can care for you. We are the biggest and best-equipped US military medical facility in Europe with two hundred thirty-five beds and eight hundred forty-four staff members. Do you have any questions for me?"

"Yes, Doc, I've been a fighter pilot for twenty-six years. When can I get back to flying?"

Lowering his head for a moment, then raising it and looking me in the eyes, he said, "Never! Your days of piloting an aircraft are over. Your flight surgeon will confirm it, but Air Force regulations will not allow you to fly again, at least not as a pilot. I'm sorry to have to tell you that." Hanging up my chart at the end of the bed, he walked out of the room.

Standing by the bed, Joy said, "Well, at least you won't be going to South Vietnam. Now all I have to worry about is Stan Jr. surviving flying helicopters over there."

Wiesbaden AFB Hospital

The next morning Lieutenant Colonel Alex McDonald, the 53rd Fighter Squadron commanding officer, came to my room, and we visited for a while. Then he said, "Stan, I'm releasing you from duty with the 53rd because you are being removed from flying status. You're also being transferred here to Wiesbaden Air Force Base until you are well enough to be assigned to a non-flying job. I'm really sorry." We shook hands, and then before he left the room, he said, "Let me know if there is anything I can do for you."

Over the next couple of weeks, Joy came to visit me at the hospital during the day while Penny was in school. Then she began to pack our apartment so that we could move to one in the officers' section of the Hainerburg Housing Area near the junior high school where Penny would be in the eighth grade. Once I was released from the hospital, after recovering completely from my heart attack, we stayed at the Amelia Earhart Hotel in downtown Wiesbaden for a week until a three-bedroom, two-bath apartment was available.

Between December 1953 and March 1973, Wiesbaden Air Force Base was the host base for the United States Air Force–Europe headquarters. It planned, conducted, controlled, coordinated, and supported air and space operations in Europe, parts of Asia and all of Africa except for Egypt to attain U.S. national security objectives and NATO goals.

At the 53rd Fighter Squadron, as a major, on the promotion list for Lieutenant Colonel, I had been given the additional duty of making sure all of the nuclear weapons were properly accounted for and safely secured. So, In addition to flying as a senior squadron pilot, that task required me to periodically inspect and inventory all of the nuclear weapons in the units arsenal.

One morning, the commander of all USAFE personnel, a colonel, called me at the hotel and requested a meeting at his headquarters office later that afternoon. Arriving there, and after he finished reviewing my Official Military Personnel File (OMPF) and asking how I was feeling since my heart attack, he said, "Stan, a new USAFE job has been created here in Wiesbaden, which I think you will be perfectly suited to fill the position. Officially, it's called the Director Of Nuclear Safety – Europe, and the slot calls for a Lieutenant Colonel to be in charge. Basically, you will be doing the same thing that you did for the 53rd Fighter Squadron but expanding it to include the 22nd Tactical Fighter Squadron, 23rd Tactical Fighter Squadron, and the 525th Tactical Fighter Squadron as well as all of the other USAFE units that have nuclear weapons.

"Ever since the January 1966 collision of the B-52 bomber and KC-135 tanker over Spain and the loss of four hydrogen bombs, USAFE's been under increasing congressional scrutiny relating to nuclear weapons storage, security, and deployment. The accident has been a diplomatic nightmare. Even though you can no longer fly, we need someone that's got extensive flying experience to oversee the program because of the complexity of multi-country overflights that are now being restricted by most of our NATO allies. You will have an office and staff in the headquarters building and report directly to the commander of USAFE, General Horace M. Wade. Do you want the job?"

Sitting there a moment, I finally said with confidence, "Yes, sir. I'd like to help out."

Two days later, I went to the office on the third floor and met my staff consisting of a young captain, first lieutenant, and a chief master sergeant, as well as a middle-aged German woman named Freida, who was the office secretary and typist. I called the Chief of

Staff for General Wade and set up an appointment to meet him the next morning.

The four-star general was a straightforward, no-nonsense command pilot who joined the Army Air Corp, in 1937 at Randolph field. He was pleased to know that before coming to Bitburg, I had set up the pilot instructor training program at Randolph.

After visiting for fifteen minutes, General Wade said, "Stan, there's no need for you to check-in daily with my Chief of Staff or me unless you run into a problem somewhere so, let us know if you need any help. You'll be notified when there are any staff meetings you need to attend. You'll also be required to attend some aviation conferences that pertain to nuclear weapons issues. Some of them are going to be back in the United States at various Air Force bases and at the Pentagon."

Standing up, I saluted him and left his office returning to mine. Because of the extreme secrecy involved with the 66,500 nuclear weapons stockpiles, their locations, and tactical distribution, there was no sign or any indication on my office door as to what we did.

Broken Arrow

The USAF report, classified SECRET, began with, *"The recent Broken Arrow accident over Spain serves as a grim reminder of the eternal vigilance of nuclear safety practices and preparation for any eventuality. This article provides valuable information that may be used as a guide for all echelons for their review of procedures and preparations."*

On January 17, 1966, a B-52G bomber of the United States Air Force's Strategic Air Command (SAC) collided with a KC-135 tanker during mid-air refueling at 31,000 feet over the Mediterranean Sea,

Staff for General Wade and set up an appointment to meet him the next morning.

The four-star general was a straightforward, no-nonsense command pilot who joined the Army Air Corp, in 1937 at Randolph field. He was pleased to know that before coming to Bitburg, I had set up the pilot instructor training program at Randolph.

After visiting for fifteen minutes, General Wade said, "Stan, there's no need for you to check-in daily with my Chief of Staff or me unless you run into a problem somewhere so, let us know if you need any help. You'll be notified when there are any staff meetings you need to attend. You'll also be required to attend some aviation conferences that pertain to nuclear weapons issues. Some of them are going to be back in the United States at various Air Force bases and at the Pentagon."

Standing up, I saluted him and left his office returning to mine. Because of the extreme secrecy involved with the 66,500 nuclear weapons stockpiles, their locations, and tactical distribution, there was no sign or any indication on my office door as to what we did.

Broken Arrow

The USAF report, classified SECRET, began with, *"The recent Broken Arrow accident over Spain serves as a grim reminder of the eternal vigilance of nuclear safety practices and preparation for any eventuality. This article provides valuable information that may be used as a guide for all echelons for their review of procedures and preparations."*

On January 17, 1966, a B-52G bomber of the United States Air Force's Strategic Air Command (SAC) collided with a KC-135 tanker during mid-air refueling at 31,000 feet over the Mediterranean Sea,

nel, called me at the hotel and requested a meeting at his headquarters office later that afternoon. Arriving there, and after he finished reviewing my Official Military Personnel File (OMPF) and asking how I was feeling since my heart attack, he said, "Stan, a new USAFE job has been created here in Wiesbaden, which I think you will be perfectly suited to fill the position. Officially, it's called the Director Of Nuclear Safety – Europe, and the slot calls for a Lieutenant Colonel to be in charge. Basically, you will be doing the same thing that you did for the 53rd Fighter Squadron but expanding it to include the 22nd Tactical Fighter Squadron, 23rd Tactical Fighter Squadron, and the 525th Tactical Fighter Squadron as well as all of the other USAFE units that have nuclear weapons.

"Ever since the January 1966 collision of the B-52 bomber and KC-135 tanker over Spain and the loss of four hydrogen bombs, USAFE's been under increasing congressional scrutiny relating to nuclear weapons storage, security, and deployment. The accident has been a diplomatic nightmare. Even though you can no longer fly, we need someone that's got extensive flying experience to oversee the program because of the complexity of multi-country overflights that are now being restricted by most of our NATO allies. You will have an office and staff in the headquarters building and report directly to the commander of USAFE, General Horace M. Wade. Do you want the job?"

Sitting there a moment, I finally said with confidence, "Yes, sir. I'd like to help out."

Two days later, I went to the office on the third floor and met my staff consisting of a young captain, first lieutenant, and a chief master sergeant, as well as a middle-aged German woman named Freida, who was the office secretary and typist. I called the Chief of

off the coast of Spain. The KC-135 was completely destroyed when its fuel load exploded, killing all four crew members. The B-52G broke apart, killing three of the seven crew members aboard. Immediately a USAFE worldwide "Broken Arrow" message was transmitted to all United States military commands alerting them to the accidental crash that involved nuclear warheads and the non-nuclear detonation and burning of several nuclear weapons.

Of the four Mk-28 hydrogen bombs the B-52G carried, three were found on land near the small fishing village of Palomares in the municipality of Cuevas del Almanzora, Almería, Spain. The non-nuclear explosives in two of the weapons detonated upon impact with the ground, resulting in the contamination of a three-quarter-square-mile area by highly toxic and radioactive plutonium. The fourth, which fell into the Mediterranean Sea, was finally recovered intact after an exhaustive two and one-half month-long search.[24]

Once my family and I moved into our new apartment, our lives settled into a daily routine of my driving the VW beetle to work then home and Joy taking Penny to junior high school and back home in the Porsche. At first, in the evenings, I needed to read the numerous volumes of *Procedures and Practices of USAF Nuclear Weapons*, which were classified material I kept in a locked safe installed in my apartment.

On the weekends Penny usually had a friend stay over or she stayed at their home. Joy and I frequently met friends at the Wiesbaden Officers' Club for dinner and cocktails. In the basement of the "O" club was a large Mexican restaurant which served really good food, including all of our favorite dishes. Military officers from around West Germany came to eat the Mexican food, and the club had a dozen hotel-style rooms where officers and their families could stay. Since it was the only Mexican restaurant for hundreds of miles around Wiesbaden, the place was packed every night.

Our quiet life was interrupted one evening when General Wade's Chief of Staff called me and told me I needed to attend an urgent Pentagon briefing in two days that would affect the nuclear capabilities and mission of USAFE. After packing my B-4 bag and ensuring that I was carrying a small bottle of white nitroglycerine tablets in my jacket, Joy drove me to Rhein-Main AFB near Frankfurt so that I could board a commercial flight to Washington D.C.

Late in the afternoon of April 5, 1968, after an eight and one-half hour flight, we flew into Washington National Airport, and I was stunned and appalled when I saw multiple plumes of black smoke rising in the central area of Washington, D.C., around the White House, Congress, and the Washington Monument. At 6:00 p.m. the evening before, Reverend Martin Luther King, Jr. had been shot and killed while standing on the balcony of the Lorraine Motel in Memphis, Tennessee. His assassination set off a wave of rioting, burning, and destruction by roving bands of angry black people. The national guard was mobilized, and thousands of soldiers were dispersed around the city to protect the nation's capital and its institutions.

Riding in a taxi to the Mayflower Hotel on Connecticut Ave, we were stopped at several checkpoint barriers manned by soldiers and questioned about where we were going. I was in my Air Force uniform, so we were quickly waved through, finally arriving at the hotel. I was on a trip to the Pentagon to attend a hastily arranged three-day conference of nuclear experts and scientists to discuss the best practices and procedures for storing and deploying weapons after another major accident happened three months earlier. What prompted the emergency meeting was "The Thule Incident" in Greenland.

On January 21, 1968, an aircraft accident involving a USAF B-52 bomber occurred near Thule Air Base in the Danish territory of Greenland. The aircraft was carrying four B28FI thermonuclear bombs on a Cold War "Chrome Dome" alert mission over Baffin Bay when a cabin fire forced the crew to abandon the aircraft before they could carry out an emergency landing at Thule Air Base. Six crew members ejected safely, but one who did not have an ejection seat was killed while trying to bail out. The bomber crashed onto sea ice in North Star Bay, Greenland, causing the conventional explosives aboard to detonate and the nuclear payload to rupture and disperse, which resulted in radioactive contamination around the debris field.

The United States and Denmark launched an intensive clean-up and recovery operation, but the second stage of one of the nuclear weapons (containing the nuclear critical mass) could not be accounted for after the operation was completed. USAF Strategic Air Command "Chrome Dome" operations were immediately discontinued after the accident, which highlighted the safety and political risks of the missions. Safety procedures were reviewed, and more stable explosives were developed for use in future nuclear weapons.

After lengthy meetings at the Pentagon, where the worldwide illicit dispersal of nuclear weapons was discussed, orders were issued by Secretary of Defense Melvin R. Laird, an appointee of President Richard M. Nixon, to remove them to secret consolidated sites in Europe known only to a few senior commanders and high-level government officials of the NATO countries. Most were going to be surreptitiously stored in USAFE bunkers located in West Germany.

My job when I returned to Wiesbaden was to coordinate the covert transportation of the nuclear weapons from their various European locations and bring them to the designated consolidated arsenals. The task required that I receive a Top Secret security clearance, including a Single Scope Background Investigation (SSBI) by the FBI. Additionally, I received a Sensitive Compartmented Information (SCI) designation, which added additional controls on information dissemination by me to senior commanders.

I had to let Freida go, the German civilian office secretary and typist. She was replaced by a female USAF Staff sergeant clerk-typist with a secret security clearance. Only a small number of USAFE, military officers, including General Horace M. Wade, knew what was happening. It took several months to move everything in heavily guarded unmarked trucks at night, but eventually, all the nuclear weapons were relocated. I spent many sleepless nights overseeing their movement in remote areas of North-Rhine Westphalia and Southern Bavaria. Joy was not happy with my being gone so much, especially after having a heart attack. But finally, everything was finished, and I was able to go back to a normal office routine.

Late one morning, I was summoned to General Wade's office, where he presented me with an Air Force Commendation Medal (AFCM) for my efforts to see that the movements of the nuclear weapons went off smoothly. His Chief of Staff had called Joy and asked her to attend the awards and decoration ceremony, so she was present when General Wade pinned the medal on my uniform. After the brief meeting, Joy and I went to the Officers' Club and had lunch. Other than pinning my Lieutenant Colonel's rank on my collar, this was the first time she participated in an official Air Force event. One week later, I received PCS orders transferring me to the 12th Air Force at Connally Air Force Base in Waco, Texas.

Once again, Joy packed everything in the apartment as we prepared to move back to the United States and Texas. I spent two weeks briefing my replacement on the duties of the USAFE Director of Nuclear Safety, which was my official title. Reluctantly, I sold Joy's beloved Porsche 912 and my VW bug, and the movers came and loaded our furniture and personal effects. Then from Rhein-Main airport in Frankfurt, Joy, Penny, and I returned to the United States on an American Airlines Boeing 707, arriving nine hours later at New York's LaGuardia Airport. From there, we flew to Dallas, Texas, where we stayed a few days at Joy's aunts' (Louise and Hazel) apartment while I arranged the purchase of a 1970 burgundy-colored, two-door hardtop Pontiac Grand Prix.

CHAPTER 20

WACO, TEXAS

After visiting for several days with Joy's aunts, we loaded our new car and drove to Waco, and James Connally Air Force Base, where I became the Director of Safety for the Twelfth Air Force. Its mission was to provide training for tactical aircrews to bring them up to a state of combat readiness capable of conducting joint air operations in South Vietnam. It was also the primary source for tactical fighter, reconnaissance, and airlift forces deployed to the Southeast Asia war zone.

We moved into a house on base, and Penny started school at Connally High School. Rather than sitting at home each day, Joy wanted to return to teaching, so she applied for a 5th grade teaching position at nearby Connally Elementary and was immediately hired because a teacher had recently left.

Over a long weekend, we drove to the ranch in Sterling City to see Sallie, Mac, and their kids. After visiting in their kitchen for a while, Joy asked, "Where is our little dog, Pug?"

Sallie said, "Joy, I hate to tell you this, but she disappeared the day after you left her with us and hasn't been seen since. In the last three years, Mac and I have periodically driven all the pastures and have not found her. I'm really sorry. We are so far out in the country that she could only have been carried off by coyotes because our nearest neighbor is twenty miles away."

Joy Corvin and Lt. Col. Stan Corvin, Sr.

Early the next morning, I went with Mac on his morning rounds, checking livestock. At mid-morning, we drove to the feed store in town, and he got twenty bags of Purina™ cattle feed cubes. We went by the truck stop near the edge of town, sat down on the round stools at the counter, and ordered hot coffee and pie from the waitress.

The owner, Earl Brandt, came over to us and said, "Mac, didn't you and Sallie used to have a little black Pekingese dog?"

"We did, Earl, but she disappeared three years ago, and we haven't seen her since. Why do you ask?"

He said, "Well, this morning, a trucker stopped in to refuel and said he found a little black dog at a rest area near Garden City, and he dropped her off here. She might be your missing dog."

We all walked back to Earl's office, and sleeping on a towel was Pug. When she awoke and saw me, she excitedly ran over and was jumping on my pants leg. I picked her up, and she snuggled against my face and licked me.

Earl laughed and said, "Yep, she's your dog for sure. Will you look at that?"

After leaving the truck stop, we drove to the ranch house, and I carried Pug inside. When Joy saw her, she ran over, scooped the dog from my arms, and hugged her tightly. Over the next thirty minutes, we talked about how Pug could have walked over twenty miles to the nearest paved road without being killed and eaten by the numerous coyotes, bobcats, and cougars living in the ravines and dense mesquite covered pastures. She obviously had been well cared for by the good condition of her shiny, clean black fur covering her body. But who could have looked after the little Pekingese for three years? In the end, we never found out, and Pug lived with Joy and me for seven more years before her eyesight was gone, and she was accidentally run over by a car on the street in front of our home.

Pug and Her Litter of Puppies

After we had been at Connally AFB for about a year, The Twelfth Air Force moved to Bergstrom AFB, Texas, during the Vietnam War. As part of the permanent party closing the base, I stayed in Waco at the downtown headquarters complex located near 25th Street and Windsor Ave. The move was the result of a Base Realignment and Closure (BRAC), a process to increase the United States Department of Defense efficiency by planning the end of the Cold War closure of military installations. I worked with local economic development staff to begin the transfer of James Connally Air Force Base to the city of Waco and the newly formed Texas State Technical Institute who was already located on the base.

One person who was assisting with the transfer of the base housing to civilian owners was Mrs. Dolly Kelly, a well known Waco realtor. She had worked for four years with Mr. Truett Smith, the mayor of Waco, and then was a partner in their Sanger Suburban Realtors company. Dolly helped us find our new home on Lakeshore Drive a block away from Lake Waco, and we became close friends, frequently socializing at our home or hers.

After Penny graduated from Connally High School, she moved to Dallas and, for a while, lived with Aunt Louise and Aunt Hazel while she attended nursing school at El Centro College in Dallas. In her sophomore year, she moved into an apartment with two other nursing students. After we moved into our new home, Joy was hired as a fifth-grade elementary school teacher at Mountainview Elementary, only a few blocks away.

School Photo of Joy Corvin, 1971

Stan Jr. was in the United States Army serving in Vietnam as a helicopter pilot with the rank of warrant officer. After an eighteen-month tour of duty in the war-torn country, he was assigned to a helicopter unit in Schweinfurt, West Germany, and was promoted to first lieutenant. One year later, he was promoted to captain. Then the following year, he volunteered to go back to South Vietnam to fly helicopters on Top-Secret covert missions for the Central Intelligence Agency (CIA).

I was nearing the end of my career with thirty-two years of active-duty service and had been promoted to colonel when Stan Jr. called me from Love Field in Dallas and asked me to come pick him up. He was on his way to his new assignment but had a few days to spend with Joy and me before he left for Fort Rucker, Alabama, for additional training in twin-engine helicopters. After the training he was going to Danang, South Vietnam, to fly for the CIA. When he told me that I was stunned.

"Your mother isn't going to like that at all, so I don't think you need to tell her what you'll be doing. Make something up. Okay?"

"Alright, Dad, I will."

I picked him up at the airport and was surprised at how big he was, at six feet tall and two hundred pounds. Apparently, the German beer and bratwurst had added a few pounds to his weight. We drove back to Waco to our new home and arrived at about the same time that Joy did after teaching school that day. She was thrilled to see our son but was confused about why he had just suddenly shown up. When he told her that he was going to return to Vietnam flying helicopters, she lost all color in her face, and her lips began to tremble. He quickly explained to her that he was going to have a very safe job flying VIPs around the northern part of the country and wasn't going to be exposed to any hostile fire.

With tears welling up in her eyes, she angrily said, "Stan Jr. I don't believe you!" And then she got up, went back to our bedroom and slammed the door. Later that evening, she came out of the room and chatted with him but was somber and clearly upset.

The next morning I stayed home from work, and he and I went to a local car dealership where he bought a two-year-old yellow and white Chevy Cheyenne 10 pickup. With a 454 cubic inch engine, it was a very fast truck which he, unfortunately, discovered three days later when he received a speeding ticket in Mississippi going one hundred ten miles per hour on Interstate 10 near Gulfport. After completing his multi-engine helicopter training, he left his pickup with me when he went to South Vietnam.

Over the next eighteen months, we occasionally received letters from Stan Jr., who was stationed in Danang, South Vietnam, flying helicopters for the CIA. Many times, late at night, I heard Joy quietly sobbing next to me in the bed and held her until she went to sleep. She faithfully wrote him letters every week and once a month sent him a tightly packed care package that usually contained homemade cookies, a variety of canned goodies, and assorted things she thought he might like. Then the letters stopped coming, and her anxiety level increased dramatically.

One day seventeen months after Stan Jr. deployed, Joy, asked, "Stan, do you think he's okay? Won't they let us know if he's hurt or God forbid that he's been killed?"

Holding her, I said, "Yes, they will let us know but probably only if he's been killed. Before leaving, Stan Jr. told me that he intended to sign a waiver of his family being notified if he was wounded and only if he has been killed. So, what we don't want to see is a U.S. Army sedan drive up to our house, and two officers walk to our door."

With tears welling up in her eyes, she angrily said, "Stan Jr. I don't believe you!" And then she got up, went back to our bedroom and slammed the door. Later that evening, she came out of the room and chatted with him but was somber and clearly upset.

The next morning I stayed home from work, and he and I went to a local car dealership where he bought a two-year-old yellow and white Chevy Cheyenne 10 pickup. With a 454 cubic inch engine, it was a very fast truck which he, unfortunately, discovered three days later when he received a speeding ticket in Mississippi going one hundred ten miles per hour on Interstate 10 near Gulfport. After completing his multi-engine helicopter training, he left his pickup with me when he went to South Vietnam.

Over the next eighteen months, we occasionally received letters from Stan Jr., who was stationed in Danang, South Vietnam, flying helicopters for the CIA. Many times, late at night, I heard Joy quietly sobbing next to me in the bed and held her until she went to sleep. She faithfully wrote him letters every week and once a month sent him a tightly packed care package that usually contained homemade cookies, a variety of canned goodies, and assorted things she thought he might like. Then the letters stopped coming, and her anxiety level increased dramatically.

One day seventeen months after Stan Jr. deployed, Joy, asked, "Stan, do you think he's okay? Won't they let us know if he's hurt or God forbid that he's been killed?"

Holding her, I said, "Yes, they will let us know but probably only if he's been killed. Before leaving, Stan Jr. told me that he intended to sign a waiver of his family being notified if he was wounded and only if he has been killed. So, what we don't want to see is a U.S. Army sedan drive up to our house, and two officers walk to our door."

Stan Jr. was in the United States Army serving in Vietnam as a helicopter pilot with the rank of warrant officer. After an eighteen-month tour of duty in the war-torn country, he was assigned to a helicopter unit in Schweinfurt, West Germany, and was promoted to first lieutenant. One year later, he was promoted to captain. Then the following year, he volunteered to go back to South Vietnam to fly helicopters on Top-Secret covert missions for the Central Intelligence Agency (CIA).

I was nearing the end of my career with thirty-two years of active-duty service and had been promoted to colonel when Stan Jr. called me from Love Field in Dallas and asked me to come pick him up. He was on his way to his new assignment but had a few days to spend with Joy and me before he left for Fort Rucker, Alabama, for additional training in twin-engine helicopters. After the training he was going to Danang, South Vietnam, to fly for the CIA. When he told me that I was stunned.

"Your mother isn't going to like that at all, so I don't think you need to tell her what you'll be doing. Make something up. Okay?"

"Alright, Dad, I will."

I picked him up at the airport and was surprised at how big he was, at six feet tall and two hundred pounds. Apparently, the German beer and bratwurst had added a few pounds to his weight. We drove back to Waco to our new home and arrived at about the same time that Joy did after teaching school that day. She was thrilled to see our son but was confused about why he had just suddenly shown up. When he told her that he was going to return to Vietnam flying helicopters, she lost all color in her face, and her lips began to tremble. He quickly explained to her that he was going to have a very safe job flying VIPs around the northern part of the country and wasn't going to be exposed to any hostile fire.

Looking horrified, Joy began to cry and ran to the bedroom.

A few weeks later, we were watching Johnny Carson's "The Tonight Show" when the telephone rang. Joy answered it, and I heard her say, "Stan Jr., are you okay?" There was a pause, and she handed the phone to me, unable to talk.

"Are you okay, son?" I asked.

"Yes, I am, Dad, but I'm in a hospital in Camp Zama, Japan, after being slightly wounded trying to save an American fighter pilot who had been shot down at Khe Sahn. But the good news is I'll heal okay and come home in a few months."

Breathing a sigh of relief, I replied, "Son, when you get home, we'll go fishing at Lake Waco, and drink some beer." I hung up the telephone and went over to Joy, but she shook me off and was inconsolable. "Look, honey, he's safe in Japan in a hospital and out of the war zone. He'll come home soon, and you won't have to worry anymore."

Sniffling, she said, "I guess you're right. We are lucky that he's alive, but he's not going to receive the letters you and Penny and I just mailed him."

"Don't worry. They'll be forwarded to him in Japan or sent back to us here in Texas," I said. (See Appendix A.)

Over the next several months we visited with Stan Jr. on the telephone. Then one evening, he called and said, "I'm being discharged from the hospital tomorrow and will arrive in Dallas in a couple of days on a TWA 747 flight coming in from Los Angeles LAX airport. Can someone pick me up at Love Field?"

"Of course, son, we'll be there." Two days later, after some confusion about when he would arrive, Penny picked him up and drove him to our home in Waco.

We heard her Pontiac GTO pull into the driveway at the back of the house, and Joy and I ran out to greet them. Stan Jr. got out of the car wearing a loosely fitting khaki uniform and a big white gauze eye patch on his right eye. He had a crutch tucked under each arm and was walking very slowly. I was astonished when I saw him. He had lost fifty pounds and could barely move and was limping badly. Joy and I gently hugged him and helped get him inside our home and to the den where he stretched out on the sofa.

Sipping a Budweiser™ beer, he quietly said, "I'm going to be okay, but it's going to take some time for the wounds to heal. I was shot by an AK-47 twice in the upper chest, twice in the stomach and once in the right cheek of my butt. Shrapnel hit my right eye, and I had surgery on it to remove the pieces. But the ophthalmologists say it is going to be okay. Can I stay here until I'm healed?" he asked.

"Of course!" his mother and I said in unison. "We'll set you up in the guest bedroom." Joy said. Stan Jr. looked worn-out and exhausted, as we helped him back to the bedroom, where he collapsed on the king size mattress.

Since Penny had recently graduated from nursing school, as a registered nurse, while gently picking up his wrist she asked, "Why is your right hand so swollen and your knuckles badly scraped?"

He said, "I hit a hippie at the Los Angles LAX airport this morning when he spit in my face and bandaged right eye; however, I don't think my fingers are broken." But he could barely wiggle them.

Penny said, "I've got a medical kit in my car, so let me clean and wrap them. Also, let me take a look at your other wounds and see if I need to change the bandages." Then she went to her car; returned to the bedroom with a large black bag and motioned us out, and closed the door.

Thirty minutes later, she came out and said that her brother was sleeping. Sitting down, she shakily said, "He shouldn't be alive! I've never seen anything like it. He lost half of his blood supply lying in a dirty, muddy rice paddy fighting off the enemy for thirteen hours. It's a miracle he survived!" Then she began to cry, and I went over and put my arm around her shoulder to comfort her.

Over the next few weeks, we learned that he was shot down twice in ten minutes, first in his helicopter and then in a rescue one trying to save an American fighter pilot who had bailed out of his F-4 Phantom jet and landed in the middle of 12,500 North Vietnam Army soldiers. The NVA had taken over the former Marine and Special Forces base at Khe Sahn in the Ashau Valley in the northwest corner of the country. All he would say is that had it not been for three U.S. Air Force A1-E "Spads" providing close air support for thirteen hours, he wouldn't be alive now.

Eventually, he recovered and was assigned to HHC, 3rd Brigade, 2nd Armored Division at Fort Hood as a legal officer in charge of court-martials of soldiers who committed serious crimes. With the Vietnam War winding down and him having over 7,400 hours flying time, he wasn't going to be piloting helicopters for many years. As an infantry branch captain, he was likely to be given a company to command sometime in the future. Renting an apartment near Lake Waco, he drove to his office on Fort Hood each workday.

Colonel Ed Skelton

One Friday evening, I received a telephone call from my close friend Colonel Ed Skelton informing me that he had just returned from

South Vietnam and was being assigned to Randolph AFB. He asked me to meet him at the Officers' Club stag bar the next afternoon. I said I would like that and then called Stan Jr. and asked him if he wanted to ride down there with me, and he said yes.

Although Ed and I talked occasionally, we had not seen each other for four years. I remembered the time he and three pilots delivered four new reconnaissance RF-4E Phantoms to the German Air Force in 1969 at Bitburg Air Force Base. A hastily planned airshow was announced, and several thousand German civilians, dignitaries, and Luftwaffe generals were invited to the airfield.

Before Ed's flight landed, he called the tower and asked permission for one aircraft to make a low-level pass over the 10,026-foot runway on a heading of 240°. The tower gave him permission, and a public address announcer told the assembled audience in German and English to watch for a jet to fly down the runway. I had brought Joy, and she joined me as we sat in VIP bleachers. Then, we began to hear an approaching jet coming from the east. Suddenly, it appeared very low over the asphalt runway, inverted, and with its landing gear extended upward. Barely flying above the jet aircraft's stall speed, Ed flew the length of the runway with his verticle stabilizer only a few feet above the ground. At the end of the runway, he swiftly accelerated, rotated 180° upright, raised his landing gear, and with his afterburners roaring, disappeared into the clouds. The crowd, especially the Germans, went wild, cheering, whistling and applauding.

A few minutes later, we heard the sound of several jets entering the traffic pattern. They landed in a two-by-two right echelon formation and taxied to the parking area near the VIP bleachers; then shut down their engines. Raising their canopies at the same time, a short fat pilot wearing Rayban sunglasses climbed down from the front seat of the lead jet, removed his helmet, lit a cigar, and waved at the crowd. It was Colonel Eddie L. Skelton, who had provided the thrilling display of aerobatic skill. For a moment, the crowd was silent, expecting to see a tall, lean, handsome American fighter pilot. Then the Americans began to applaud loudly, and the Germans did too as they whistled and cheered. The memory caused me to chuckle, and I looked forward to seeing my life-long friend the next day.

Saturday afternoon, September 9, 1972, Stan Jr. and I drove to Randolph Air Force Base and went to the Officers' Club stag bar. We walked into the entrance and waited for our eyes to adjust to the dimly lit room.

"Stan, come over here and join us," Ed yelled, waving his hand.

We walked to his table and were greeted by him and four other pilots sitting there. Everyone stood up, shaking hands with us. Ed looked at Stan Jr. and said, "You were a skinny little kid with big ears the last time I saw you."

My son laughed and said, "I'm all grown-up now, sir, and my ears have shrunk." Then he looked at Ed curiously as if trying to remember something.

We sat down, and I ordered a round of beers for everybody at the table. After the waitress delivered the ice-cold mugs, Ed turned to Stan Jr. and said, "Your dad tells me that you are an Army captain now and a helicopter pilot."

"Yes, sir. I am, or at least was, because I'm now stationed at Fort Hood as a brigade legal officer. I returned from Vietnam this past July, where I flew Hueys out of Danang in I Corp."

Ed laughed, saying, "You Army helicopter pilots were crazy as hell over there! I know because my guys and I spent all one day keeping the NVA off eight of you that had been shot down in two helicopters in the Ashau Valley near Khe Sahn during the Easter Invasion!"

Stan Jr.'s eyes widened, and after slowly sipping his beer, he asked, "Were you Sandy 6, flying an A-1E Spad on April 29th?"

Ed looked at him in surprise, saying, "Yes, but how in the world could you possibly know that?"

Stan Jr. hoarsely said, "Colonel Skelton, I was Coachman 22!" No one said a word for a few seconds.

"You mean I was talking to you on the ground?" Ed asked incredulously.

"Yes, sir! We talked all day on the guard frequency of my survival radio, as you and your guys kept the NVA from capturing and killing my crew and me, along with my commanding officer and his three crew members."

Ed sat there in stunned silence and then said, "Well, I'll be damned!" Then he rose and went over to my son, and they hugged.

Stan Jr. whispered, "Thank you, sir. I wanted to say that to you when I was finally rescued, but I left the radio in the rice paddy after we got picked up."

Ed leaned back, still holding my son's arms, looked at him, and with tears in his eyes said, "Son, you are very welcome, and I'm glad my guys and I were able to help you and the others." Returning to their chairs, they began to tell the story, and most of the other pilots in the bar pulled up chairs around the table to hear the amazing story. Soon, there wasn't a dry eye in the room.

A1-E Spads in South Vietnam

A1-E Spads over South China Sea

Front row: Col. Ed Skelton third from left with his Spad pilots

Sitting there with my son and my best friend, I was overwhelmed by emotion at the events they described and got choked up as the story unfolded, thinking back to the time Ed saved my life on Iwo Jima as he and I fought off the Japanese banzai soldiers so many years ago.

Later, food was served, and we partied into the night. Stan Jr. and I ended up staying at the BOQ, where we got a room together and finally went to bed. I had called Joy in the afternoon and told her we would return home the next day. She was astonished when I summarized their story.

Then laughing, through her tears, she said emphatically, "That twerp. I knew he wasn't flying VIPs!" We were both amazed at the coincidence that my life-long best friend had saved our son's life in South Vietnam on April 29, 1972.

We drove home on Sunday, and both returned to work Monday

morning. Over the next two years, eventually, I completely closed down James Connally Air Force Base and Twelfth Air Force Headquarters in downtown Waco. Joy, who had always been the love of my life, continued to teach fifth-grade elementary school. Finally, in 1974, I retired with thirty-three years of active duty service in the Royal Canadian Air Force, the Royal Air Force, the United States Army Air Force, and the United States Air Force.

Oh, what an adventure it had been as,
"Off I went into the wild blue yonder!"

THE END

EPILOGUE

THE EAGLE I KNEW

The eagle has landed and flies no more.
He's buried at Moriah and does not soar.
But oh my God the life he lived,
A fighter pilot, loving husband, good father to his kids.
He traveled the world seeking what's right,
Never backing down, or running, from a deadly dogfight.
He flew in two wars, and had no fear,
Although many times, Death's Door was so near.
He's gone now, and I miss him,
But you can be absolutely assured.
We'll soon meet in heaven,
Where his bi-plane is moored.
We'll fly through the Pearly Gates,
As many have already done.
And at day's end, head west,
Towards the orange setting sun.

Stan Corvin, Jr.

EPILOGUE

THE EAGLE I KNEW

The eagle has landed and flies no more.
He's buried at Moriah and does not soar.
But oh my God the life he lived,
A fighter pilot, loving husband, good father to his kids.
He traveled the world seeking what's right,
Never backing down, or running, from a deadly dogfight.
He flew in two wars, and had no fear,
Although many times, Death's Door was so near.
He's gone now, and I miss him,
But you can be absolutely assured.
We'll soon meet in heaven,
Where his bi-plane is moored.
We'll fly through the Pearly Gates,
As many have already done.
And at day's end, head west,
Towards the orange setting sun.

Stan Corvin, Jr.

ABOUT THE AUTHOR

STAN CORVIN, JR.

Born in 1945 in a small town in West Texas, Stan grew up in a military family. His father, a career United States Air Force fighter pilot from 1941 to 1974, retired as a colonel, and his mother was an elementary school teacher who frequently taught at many of the bases where they were stationed.

After attending Texas Tech University for his undergraduate studies, Stan was drafted into the U.S. Army. In basic training, he was accepted into the Army's helicopter flight school and graduated nine months later in December 1967. Serving in the U.S. Army from 1967 to 1974, he flew helicopters in Vietnam in 1968-69 as a "Loach" pilot for a "Hunter Killer" team and then as a covert operations pilot for the CIA in 1971-72 attaining the rank of captain. Stan resigned his commission in 1974 to pursue a career in banking.

In 2014, after forty years in banking and commercial lending, Stan retired, and in 2015 wrote, and published the first edition of **Vietnam Saga: Exploits of a Combat Helicopter Pilot,** a vivid personal memoir about his three years of flying during the Vietnam War including his story of being shot down twice in ten minutes at Khe Sanh trying to save an American USAF F-4 fighter pilot who had bailed out and was surrounded by 12,500 NVA soldiers. Stan survived for thirteen hours laying in a muddy rice paddy after being shot four times in the chest and stomach by an enemy AK-47!

In 2015, Stan was asked by a close friend, Major General Carl G. Schneider, to write his memoirs about flying jets in Korea and Vietnam and how he rose through the ranks from an enlisted private to a two-star general in thirty years; a feat only a few men in the history of the United States military have ever accomplished. Thus ***Jet Pioneer: A Fighter Pilot's Memoir*** was written and published.

Then in 2017, Stan wrote and published the second edition of ***Vietnam Saga: Exploits of a Combat Helicopter Pilot,*** which included expanded text and photographs.

In February 2018, Stan published **Echoes of the Hunt,** which was the first place winner of the 2019 Texas Authors Association's Book Contest for hunting adventures. Taking place in West Texas, it is a true story of Stan's ten-day stalking of a trophy mule deer. While sitting alone beside a warm fireplace and in a cold deer stand, he also recalls childhood stories of hunting adventures with his father, grandfather, and uncles.

In September 2018, Stan co-authored and published **Vietnam Abyss: A Journal of Unmerited Grace.** It is the inspiring true story of Michael J. Snook a Vietnam Veteran who descends into the darkness of chronic Post Traumatic Stress Disorder (PTSD), alcoholism, insanity and multiple confinements in a Veterans Administration psychiatric ward then later through his participation in PTSD counseling sessions and the program of Alcoholics Anonymous recovers and becomes a born-again Christian and an ordained minister.

In February 2020, Stan co-authored and published ***Attacked at Home: A Green Beret's Survival Story of the Fort Hood Shooting.*** The story is about Second Lieutenant John M. Arroyo, Jr. who on April 2, 2014, while walking to his headquarters building on Fort Hood, Texas, was shot in the throat and neck by another soldier who then went on to kill four soldiers, including himself, and wound sixteen others. It's also is about Arroyo's life beginning with his childhood in Southern California including his time spent as a tattooed member of a violent street gang, a hopeless teenage drug addict and then his enlistment in the U.S. Army where he ultimately becomes a Special Forces Green Beret and highly decorated officer after serving two tours of duty in Afghanistan and one in Iraq. The book also tells how Arroyo used his Christian faith to protect himself and his fellow Special Forces "Operators" while deployed to the Middle-East and then relied on it to recover from the massive wounds he sustained after being shot on Fort Hood, Texas.

In February 2020, Stan co-authored and published ***Attacked at Home: A Green Beret's Survival Story of the Fort Hood Shooting.*** The story is about Second Lieutenant John M. Arroyo, Jr. who on April 2, 2014, while walking to his headquarters building on Fort Hood, Texas, was shot in the throat and neck by another soldier who then went on to kill four soldiers, including himself, and wound sixteen others. It's also is about Arroyo's life beginning with his childhood in Southern California including his time spent as a tattooed member of a violent street gang, a hopeless teenage drug addict and then his enlistment in the U.S. Army where he ultimately becomes a Special Forces Green Beret and highly decorated officer after serving two tours of duty in Afghanistan and one in Iraq. The book also tells how Arroyo used his Christian faith to protect himself and his fellow Special Forces "Operators" while deployed to the Middle-East and then relied on it to recover from the massive wounds he sustained after being shot on Fort Hood, Texas.

In September 2018, Stan co-authored and published **Vietnam Abyss: A Journal of Unmerited Grace**. It is the inspiring true story of Michael J. Snook a Vietnam Veteran who descends into the darkness of chronic Post Traumatic Stress Disorder (PTSD), alcoholism, insanity and multiple confinements in a Veterans Administration psychiatric ward then later through his participation in PTSD counseling sessions and the program of Alcoholics Anonymous recovers and becomes a born-again Christian and an ordained minister.

All of the books are available through Amazon Books, Kindle, Barnes & Noble, and audiobooks on Audible.com and iTunes.

Stan lives with his wife near Nashville, Tennessee, and they have seven adult children and sixteen grandkids.

APPENDIX A

23 April 72

Dear Stan Jr.
 We received your letter a couple of days ago and were happy to hear from you. We would have answered sooner except I have been in Dallas the past week with the people from Fleetwood Enterprises on a Southwest Mobile Home Show. Your letter sounds as if you are in the middle of things over there. There has been a lot in the newspapers and TV about the invasion. One news broadcast on TV showed Da Nang A.B. after some rockets had destroyed about 22 chopers. We are real worried about you especially your Mother and Penny. I told them not to worry

(OVER)

for we are tough people and everything always works out for us. I also said that had I been in your position I would have volunteered also. You will probably end up with the Medal of Honor. Just be as careful as you can under the circumstances. I'm very proud of you and want you to get home, so that we can fish and hunt together. We haven't heard from anyone for sometime. We wonder if you ever hear from them and how everything is proceeding. If there is anything you need or want us to do let us know.

If the S. Viets (?) can hold out for a while this may be the end of it since it appears they have committed most of their strength this time. I would like to send some of the dove politicians over there for a while. I'm going to vote for George Wallace this time since I get so mad at the others. I'll close for now and let your Mother and Penny add a note. Write and tell me about your mission and if you have any pictures of yourself send me one. Take good care of yourself your the only son that I have.

Love Dad

Dearest Stan Jr,

I was grading papers when Stan and Penny started this so will add my few lines.

Now that Penny is better, we are all well and wish you were here to drink a beer with us. The yard is so pretty now - the cannas around the patio grow about 6 inches a day and are getting blooms on them. We cooked hamburgers down there last night.

I only have six weeks (30 days) left to teach and I am really ready for it to be over. These children now are something else. I get tickled and mad at them at the same time.

Dearest Stan Jr,

    I was grading papers when Stan and Penny started this so will add my few lines.

    Now that Penny is better, we are all well and wish you were here to drink a beer with us. The yard is so pretty now - the cannas around the patio grow about 6 inches a day and are getting blooms on them. We cooked hamburgers down there last night.

    I only have six weeks (30 days) left to teach and I am really ready for it to be over. These children now are something else. I get tickled and mad at them at the same time.

If the S. Viets (?) can hold out for a while this may be the end of it since it appears they have committed most of their strength this time. I would like to send some of the dove politicians over there for a while. I'm going to vote for George Wallace this time since I get so mad at the others. I'll close for now and let your Mother and Penny add a note. Write and tell me about your mission and if you have any pictures of yourself send me one. Take good care of yourself your the only son that I have.

Love Dad

We are going to take Penny back to Dallas this afternoon. Stan brought her home with him Friday.

Honey, we watch the news and read the papers but probably still don't know exactly how it is over there. I just know that I get terribly upset and just hope and pray you will be careful.

I need to get dressed now. Please write as often as you can and take care of yourself.

All my love,
Mother

The Eagle Above

Hello Stan Jr —

I had planned to write you a letter tonight but I'll add a note anyway — I was off work all last week with the flu, but believe it or not, by Friday night about party time I was completely recovered — I came to Mother & Daddy's to recoup. but I got well before — (Did I just repeat myself — must be my age) Since I've been down here I've been reading your book "The Green Berets". It is really interesting & would appear that there is a problem in Vietnam — I'm sure my big brother will take care of it —

Since we have gotten Butch

– 2 –

home to Dallas we've found out he is fine – He forgot some of his manners while in Waco & has also developed a taste for books – Only a dog would eat my Bible, also all my sweet poems inside it – You really have to pay a high price for protection & I'm not too sure how much protection he is – I'll close now & write tomorrow – Take care & hurry home –

                Love forever,
                Penny

APPENDIX B

USAF AIR UNIVERSITY ONLINE REFERENCES

https://www.armscontrol.org/
http://www.afhra.af.mil/Information/Studies/
https://www.base-search.net/about/en/
https://fas.org/
http://www.jstor.org/
https://www.loc.gov/
http://www.au.af.mil/au/aul/lane.htm
https://www.archives.gov/
http://nsarchive.gwu.edu/
http://www.nti.org/
http://taylorandfrancis.com/

APPENDIX B

USAF AIR UNIVERSITY ONLINE REFERENCES

https://www.armscontrol.org/
http://www.afhra.af.mil/Information/Studies/
https://www.base-search.net/about/en/
https://fas.org/
http://www.jstor.org/
https://www.loc.gov/
http://www.au.af.mil/au/aul/lane.htm
https://www.archives.gov/
http://nsarchive.gwu.edu/
http://www.nti.org/
http://taylorandfrancis.com/

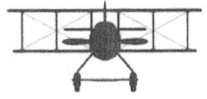

BIBLIOGRAPHY

Mark, Eduard Maximilian. *Aerial Interdiction: Air Power And The Land Battle.* Includes bibliographical references (p. ISBN 0-912799-74-9 (case).-ISBN 0-912799-73-0 (paper) 1. United States-History, Military-20th century. 2. World War, 1939-1945-Aerial operations, American. 3. Korean War, 1950-1953-Aerial operations, American. 4. Vietnamese War, 1961-1975-Aerial operations, American. 5. United States. Air Force-History-20th century. I. Title. 11. Series: Special studies (United States. Air Force. Office of Air Force History) E745.M36 1992 American wars: a historical analysis / Eduard Mark. (Special studies) and index.

Craven, Wesley Frank, and James Lea Cate, Eds. *The Army Air Forces in World War II* (7 vols.). Chicago: University of Chicago Press, 1948–1958; new imprint, Washington, D.C.: Office of Air Force History, 1983. Davis, Richard G. Carl A. Spaatz and the Air War in Europe.

Mortensen, Daniel R. A Pattern for Joint Operations: *World War II Close Air Support, North Africa.* Washington, D.C.: Office of Air Force History and U.S. Army Center of Military History, 1987. Murray, Williamson. Strategy for Defeat: The Luftwaffe, 1933.

Davis, Richard G. *Carl A. Spaatz And The Air War In Europe.* Richard G. Davis. p. cm–(General Histories) An expansion of the author's thesis. Includes bibliographical references and index. ISBN 0-912799-75-7 –ISBN 0-912799-77-3 1. Spaatz, Carl, 1891-1974. 2. Generals–United States–Biography. 3. United States. Air Force–Biography. 4. Aeronautics, Military–United States - History. 5. World War, 1939-1945–Aerial operations, American 6. World War, 1939-1945–Campaigns—Western Front.

Knaack, Marcelle S. *Encyclopedia of U.S. Air Force Aircraft And Missile Systems*. Bibliography: p. Includes index. Contents: v. 1. Post-World War II Fighters, 1945-1973. 1. Fighter planes. 2. United States. Air Force. I. United States. Office of Air Force History.

First In The Air - The Eagle Squadrons Of World WarII, Kenneth C. Kan, Air Force History and Museums Program Washington, D.C. 2007.

Foreman, John. *The Fighter Command War Diaries: The Operational History of Fighter Command, Second Tactical Air Force. 100 Group and Air Defence of Great Britain, 1939-45*. Vol. 2: September 1940 to December 1941 and Vol 3: January 1942 to June 1943. Walton-on-Thames, England: Air Research Publications, 1998 and 2001.

Greenhouse, Brereton; Stephen J. Harris, William C. Johnston, and William G.P. Rawling. *The Crucible of War 1939-1945. The Official History of the Royal Canadian Air Force, Vol. 3*: Toronto, Canada: University of Toronto Press in cooperation with the Department of National Defense and the Canadian Government Publishing Centre, Supply and Services Canada, 1994.

Schlight, John. *Help From Above: Air Force Close Air Support Of The Army 1946-1973*. John Schlight. p. cm. Includes bibliographical references and index. 1. Close air support–History–20th century. 2. United States. Air Force–History–20th century. 3. United States. Army–Aviation–History–20th century.

Stratemeyer, George E., *1890-1970 The Three Wars Of Lt. Gen. George E. Stratemeyer: His Korean War Diary.* edited by William T. Y'Blood. p. cm. includes bibliographic references and index. 1. Korean War, 1950-1953—Aerial Operations, American. 2. Korean War, 1950-1953—Personal Narratives, American. 3. Stratemeyer, George E., 1890-1970—Diaries. 4. Generals — United States—Diaries. I. Title: 3 Wars of Lieutenant General George E. Stratemeyer. II. Y'Blood, William T.

Cameron, Rebecca Hancock. *Training To Fly: Military Flight Training, 1907-1945*. Rebecca Hancock p. cm. Cameron. Includes bibliographical references and index. 1. Air pilots, Military - Training of - United States -History. 2. Flight crews -Training of - United States - History. ing - United States - History.

Sturm. Thomas A. *The USAF Scientific Advisory Board (Special Studies / Office Of Air Force History)* Reprint. Originally published: Washington, D.C.: USAF Historical Division Liaison Office, 1967. Includes bibliographical references. I. United States. USAF Scientific Advisory Board– History. 1. Title. 11. Series: Special Studies (United States. Air Force. Office of Air Force History).

Library of Congress Cataloging-in-Publication Data Meilinger, Phillip S., 1948- *Hoyt S. Vandenberg, The Life Of A General.* Bibliography: p. Includes index. I. Vandenberg, Hoyt Sanford,

1899-1954. 2. Generals -United States–Biography. 3. United States. Air Force-Biography. 4. United States-History, Military– 20th Century.

Gorn, Michael H. *Harnessing The Genie. (Air Staff Historical Study)* Bibliography: p. Includes index. 1. Aeronautics, Military– Research–United States– History. 2. Aeronautics, Military– United States–Forecasting–History. 3. United States. Air Forces– History.

Library of Congress Cataloging in Publication Data Main entry under title: *The Army Air Forces In World War II*. Vol. 1 originally prepared by the Office of Air Force History; v. 2, by the Air Historical Group; and v. 3-7, by the USAF Historical Division.

NOTES

1. Wikipedia – John Brown (Abolutionist) Description of Harpers Ferry Raid. Capture and hanging.
2. USAF Military Facts – E6B, Whiz wheel history and use.
3. Queen Mary.com/history/timeline/The War Years – The Grey Ghost.
4. Military Wiki.org/Miles_Master – Specs and Performance.
5. Aoghs.org/petroleum-in-war/roughnecks-of-sherwood-forest
6. Churchill-society-london.org.uk/thefewspeech.
7. www.bbc.co.uk/bitesize/guides/zpykxsg/revision/weather.
8. Dehavilland museum.co.uk/about-us/de-havilland-history/constant-speed-props.
9. Bendix_King.com/en/pages/bendix TR5043 radio.
10. WWII_2db.com/weapon_ Mauser Flakvierling_Antiaircraft_gun.
11. Encyclopedia.ushmm/content/en/article/operation-torch-algeria-morocco-campaign
12. Wikipedia.org/wiki/Japanese General Tadamichi_Kuribayashi_Leader of Wolves.
13. Cantwell, Gerald T., d. 1994. Gerald T. Cantwell. "Citizen Airmen : a History of the Air Force Reserve, 1946-1994" – Includes bibliographical references and index. 1. The United States. Air Force Reserve-History
14. www.airplanesofthepast.com/f86-sabre/specs.htm
15. www.nationalmuseum.af.mil/Visit/Museum-Exhibits/Fact-Sheets/Display/Article/196090/korean-war-introduction.
16. www.museumofflight.org/aircraft/antonov-2-colt
17. www.infoplease.com/fighter-planes-mig-15
18. En.wikipedia.org/wiki/Ministry_of_Aviation_Industry_(Soviet_Union)
19. www.koreanwar.org/html/units/usaf/4fiw.htm
20. Citation: National Museum of the United States Air Force – Japanese Kawanishi N1K2-Ja Shiden Kai airplane. April 17, 2015
21. www.nytimes.com/1989/08/17/obituaries/general-minoru-genda-84-dies-planned-attack-on-pearl-harbor.html
22. History of the USAF Experimental Flight Test Pilot School – FTC-TIM-AD#62. – USAF Pub. 03-01-63
23. USAF Test Pilot School History - Graduate Course Catalog page 9. Printed 2013
24. www.history.com/news/the-palomares-h-bomb-incident.